THE HISTORY AND CULTURE
OF JAPANESE FOOD

Despite the popularity of Japanese food in the West today, remarkably little is known about its history. This innovative work is the fist of its kind, is a detailed study of the food and dietary practices of the Japanese from the Palaeolithic era, beforc rice was cultivated, through the period when the distinctive Japanese culinary tradition reached its culmination (between 1640 and 1860), and on to the present day. This evolution is traced through presenting typical dishes of all periods, condiment, beverages, ingredients, methods of preparation, etiquette, the aesthetics of presentation, eating implements and cooking utensils in the social, political, and economic contexts of their consumption and use. Topics include the spread of soy sauce, the design of Japanese food, introducing the reader to home cookery and regional schools of cuisine that are virtually unknown outside Japan. It makes a unique contribution to the study of Japanese culture, and of culinary history as a whole.

Dr. Naomici Ishige has written prolifically regarding the Japanese diet. He has authored 12 books, and co-authored or edited an additional 60 works. He is currently Director General at the National Museum of Ethnology, Osaka.

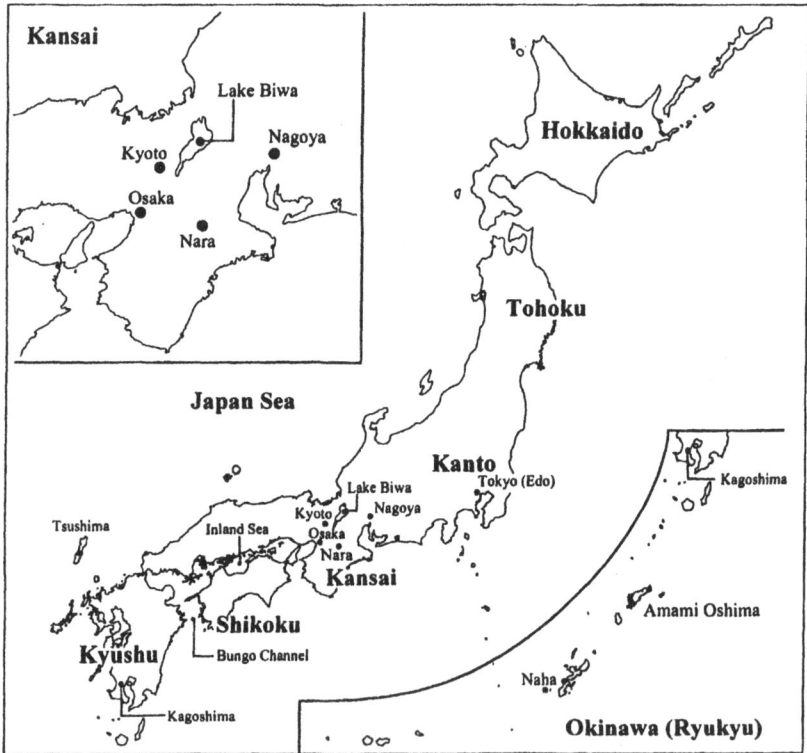

Kansai

Lake Biwa

Kyoto

Nagoya

Osaka

Nara

Hokkaido

Tohoku

Japan Sea

Kanto

Tokyo (Edo)

Kagoshima

Tsushima

Lake Biwa

Inland Sea

Kyoto

Nagoya

Osaka

Nara

Kansai

Amami Oshima

Shikoku

Bungo Channel

Kyushu

Naha

Kagoshima

Okinawa (Ryukyu)

Map of Japan

THE HISTORY AND CULTURE OF JAPANESE FOOD

NAOMICHI ISHIGE

Routledge
Taylor & Francis Group

NEW YORK AND LONDON

First published by Kegan Paul Limited
P.O. Box 256, London WC1B 3SW

This edition published 2011 by Routledge

2 Park Square, Milton Park, Abingdon, Oxfordshire OX14 4RN

711 Third Avenue, New York, NY 10017

Routledge is an imprint of the Taylor & Francis Group, an informa business

First issued in paperback 2011

British Library Cataloguing in Publication Data
Ishige, Naomichi
The history and culture of Japanese food
1.Japanese – Food 2.Food habits – Japan – History 3.Diet – Japan – History
4.Cookery – Japan 5.Cookery, Japanese 6.Japan – Social life and customs
I.Title
394.1'0952
ISBN 978-0-710-30657-9 (hbk)
ISBN 978-0-415-51539-9 (pbk)
Library of Congress Cataloging-in-Publication Data
Applied for.

PREFACE

Every kind of food carries social, historical and cultural information. A human meal consists not only of the absorption of matter as a means of supplying nutrition, but also the absorption of information that is associated with the food. Concerning Japanese food there is a great deal of information that is virtually unknown outside Japan, and that is why I have written this book for publication in English.

With the proliferation of Japanese restaurants in cities around the world since the late 1970s, it has become rather easy to enjoy Japanese cuisine without going to Japan. As the cuisine has gained popularity, many books about it have been written and published in various languages. However, the great majority of them are simply cookbooks. There has been no book designed to inform a non-Japanese audience about Japanese dietary history and how the culture of Japan is projected through its food. This book is meant to fill that vacuum.

As a cultural anthropologist, I have spent the past 20 years conducting field work on the food and diet of many peoples, mainly in Asia. On the basis of my findings, I present in this book various comparisons between the dietary cultures of Japan and other parts of Asia, especially China and Korea, which are the areas that historically have had the strongest influence on Japan.

Part One surveys the history of Japanese food and diet, from the Stone Age to the present. Part Two describes the contemporary dietary culture of Japan, from table manners to cookery to typical foods. Readers who are primarily interested in the Japanese diet of today may wish to start with Part Two.

Several people and organizations have helped me prepare this book for publication. I am particularly indebted to Stephen Suloway and Kyoto Tsushinsha for the translation and editing of my Japanese manuscript, to the Ajinomoto Foundation for Dietary Culture which provided financial support for that work, and to my long-time friend Prof. Kenneth Ruddle for his comments on the manuscript.

Naomichi Ishige
National Museum of
Ethnology, Osaka
January 2000

Map of East Asia

CONTENTS

PART TWO
THE DIETARY CULTURE OF THE JAPANESE

ILLUSTRATIONS

INTRODUCTION

THE HISTORICAL FRAMEWORK

The history of Japan is usually divided into ages and periods corresponding to changes in government. The ancient age, marked by the central authority of the imperial court and its bureaucracy, gave way in the twelfth century to the medieval age of warrior governments. The early modern age began in the sixteenth century with reunification and the emergence of the Tokugawa shogunate, and the modern age dates from the Meiji Restoration of 1868.

Compared to changes in political and economic systems, which are often linked with sudden or even revolutionary shifts in ideology and technology, changes in diet normally exhibit much gentler patterns of advance. Historians tend to take changes of political system as the dividing points for historical eras, yet a change in government does not lead to any rapid change in people's eating habits. New foodstuffs or manners of eating will not spread through a nation without a preparatory period for the adjustment of systems of production and supply. Moreover, the food tastes and preferences that are formed during childhood and youth tend to undergo a slow process of change, transforming gradually as they are transmitted from generation to generation. Therefore, divisions in the history of dietary life differ from the periods into which historical events are generally classified.

Rather than the periodization used by historians, this book adopts an original system conceived by the author as a practical

1

framework for investigating the dietary history of the Japanese (see Table 1, page 4).

In palaeolithic and neolithic times, the society of the Japanese islands was based on hunting and gathering, and the diet consisted largely of acorns and other nuts, fish and shellfish, and wild game. The cultivation of rice and other crops began and gradually spread through the islands between about 400 BCE and CE 250, which is here called the Early Agriculture Period.

The long interval between the sixth and fifteenth centuries, stretching across most of the ancient and medieval ages, is viewed as the Formative Period of the dietary culture of Japan. Various influences which were absorbed from the Asian continent during the first part of the period were gradually adapted and assimilated into a stable indigenous cuisine.

The period spanning the sixteenth and the first half of the seventeenth centuries (which historians would term the close of the medieval and beginning of the early modern ages) is surveyed as a separate era in Chapter 4, The Age of Change. This is the time when many aspects of dietary culture were altered as a result of external influences introduced through trade with China and western Europe. It corresponds to the social changes accompanying the collapse of the medieval order and reorganization of the feudal system.

Thereafter, the distinctive Japanese culinary tradition that has continued to the present day reached its culmination between about 1640 and 1860, the period of national isolation when foreign influence was extremely limited. This era is dealt with in the Chapter 5, The Maturing of Traditional Japanese Cuisine.

Finally, since the reopening of the country in the mid-nineteenth century, Japanese society has progressively modernized in line with the norms of Western civilization, a process that initiated great changes in food culture which continue today. It is described in Chapter 6, Changes of the Modern Age.

Part Two presents the food culture that is found today in Japan. Historical background is included, but the focus is on specific aspects of the dining experience. *Bon appétit!*

JAPANESE PRONUNCIATION AND SPELLING

The vowel sounds of romanized Japanese are: *a* as in father, *e* as in bed, *i* like the *e* in equal, *o* as in note, and *u* like the *oo* in boot. When vowels occur next to each other, each is pronounced with no break between the sounds. A macron above a vowel–*ô*, *û*, *â*–indicates that the basic sound is elongated. (Macrons are not used for proper names in this book.)

A consonant always marks the start of a new syllable. There is never a consonant sound at the end of a syllable, although some syllables end with a written *n*, which indicates that the preceding vowel is nasalized. Consonants are otherwise pronounced essentially the same as in English. Each syllable of a word is given equal stress.

Japanese personal names are written in the traditional manner, last name first.

Periods of Japanese Dietary Culture

DIETARY PERIOD		HISTORICAL PERIOD		
− 400 BCE	**Hunting and Gathering**		− 8000 BCE	Paleolithic Age
		Jômon (Neolithic) Middle Jômon 3500 – 2000	c.8000 – c.400 BCE	Prehistoric Age
400 BCE – CE 250	**Early Agriculture**	Yayoi	c. 400 BCE – c. CE 250	
		Kofun	c. 250 – 710	Ancient Age
		Nara	710 – 794	
	Formative	Heian	794 – 1192	
500 – 1500	**Period**	Kamakura	1192 – 1336	
		N & Southern Courts	1336 – 1392	Medieval Age
		Muromachi Civil Wars 1467 – 1568	1392 – 1568	
	Age of			
1500 – 1641	**Change**	Momoyama	1568 – 1600	Early Modern Age
		Edo	1600 – 1868	
	Maturing of			
1641 – 1868	**Traditional Cuisine**			
		Meiji	1868 – 1912	Modern Age
	Modern	Taishô/Shôwa	1912 – 1989	
1868 –	**Period**	Postwar 1946 –		

PART ONE

The Dietary History of Japan

CHAPTER 1

THE PREHISTORIC ERA

1.1   The Paleolithic Age

The Japanese archipelago forms an arc stretching from north to south near the northeast edge of the Asian continent. The bulk of the land area is made up by the four large islands of Hokkaido, Honshu, Shikoku and Kyushu. The country stretches some 3,500 kilometres from the northern tip of Hokkaido near the Sakhalin peninsula of Russia, to the southernmost island in the Okinawa group near Taiwan. A narrow strait separates the islands of Tsushima, off the northwest coast of Kyushu, from the Korean Peninsula.

During the glacial epoch, when the land surface was mostly frozen and the sea level receded, the archipelago was a single landform linked to the continent. Land bridges connected present-day Hokkaido to Siberia and Kyushu to Korea, and what is now the Japan Sea lay entirely inland. During that era, animals and humans could migrate freely from the main part of the continent.

Human habitation of the Japanese land area is known to date back as far as 600,000 years. Some 3,000 palaeolithic sites have been discovered, most of them from 30,000 to 10,000 years old, classified as late palaeolithic. The remains unearthed from those sites are limited to scant amounts of stone tools and stone shards from toolmaking. Land animals no doubt made up a large part of the diet of palaeolithic people, as the subarctic climate made edible plants scarce and fishing techniques had not developed. It is believed that the people of the time erected small, temporary shelters and lived in nomadic fashion, perhaps carrying light tents as they roamed over broad areas, hunting game or catching fish which ran upstream in season.

As virtually no remains of animal or vegetable foodstuffs have been discovered with the stone tool finds, we know very little about what palaeolithic people ate or how they prepared their food. Analysis of organic matter adhering to a 140,000-year-old stone tool discovered recently in Miyazaki Prefecture established that it is consistent with the fatty acid composition of the Naumann elephant, indicating that the implement was used to dismember such an animal [Nakano 1989:120–121]. In future, similar typological analyses of fatty acid traces, along with reconstruction of the palaeo-environment, may well yield an increasing amount of materials that would inform us about the human diet in palaeolithic times.

Groups of flame-scorched natural stones, about the size of a fist or slightly smaller, have been unearthed at palaeolithic sites in the Kanto region. They are believed to have been used for cooking, as there was organic matter of animal origin adhering to some of those scorched stones. We know of the use of earthen ovens on Pacific islands for cooking meat and fish and taro, yams or breadfruit, by placing the food on rocks and covering it with banana leaves and soil. This method was also utilized in palaeolithic Europe.

Scorched rocks from the neolithic (Jômon) period have also been found. Stones remained in occasional use for cooking even after the spread of earthenware and pans, and some techniques have been passed down to the present. For example, fisherfolk on the small island of Awashima in the Japan Sea use stones to prepare lunch along the shore. Freshly caught small fish are roasted over an open fire and then placed in a cylindrical *bentô* (portable meal) box made of lacquered tree bark (called a *wappa*). Water is poured over the fish, and it is momentarily boiled by adding a stone heated in the open fire. Miso is then dissolved in the fish broth to complete a version of the staple miso soup without using a pot.

Around 8000BCE, or approximately 400 human generations ago, the inhabitants of the archipelago experienced a major climatic shift. With the change from the cold, dry climate of the glacial epoch to the warm, humid climate of the later ice age, the conifer forests and steppe lands which had covered all Japan were restricted to northern and upland regions. In their place, luxuriant temperate forests began to cover the lowlands of the archipelago. As a result, large herbivores such as the mammoth, reindeer, bison and horse disappeared, and the range of cold-water fishes such as trout and salmon was limited to the north. The land bridges disappeared, leaving Japan separated from the Asian continent by the Japan Sea, and broken into different islands. Receiving warm ocean currents from the south and cold currents from the north along both the Pacific Ocean and Japan Sea coasts, the Japanese archipelago lies in one of the finest fishing regions of the world.

These climatic changes naturally changed the way people lived. Remains from about 8000BCE of shell mounds, graves, and home sites with holes for stout pillars indicate the start of the shift from a nomadic lifestyle to domiciled settlement. Indeed a uniform pattern of settlement began about the same time throughout the middle latitudes of the planet in areas where temperate forests were advancing, including Europe, West Asia, China and North America as well as Japan.

The economic basis of domiciliation in Japan consisted mainly in the gathering of carbohydrate-rich nuts growing in temperate forest zones, including acorns, walnuts and chestnuts. Hunting of deer and boar was also important. Moreover, as the sea level rose and the coastlines approached the forests, it became possible to select home sites that would allow regular harvesting of nuts and game from the forest as well as fish and shellfish from the ocean.

1.2 The Advent of Earthenware

Archaeologists regard the appearance of earthenware as the demarcation between palaeolithic and neolithic Japan. Due to the presence at most neolithic sites of earthenware displaying surface decorations that were impressed with twisted cords, the neolithic era of Japan is referred to as the *jômon* (cord-marked) period. Jômon earthenware is the oldest that has been discovered anywhere in the world, having been traced by carbon dating to as early as

9

14,500BCE. Scholars are divided on the question of whether such early use of pottery was a cultural feature developed exclusively in Japan, or was transmitted from an ancient, as yet unrediscovered culture in Siberia.

The use of earthenware allows food to be cooked by boiling. Since some of the earliest Jômon-period vessels bear marks from the application of fire, the earthenware pots were probably used more as cooking utensils than as storage vessels. Through boiling, food can be softened for eating, poisons can be removed, and astringent or bitter tastes can be altered. Boiling also makes even the tiniest shellfish or seeds edible. Furthermore, through retention of the nutrition and flavour dissolved in broth, it allows new developments in cooking which were not possible with the older technique of baking in earthen ovens.

The use of earthenware led to more active utilization of vegetable food resources. The population of the Japanese islands is estimated to have grown from about 20,000 at the start of the Jômon period to 260,000 at the end of the middle Jômon period in 2000BCE [Koyama 1984:173]. To allow such an increase, new food resources must have been developed. The most common staple foods in Jômon times were various types of acorns, horse chestnuts, Japanese chestnuts, and walnuts. Most acorns contain tannin which makes them too bitter to be eaten raw. The bitterness can be removed from some types by pulverizing and soaking them in water, perhaps in a fine-meshed basket, whereas others must be boiled before they are soaked. It was through such procedures that acorns would initially have become part of the diet.

Although acorns have been found at some of the earliest Jômon sites, chestnuts and walnuts, which can be eaten raw, predominate. At sites from the middle Jômon period, when the population had increased, there are sharply larger amounts of high-tannin acorns and horse chestnuts which require preparation to remove harshness. These were typically stored in pits beside the homes. Horse chestnuts, which contain non-water-soluble saponin and aloin, must be neutralized with alkali to make them edible. We suppose that the bitterness was removed by boiling them together with substantial quantities of ash, a technique that survives today as a folk custom in certain areas of Japan. Homes with ovens fitted with special apparatus for collecting ash have been found at various sites.

The yields from these nuts were extremely high. Koyama Shûzô has calculated that for one kind of acorn, the yield from 100 ha would be 65 kilograms. In terms of food energy available from a standard plot of land, that amounts to one-eighth the nutritional value of paddy rice (the most productive agricultural crop), and 500 times that of the wild boar, which was then the most commonly hunted animal. Whereas the population merely subsisted during palaeolithic and early Jômon times by relying on the catch from hunting, it multiplied with the subsequent shift toward vegetable resources, mainly nuts.

It was during the era when nuts came to be eaten in great quantity that Jômon pottery evolved considerably and began to be made in many sizes and shapes. This differentiation no doubt signifies the diversification of cooking and eating methods. It is believed that shallow bowls were used for kneading starches made from nuts and wild rhizomes, while decorated vessels were used for serving food. Discoveries have included pieces of starch which are thought to have been kneaded into a cookie-like shape and buried in oven ashes for baking. Another probable cooking method was boiling round dumplings of starch in pots. There may well have been one-pot meals of such starches boiled together with meat, fish, shellfish or wild plants. It is also likely that mixtures of starch and water were boiled in pots and eaten in paste form.

Shell middens are a common feature of Jômon sites, indicating that marine resources were a major part of the diet. Although coastal fishes were often eaten, the larger role was played by shellfish, which were easily gathered and were steadily and amply available. Analysis of the accumulation patterns of these refuse heaps shows that people frequently collected and discarded shells in large quantities, exceeding the amount that could be eaten at one time. While it is a chore to pry open a living mollusk, it is easy to extract the meat after boiling. Presumably during the gathering season large amounts of shellfish were boiled en masse, and the cooked meat was dried and later used for trading with communities located far inland. The broth obtained from such a procedure would naturally have been enjoyed as soup.

Sites from the late Jômon period (2000-400 BCE) have yielded earthenware vessels that were used exclusively for making salt by boiling down sea water. Salt may also have been produced through a method that is known to have been used in Japan until recently, whereby sea water is repeatedly poured over seaweed and evaporated, then the seaweed is washed with salt water and that salt-rich water is boiled down. Poetry from the eighth century CE speaks of burning seaweed to make salt. The process referred to likely involved pouring sea water over seaweed and drying it many times, then burning it to obtain a mixture of salt and ash. Although there is no archaeological evidence for it, this method may have been used in Jômon times as well. It is also likely that in coastal areas sea water was added for flavour when boiling food. As rock salt is not made in Japan and there are no salt lakes or salt springs, inland areas always relied on salt made from sea water. Thus since ancient times salt has been a vital and precious trading commodity.

Besides salt, Japanese pepper (*sanshô*; *Zanthoxylum piperitum*) has also been found at Jômon sites and was presumably used as a seasoning, much as it is today. This spice, made from the leaves and nuts of a tree that originated in Japan, is widely used to add a tangy zest to Japanese dishes.

1.3   Jômon Society and Dietary Culture

The neolithic revolution that began in Mesopotamia was named for the advent of stone tools made by grinding rather than chipping, and yet it involved much more than technological reform in the sphere of toolmaking. It also signifies the shifts in society that accompanied changes in food production, that is, the change from hunter-gatherer society to agricultural and pastoral society. In Japan, neolithic or Jômon society had a somewhat different character than the contemporary societies that evolved in the heartland of the Eurasian continent. While it possessed technological elements such as polished stone toolmaking and earthenware pottery which were common to neolithic peoples elsewhere in the world, Jômon society did   not   practise   either   intensive   land   cultivation   or   the domestication and breeding of livestock. It was a neolithic society of hunter-gatherers.

Though Jômon society was not agricultural it was not entirely without cultivated crops. Excavations have established the use by the third millennium BCE of grains including buckwheat, wheat and millet (*awa*; *Setaria italica*), as well as the *ryokutô* bean (*Vigno radiata*), perilla mint (*egoma*; *P. frutescens*), and gourds used both as containers and food. The grains would later be systematically cultivated, initially in slash-and-burn fashion. Some scholars have interpreted the discovery of grain at Jômon sites to mean that slash-and-burn agriculture was practised in Jômon times. However, as both the quantities of grain and the number of sites where it has been discovered are very small, it is unreasonable to view crop production as part of the economic foundation of Jômon society. There is a considerable likelihood that the grains found at Jômon sites were transmitted from the area spanning the Korean Peninsula and nearby Siberian coast. We must presume either that attempts at cultivating the transmitted grains proved unsuccessful owing to the insufficient technological knowledge of the time and were abandoned; or that grain cultivation was practised in Jômon times using extremely non-intensive techniques, on a scale that was minute by comparison to the gathering of wild plants, and the cultivated lands were quite localized. The non-grain plants were probably cultivated in kitchen gardens next to the homes, and used in small quantities to add variety to meals, rather than as main foods. The gourds, of which only a few relics have been found, are likely to have served mainly as containers. More than a thousand Jômon sites have been surveyed to date and the research results, taken comprehensively, make clear that Jômon society was one of hunter-gatherers.

The sole domesticated animal of the Jômon era was the dog. Jômon culture was from the beginning marked by use of the bow and arrow and the raising of dogs. Deer and wild boar were the main hunting prey. The skeletal remains of some 70 types of mammals have been found at Jômon sites, but at most sites more than 90 per cent of the bones are from deer and wild boar. They were chased down with the aid of hunting dogs, which have survived in continuous lines for at least 10,000 years until today.

That hunters treated their dogs as precious companions is suggested by the discovery of many dog burial sites.

It is said that many Japanese can name more than twenty kinds of edible fishes, while a European or American can rarely name more than ten. Statistically, the Japanese today eat more fish than any other nation. A Buddhism-related taboo on eating the flesh of mammals (see Chapter 3) made fish the predominant animal foodstuff for several centuries, and this undoubtedly played a role in making Japan into the nation of fish lovers it is today. Yet the custom of eating much fish dates from Jômon times.

The convoluted shapes of the Japanese islands make for extraordinarily long coastlines. In addition, during the fifth and sixth millennia BCE the sea level was some five metres higher than it is today, submerging many of today's plains and bringing the sea in convoluted patterns up to the foot of today's tablelands, creating ideal conditions for fishing. Moreover, the seas around Japan, where the warm Japan current from the south and the cold Kurile current from the north come together, contain more species of fish than all but a very few areas of the world.

Bone fishing hooks, harpoons made from deer bones or antlers, and sinkers for fishing nets have been discovered in Jômon shell mounds, and certainly traps for catching various types of fish existed, although no traces remain as they were made from vegetable materials. The bones of 71 species of fish have been found in Jômon shell mounds. Open-sea fishery developed in the Tohoku region, where dugout canoes were ridden into the offing to harpoon bluefin tuna and bonito, and fishing was done with large hooks. It is likely that the stimulus for the development of a fishing industry for large migratory fishes was that they were easy to preserve and so were valued as trade commodities. Tuna and bonito meat keep well after being boiled and then steamed and dried in the sun until hard. They are kept today in that form, called *namari* or *namari-bushi*, and typically eaten after being boiled with vegetables. *Katsuo-bushi*, bonito that is smoked after boiling, turns as hard as wood and keeps for years. Today *katsuo-bushi* is commonly used to make soup stock (*dashi*), by placing shavings in boiling water to extract the essence (see Section 9.1). In ancient times, apart from being used for stock, *katsuo-bushi* was jerked for gnawing.

Among many peoples, fishing in the open sea is viewed as men's work, while women gather shellfish along the coast. The same was probably true for Jômon people. Some 60 per cent of the known Jômon shell mounds are concentrated in the Kanto region, which at the time had a very high number of natural inlets and was surrounded by extensive shoals. The tide ebbed a considerable distance each day, allowing easy picking of shellfish. Jômon shell mounds have yielded 354 species, a large proportion of which were clams (*Meretrix lusoria, Ruditapes philippinarum, Mactra veneriformis*). Investigation of the patterns of accumulation often reveals that extremely large quantities of shells were discarded at one time, presumably after the meat was boiled and extracted for drying and preservation. The discovery at shell mounds of obsidian tools produced in mountain areas as distant as 100 kilometres suggests that dried shellfish were carried inland for trade.

Peoples who subsist on diets composed largely of game and fish are known in general to have low levels of tooth decay, and yet inspection of the teeth of the Jômon people has revealed a fairly high incidence of decay. That is an indication of the large quantities of carbohydrates they ingested, notably from acorns, as described above.

The lifestyle at the beginning of the Jômon period, as in palaeolithic times, seems to have been that of the band or horde, consisting of several families living as a social unit without fixed abode and roaming over a specific territory according to seasonal changes in the food supply. Fixed hamlets were formed as the lifestyle shifted to reliance on the gathering of acorns as the predominant foodstuff. During the middle Jômon period, the Kanto region reached a population of three persons per square kilometre, an extraordinary level for a hunter–gatherer society, and was dotted with hamlets of 30 to 100 persons. Earthenware displaying the same patterns of decoration has been found at sites located across a wide range. As with other peoples of the world, we may suppose that among Jômon people the making of pottery was women's work. The range in which a given style of pottery occurs may be taken as denoting a single cultural area, and also an area in which marital relations could be established among the inhabitants. It may further be supposed that in such a cultural area the same dialect would be spoken and similar religious ceremonies would be practised. While it seems likely that such broad-based social units linking many villages were formed, archaeological findings to date show no evidence of social class divisions, and it is thought that equal rights were held by all. From that we may conclude that Jômon people were at the stage of tribal society, and the Japanese islands were inhabited by many tribes.

CHAPTER 2

THE ESTABLISHMENT OF A RICE-GROWING SOCIETY

2.1   A Crop Held in Special Regard

As wet rice cultivation took hold from the third century BCE, Japan turned into an agricultural society. This is the most significant event in the history of Japanese food.

Since that time, rice has held the central place in the culinary value system of the Japanese. Above all other foods, rice has steadily been regarded as special and highly significant, and matters of rice production and distribution were always the key point of the traditional social economy. This special esteem for rice continues today, as will be seen below.

At present, Japan has a remarkably low rate of self-sufficiency for major agricultural products. According to 1987 statistics, the nation relies on imports for more than half of the food energy ingested by the population, with just 49 per cent provided by domestic products. Even so, for their staple food, rice, the Japanese maintain production capacity at a level substantially higher than demand. As a result of government controls designed to prevent excess production, national production stands somewhat higher than 100 per cent of demand. To ensure stable supplies and prices, rice distribution is also kept at uniform quantities through national regulations. Behind the adoption of those laws lies the traditional value sense that rice is the most important of all foodstuffs, and that guaranteed self-sufficiency in rice is the pivot of agriculture policy.

Policies that hold rice in special regard are nothing new. Ever since Japan was first administered as a nation in the fifth century, ways to augment the rice harvest have been the keystone of agriculture policy. Until the latter part of the nineteenth century, when the forms of the modern state were adopted, taxes were collected from farmers in the form of rice rather than cash. The mentality that reflected the position of rice as the underpinning of the national economy has carried over to present-day governments, which continue to regard rice as a special commodity.

In times past, under the harsh taxation of feudal lords, there were many farmers who delivered the bulk of their rice production as tax and actually did not have sufficient rice for their daily meals. Still, during festival times it was customary for even the poorest people to eat meals of rice as well as ceremonial rice cakes (*mochi*; see Section 9.10) and to drink sake (brewed from rice). The New Year holiday and many other annual events and festivals derive from ceremonies connected with rice farming.

Traditional rice-related festivals occur mainly during the months of May, July–August, and October–November. In May, with the transplanting of seedlings to the paddies, a rice–planting festival marked the start of the year's production in the field. Frequently the farming work at planting time was itself made festive, with maidens in local folk costume singing to musical accompaniments as they planted seedlings. Today, those customs have mostly disappeared and the operation is usually carried out with machinery.

The emperor or empress of ancient times was considered to be a divinity as well as a sovereign, and functioned as the supreme priest of Shinto. As a vestige of that role, today's emperor performs a ritual rice planting each spring at a paddy within the palace grounds, as a prayer for the success of the year's rice crop throughout Japan. The festivals of July and August, the time when insects often blight the rice, are ritual prayers for protecting the crop. The festivals of October and November are harvest festivals. As a part of the formal enthronement ceremonies, a new emperor performs a special ritual offering of food at harvest time, called the *Ônie-no-matsuri* (or *Daijôsai*). Its mystical significance involves the transmission to the new emperor of an immortal spirit which supplements the sacred imperial power. That spirit is believed to weaken after the death or abdication of the predecessor, and to be reinvigorated as the new emperor partakes of rice and sake prepared from the freshly harvested first crop of his tenure. Thus the spirit of the rice plant is invoked to renew the spirit of the divine sovereign that is said to dwell in the new emperor.

The belief that rice is a plant in which a spirit dwells is found not only in Japan but also in Southeast Asian regions of wet rice cultivation, where the plant spirit is venerated through ritual involving the year's first-harvested ears of rice. In Southeast Asia and Japan it was commonly believed that disrespectful behaviour toward the spirit of the rice plant, believed especially to dwell in the first-harvested grains of rice, will cause people to waste away because the rice they eat will yield no nutrition and the seeds they plant will be barren. It appears that such ideas spread through all rice-growing regions in ancient times, but were displaced in China by the advent of other religions, while remaining in Southeast Asia and Japan. In present-day Japan, however, the folkway that ascribes trouble to the rude handling of rice only barely survives among the older generation, and so the idea of the spirit of the rice plant is being abandoned.

The physical factors that make rice an excellent staple undoubtedly help to account for the disposition of Asian peoples to view it as special among foods. Both agriculturally and nutritionally, rice is an ideal food for monsoon Asia. It provides the highest yield per unit area of all crops cultivated in the region. It grows in summer in the high-temperature, high-precipitation monsoon belt. Rice cultivation in paddies is a highly rational farming system in various respects. The paddy soil is covered with water during the growing period, with the result that soil disperses slowly with little loss of fertility, and fertilizers are not required because nutrients are supplied with the flow of irrigation water. Furthermore, in contrast to most dry land farming, soil erosion is not a problem, and the same field can be used year after year with no ill effects from continuous cultivation.

From the nutritional standpoint, rice is an outstanding crop not only as a source of calories, but also as a protein supply. When rice is compared to wheat for aggregate amount of vegetable protein, wheat is slightly higher. Yet rice outperforms wheat in a comparison of the balance of essential amino acids, that is, in protein value.

If the protein required to maintain the human body is ingested solely from rice, a person weighing 70 kilograms must eat about 0.8 kilograms (uncooked) of rice per day. Eating such a large quantity of rice burdens the stomach and may cause it to enlarge, yet it is possible, and it was not unusual for Japanese farmers to eat 1.5 kilograms of rice a day during their busiest, most labour-intensive season. On the other hand, if bread made from wheat were to be used as the sole source of protein, about three kilograms would have to be eaten in a day, and such a large amount would be so bulky as to be impossible in actual practice. Accordingly, a bread diet must be supplemented with foods such as meat and dairy products which contain large amounts of lysine and tryptophan, the essential amino acids in which wheat is deficient. Eaten together with such rich sources of animal protein, bread becomes necessary only for its calorie-providing carbohydrate content, and since meat and dairy products contain high-calorie fats, it is not necessary to eat large amounts of bread.

The damp climate of monsoon Asia is ill–suited to the breeding of cattle or sheep, and hence a pastoral lifestyle was not adopted. Nor was it customary to consume milk from domestic animals. The main domestic animal raised for food was the pig. To a remarkable degree, protein was ingested from rice rather than from meat or milk. Large quantities of rice were eaten as the major source of both carbohydrates and protein, for rice alone can give the body everything it requires apart from certain vitamins and minerals. Thus, if an adequate supply of rice can be guaranteed, the problem of sustenance is largely solved. That is why rice was regarded as an extraordinary foodstuff.

Calculations based on national statistics for Japan in 1873 – when there had as yet been virtually none of the Western influence on dietary patterns that accompanied modernization – show that rice was the dominant source of both calories and protein. Specifically, on a per capita daily basis, rice provided 1,148 kilocalories, or 65.5 per cent of calories received from staple crops (grains and potatoes), as well as 23.1 grams of protein [Koyama and

Gotô 1985:491–2]. Such thorough reliance on rice was the chief feature of the Japanese diet from the introduction of rice cultivation some two millennia ago up to the 1960s, a time of great change in eating patterns, when large amounts of meat, dairy products and fats and oils began to be eaten, and both the amount of rice consumed and its importance as a protein source began to decline.

2.2   Dissemination and Development of Rice

There are two species of cultivated rice, *Oryza glaberrima* which originated in Africa around the Niger River and is still grown in some parts of the region, and *O. sativa* which originated in Asia and has been disseminated throughout the world. *O. sativa* was formerly thought to have originated on the Indian subcontinent, but Japanese researchers have constructed an influential theory of its origin in the mountainous region stretching through Assam, northern Burma and the Chinese province of Yunnan. Along the east coast of China, traces of rice from about 5000 BCE were found in recent excavations at Hemudu on the southern shore of Hangzhou Bay, and this has led some Chinese scholars to assert that rice originated in China [Chen and Watabe 1989:9–46].

In any case, there is no doubt that rice was brought from China into Japan and Korea, where wild rice species have not been found and rice farming began relatively late. Many neolithic settlements that developed on the basis of rice cultivation, dating from the fourth millennium BCE onward, have been found along the middle and lower reaches of the Yangtze River. The same sites have also yielded the bones of livestock including cattle and water buffalo, which could have been used for farm work, and also pigs. The technique of wet rice cultivation is thought to have been perfected in the Yangtze delta area during the several centuries prior to 1000 BCE, a time when stone and bronze tools were in simultaneous use. Although rice cultivation is spreading across northern China today, thanks to the development of strains that grow in cold climates, the historical rice-growing region of China lies south of the Yellow River basin. In ancient times, the main food crop of the north was millet, both the foxtail and common varieties.

Stone tools of the same types used in the Yangtze delta area before 1000 BCE have been found at southern Korean sites dating from between 800 and 0 BCE, and at Japanese sites from the early part of the Yayoi period (beginning about 400 BCE). They include several types of stone adzes, as well as stone knives that are thought to have been used to harvest rice [Ishige 1968:130–150]. This leads to the supposition that rice cultivation was transmitted from the Yangtze delta to southern Korea and Japan. There are two theories of how this might have occurred. One is that immigrants navigated the East China Sea and settled on both the southern Korean Peninsula and northern Kyushu, and began growing rice in their new locations. The second theory is that rice growing was first introduced to southern Korea, either from the Yangtze delta area or from the lower reaches of the Huai River basin somewhat further north, and was later brought to northern Kyushu as people living in Korea crossed the Korea Strait.

The tools used for fabrication in the early rice-growing culture of Japan were mainly stone, although bronze and iron were used for contemporary weapons, ritual implements, and handicraft tools. It has been proved that bronze and iron culture originated in northern China. The idea has been put forth that in the southern part of the Korean Peninsula there was a blending of the metal-tool culture that was spreading southward and the rice-growing culture that was spreading northward. That would support the theory that key cultural influences reached Japan from Korea. However, storehouses for harvested rice that have been found at early rice-growing settlements in Japan are architecturally distinctive in that they stand atop high posts. Examples of that *takakura* form are still in use today on islands south of Kyushu and in the Okinawa group. The same architectural form existed in the Yangtze delta in ancient times, and is found today throughout Southeast Asia, but is unknown on the Korean Peninsula. These facts offer support for the idea that rice cultivation was introduced directly from the Yangtze delta to Japan.

The arrival of rice growing in Japan doubtless was not a singular event, for rice must have been carried along with many of the waves of immigrants. There was immigration from southern Korea as well as from the Yangtze delta region, and the culture of Japan during its early rice-growing period is very likely to have taken shape through the overlap and fusion of the cultures of those two regions.

Early agriculture in Japan was not limited to rice. Other crops that have been found in excavations include millet (*kibi*), foxtail millet (*awa*), barley, wheat, and Deccan grass; soybeans and adzuki beans (*Vigna angularis*); melons of both fruit and vegetable types; and peaches. Some of those, such as peaches and melons, are thought to have been introduced from China, whereas others such as barley, adzuki beans and buckwheat are thought to have come by way of the Korean Peninsula. In sum, it seems that at the time of the arrival of rice growing, crops from those two regions came together in Japan to make up a discrete agricultural complex.

The early agricultural era of Japan was named the Yayoi period after the Tokyo neighbourhood where archaeologists first discovered the distinctive earthenware of the period. Early Yayoi sites are concentrated in northern Kyushu, and consist of hamlets with paddies located close by. Wet rice cultivation was soon transmitted as far as the Kansai district (around present-day Osaka and Kyoto), but thereafter Yayoi culture was static in terms of territorial expansion. For a time, western Japan expressed the Yayoi age while eastern Japan remained at the level of Jômon culture. It may be that Yayoi culture, with its economic basis in rice growing, could not spread to eastern Japan until new rice varieties suited to the colder eastern climate were developed. The Jômon-period population lived mainly in the east and north, as far west as the mountainous Chûbu region of central Honshu (north and east of present-day Nagoya) where the forests contained many acorn-bearing trees. The western part of the archipelago, where the population was comparatively quite sparse, was on the fringes of Jômon culture. There, where the warm climate was suitable for growing rice and there were few indigenous people who might tend to reject an outside culture, it was easy for a new culture to propagate. In the east, where a stable culture centred on acorn gathering was flourishing, there was very little incentive to hazard a switch to an unknown lifestyle of agriculturalism. These dynamics might have delayed the propagation of Yayoi culture to eastern Japan.

Use of wild plants as important foodstuffs did not cease with the beginning of Yayoi culture. Acorns have been unearthed from 168 Yayoi sites, while rice has been found at only 128 [Terasawa and Terasawa 1981:69]. Yet the fact that rice has not been found at a site does not necessarily mean that its inhabitants did not grow it, for grains of rice are harder to find than acorns. Moreover, Jômon-style acorn gathering would have continued during the Yayoi period in order to make up for bad harvests or shortfalls in rice production. In the initial phase of rice growing, considerable risk would have been involved in relying completely on it for survival.

The range of wet rice cultivation expanded as far as the northern tip of Honshu by CE 0. Yet it penetrated neither the northern island of Hokkaido nor the Ryukyu (Okinawa) island chain south of Kyushu, areas that retained gathering economies well beyond the Jômon period. Thus it was in the heartland of the Japanese archipelago – the islands of Honshu, Shikoku and Kyushu – that the Yayoi period brought the formation of an agricultural society based on wet rice cultivation. Meanwhile, the outlying islands inhabited by different ethnic groups – the Ainu of Hokkaido and the Okinawans of the Ryukyus – maintained lifestyles that did not rely on rice growing, and persevered along their own cultural tracks which differed from that of the Japanese mainstream.

Farm implements used in the earliest wet rice cultivation included wooden hoes and shovels. These were fabricated with stone tools, and stone knives were used to reap the ears of rice. At first, natural wetlands were utilized as paddies, but the area of natural landforms that could be used for cultivation would have been limited, and no doubt would have sustained damage from droughts and floods with some frequency. The breakthrough from that stage of unstable agriculture, and the accompanying rapid increase in productivity, seems to have come as iron farming tools began to spread at about the beginning of the Common Era. With iron tools it became possible to build the storage reservoirs and canals necessary for large-scale artificial irrigation, and hence to open up fields in areas other than low-lying wetlands, leading to stable rice production without undue influence from variations in precipitation.

Developments in agriculture were reflected in the population trend. The population of all Japan in the middle Yayoi period (about CE 0) has been estimated at 600,000, about twice as high as the peak of the Jômon period. Between 200 BCE and CE 0 alone, the population is believed to have tripled. Such rapid increase is unparallelled throughout Japanese history, with the exception of the fivefold growth seen during the late nineteenth and twentieth centuries. Thus the Japanese experience matches the population pattern observed in societies throughout the world, in which the peaks of growth occur during the agricultural and industrial revolutions. The Yayoi period was indeed the time of the agricultural revolution in Japan.

There was especially remarkable growth in western Japan, where the Yayoi population reached some twenty times the level of the Jômon period. Favoured by geographical conditions that promoted the rapid adoption of rice and metal culture and the introduction of Chinese and Korean civilization, western Japan achieved a level of development surpassing that of the east. An economy based on surplus agricultural production brought the emergence of groups of specialized artisans who worked full-time at making stone and metal tools. As divisions of labour appeared, social stratification developed. Small villages combined into larger politico-religious units, and a number of chiefdoms were organized in western Japan. According to the Han Chinese chronicle that provides the earliest written mention of Japan, it comprised 100 small independent states during the first century BCE.

The *Wei zhi* chronicle of the Chinese Wei kingdom records that in CE 239 an envoy of the queen who ruled the most powerful of the chiefdoms in Japan visited the Wei court, and that a Wei envoy had visited Japan. Scholars have debated for more than a century, without resolution, the question of whether her queendom lay in northern Kyushu or around Nara, where the capitals of Yamato were situated during the later era of unification. The Wei chronicle also notes that she acted as a shamaness and reigned with religiously styled authority over a society which was stratified into a governing class, the general citizenry, and slaves. The same document includes the earliest account of Japanese dietary culture. From it we know that among the Japanese of the third century: 'there are people who are specialized in diving into the water for fish and shellfish'; 'rice and millet are cultivated'; 'as the climate is warm, raw vegetables are eaten in both summer and winter'; 'they have ginger, citrus fruits, *sanshô* pepper and *myôga* ginger, but do not know how to use them in cooking'; 'at meals they eat with their fingers from a small dish with attached base'; and 'they are fond of drinking wine'.

A giant tomb was constructed on the death of that queen, according to the Chinese source. By the fourth century, massive earthen tumuli were commonly constructed for the burial of the central government royalty and local chieftains, together with weaponry and personal ornaments. The Japanese term for these tumuli has become the name of the Kofun period of history, spanning the years from 250 to 552.

The Kofun period was also marked by a unified state. A government in Yamato (near present-day Nara) came to hold sway in both military and civil matters over the many small local states, and the expansion of its authority furthered the process of national unification on the main islands of Honshu, Shikoku and Kyushu. The modern Japanese imperial line is officially claimed to descend directly from the Yamato royalty. Yamato mounted an invasion of Korea in the latter part of the fourth century and established a colony in the southern part of the peninsula. During the fifth century the Yamato court sent several emissaries to the Chinese capital. It also intervened politically on the continent during this period, a time when China was unstable and three Korean kingdoms were fighting for supremacy. Meanwhile, Japan received successive waves of immigrants who were fleeing the turmoil in southern China and Korea. They brought with them the written language of China and various types of technology. By the sixth century, Japan had absorbed in large measure the mainstream civilization of East Asia.

2.3   Rice Cooking

The main types of rice produced in Asia are *japonica* and *indica*. The *japonica* plants are shorter and flourish in cool climates. Their grain is short and somewhat rounded and has a rather sticky texture when cooked. The *indica* plants, which are suited to tropical climates and do poorly in cool weather, yield a long, narrow grain that is not sticky when cooked. *Japonica* rice traditionally has been cultivated in Japan, Korea, central China and northern Indochina. *Indica* is grown in southern China, India and much of Southeast Asia. A third type, *javanica*, with characteristics between those of the other two, predominates in Indonesia.

Although excavations near the Yangtze River delta have established that both *japonica* and *indica* rice were grown there in neolithic times, only the former was transmitted to Japan. There is no evidence that the *indica* type was cultivated in prehistoric Japan. It was introduced many times from the eleventh century onward, but never cultivated on a large scale. Including extinct strains, some 2,000 varieties of rice have been cultivated in Japan up to the present, and the great majority are the *japonica* type. Varieties are differentiated mainly to match the environments and technical requirements of different growing areas, with taste as another important factor. The Japanese tend to think that cooked *indica* rice 'falls apart, lacks flavour and has a disagreeable smell', and hence rate it as inferior to *japonica*. When the Japanese population grew rapidly in the late nineteenth century, in the absence of efforts to increase domestic rice production, *indica* rice was imported from China and Southeast Asia, but it was considered food for the poor. Conversely, in areas where *indica* predominates, *japonica* rice is considered inferior. When Japanese businessmen stationed in Southeast Asia ask their servants to buy *japonica* rice at the market, the response is, 'You are rich, why should you eat tasteless rice?'

Regardless of type, rice is eaten plain in East Asia. It is boiled in water alone and served without flavouring. In India and regions further west, rice may be eaten plain but often, after it is washed, it is sautéed in oil or flavoured with salt before boiling. Spices, meat and vegetables may also be added for a pilaf or paella. Those styles of rice cooking are generally found in areas where dairy products are commonly eaten, where butter is often used in cooking, including rice cooking. In non-pastoral East Asia rice is usually eaten plain and, as the main protein source, it is traditionally consumed in large quantities at every meal. The customary lack of flavouring allows large quantities to be eaten more easily. Likewise, where wheat is the main protein source, bread that is only lightly salted can be eaten in large quantities much more easily than cake.

Plain rice cooking can be broadly classified into three methods. One method is to cook the washed rice in a large amount of water and pour some water off after it has begun to boil. If it is left to cook completely in the large amount of water, the starch will be entirely gelatinized and it will turn into a gruel. Instead, some of the boiling water is discarded and the remainder is set over a low flame, so that part of the water is absorbed by the rice and part evaporates as steam. Cooked rice with a non-sticky texture can be quickly and easily prepared by this method, although some nutrients are lost by throwing away part of the viscous water which contains dissolved elements of the rice. This method is used notably in places where *indica* rice predominates, including most areas of Southeast Asia and the southern and northern regions of China. (Although the north of China traditionally was not a rice growing region, since ancient times it has consumed large quantities of rice brought from the Yangtze basin via the Grand Canal.) *Indica* rice is not very sticky, and this technique makes it still less so.

A second method is to boil the rice completely without pouring some water off midway as above. When a large amount of water is used, the result is not solid grains of rice, but a runny gruel. As its water content is high, rice gruel offers proportionally less nutrition by volume, and since it can be swallowed without chewing, it is popularly served at breakfast when the appetite is not so strong. Rice gruel was the customary breakfast of city dwellers in the rice-growing regions of China and of the Korean upper class. Chinese farmers normally eat granular cooked rice for breakfast because rice gruel is thought to provide insufficient energy for heavy labour. Until recently in parts of western Japan the customary breakfast, even for farm workers, was tea gruel (*chagayu*) made by boiling rice in water with salt and a cloth bag of low-grade green tea. Tea gruel was a means for economizing on rice, by using the high water content to provide a sense of fullness in the stomach. In general, the Japanese view rice gruel as food for the ill, because it is easily digestible.

Alternatively, the quantity of water may be precisely adjusted to match the amount of rice, so that the rice absorbs it all and is cooked into soft solid grains. For that purpose, it is necessary not only to set the proportions of rice and water, but also to regulate the heat properly. For *japonica* rice the standard measure is 1.2 to 1.3 parts water per one part rice, although somewhat less water is needed for freshly harvested rice, and somewhat more for rice that is drier than normal. Certain varieties have slightly different requirements. The rice should cook over high heat during the first stage when water is circulating in the pot and gelatinizing the starch content, and the heat should be reduced to avoid scorching during the latter stage when most of the water has been absorbed by the rice. This complex technique is considered the best way to cook *japonica* rice to the sticky texture that is preferred in Japan. It is also used in the Philippines, Korea, and the Yangtze River basin.

The third way to cook rice is by steaming, in order to prepare glutinous rice. Both the *indica* and *japonica* types of rice include glutinous varieties which contain a different sort of starch than non-glutinous rice. When glutinous rice is heated after absorbing water, the starch quickly becomes pasty. If it is cooked in a pot, the bottom portion of the rice that receives the heat first turns pasty and sticks fast together. That hinders convection, preventing the rice grains from circulating with the water and limiting the amount of heat they receive, and the result is a layer of scorched rice on the bottom of the pot with half-cooked rice above. Therefore glutinous rice is always cooked in a rice steamer, after first being soaked in water until an appropriate amount is absorbed. In Japan and other places, glutinous rice is generally eaten not as a daily food but on special occasions, after being processed into a cake form. Glutinous rice cooked in a steamer serves as the daily staple in the northern–Indochina region that spans the Shan State in Burma, north and northeast Thailand, Laos, and tribal areas of Yunnan in China.

Archaeologists think the second method of rice cooking was used in Japan during the Yayoi period. Various examples of Yayoi unglazed earthenware have been found with soot on the outside and rice grains stuck to the inside, suggesting that the cooking technique was similar to that used in Japan today. From the Kofun period, however, the remains of home sites from the fifth century onward include many steamers made of hard earthenware. An eighth-century poet described an impoverished life with lines to this effect: 'Cobwebs fill the steamer / Cooking rice has been forgotten.' It is known that rice was usually eaten steamed until about the twelfth century. Yet from the thirteenth century to the present, the Japanese have customarily boiled their rice by the second method. What are we to make of this? A simple explanation could be that glutinous rice was introduced around the fifth century and as it became the standard, steamer cooking became the rule; then in the thirteenth century non-glutinous rice once again became the common staple. Or it may be that both normal and glutinous rice were eaten in Japan from the start, and until the technique for making hard earthenware was brought in from Korea, glutinous rice was cooked in wooden steamers like those used today in Indochina, which were placed over earthen pots filled with water, but the wooden material rotted away and left no trace for archaeologists. Prehistoric rice has been found in charcoal state, but since it is difficult to analyze the starch scientifically, it has not been convincingly identified as glutinous or non-glutinous rice. Significantly, it is glutinous rice that is prepared for traditional festivals and annual events. Considering that ancient customs which have disappeared from modern daily life are temporarily revived at festival times, as ceremonies in general have the character of reduplicating and reproducing times past, it seems reasonable to interpret the ritual meals as vestiges of a former diet of glutinous rice. When rice is steamed together with adzuki beans it takes on a reddish tint, and crimson glutinous rice is eaten during ceremonies and on festive occasions. As in China and Korea, the colour that symbolizes festivity is red.

Brown rice is popular nowadays among those who follow the natural foods movement, in Japan as well as in Europe and America. Brown rice is rice from which only the hull has been removed, with little or no further polishing. Polishing the rice removes the outer, darkish bran layer which is rich in vitamin B1, and makes the rice pure white. In former times the supplementary foods of the Japanese diet provided very little vitamin B1, and the resulting deficiency made beriberi so common that it was considered the national disease.

Well-polished rice was considered tastier, and thus tended to be eaten by wealthy people from the higher classes, and in the city as opposed to the countryside. Recorded cases of beriberi became numerous from the latter part of the seventeenth century, when population concentrations built up in large cities. For a time beriberi was known as 'the Edo sickness' (Edo is the old name for Tokyo), and was said to be cured by leaving the city for the countryside. Various historical documents provide evidence that unpolished rice had been popularly consumed up to the seventeenth century, and that white rice then became the common staple. Proponents of brown rice make much of the idea that the Japanese of the ancient and medieval ages did not suffer from beriberi because they regularly ate unpolished rice, and many food historians agree.

Yet there is no Asian nation where genuinely unpolished rice is traditionally eaten at daily meals. The genuine brown rice that is currently sold in health food stores, with only the hull removed and the seedcase intact, must be soaked for about 20 hours before it is cooked, and must cook for a long time at a higher energy cost, and hence the issue of economic efficiency would suggest that unpolished rice was not eaten on a daily basis before the time of modern pressure cookers. In addition, the results of experiments show that the body's rate of digestion for unpolished rice is remarkably poor.

With the diffusion of new hulling tools in the latter part of the seventeenth century, it became possible to remove only the hull and leave the bran on the rice, producing what is known today as brown rice. Previously the hull had been removed from the rice grains by placing them in a wooden mortar and pounding them with a long-handled wooden mallet, in much the same way as can be seen today in rural Southeast Asia. That method took off not only the hull but also a portion of the rice bran, and the product was not true unpolished rice. In other words, the same process served both to hull and to polish the rice. White rice from which the bran has been completely removed amounts to about 90 per cent of the original rice quantity, while removing the hull with a mallet yields about 95 per cent. Such was the actual nature of unpolished rice up to the late seventeenth century. Compared to white rice, it was darker coloured and slightly inferior in taste, it prevented beriberi because some of the vitamin B1 remained, and its water absorption rate was high enough to allow it to cook in a short time. It is incorrect to think that the Japanese of old ate the sort of unpolished rice that is sold in health food stores today.

2.4   Sake Brewing

Fermenting agents such as yeast convert sugar into alcohol. Many kinds of fermenting agents are found in nature, and alcoholic drink can be primitively brewed from any material with high sugar content. The simplest brewing methods use liquids with high sugar concentration as the basic ingredients, such as honey for mead, sap for palm wine, and sweet juicy fruits like the grape for fruit wine.

Kettle-shaped earthenware vessels with intricate ornamentation which have been discovered at late Jômon-period sites are believed by many archaeologists to have been used as containers for alcoholic drinks made from fruit. Whether or not there were alcoholic drinks in Jômon times is very difficult to prove. Among the wild plants found at Jômon sites, the candidates for ingredients of fruit wine would be wild grape (*Vitis coignetiae*), paper mulberry (*Broussonetia papyrifeta*), and dockmackie (*Viburnum dilatatum*), yet it is impossible to establish whether they were indeed processed into wine. In European climates where the temperature falls rapidly in the autumn, the sugar that is stored up in the fruit during the summer does not significantly deteriorate before harvest time, but in Japan where the temperature drops slowly in the autumn, the sugar changes into various types of acid and becomes unsuitable for producing fruit wine. Thus the environmental conditions in Japan are unfavourable for making fruit wine.

All of the documentary sources for Japanese history point to the conclusion that Japan had no tradition of brewing with fermented fruit before the latter part of the nineteenth century when winemaking techniques were imported from Europe. Mulberry, persimmon, myrica and apricot wines are all mentioned in various texts, but they were not fermented from the fruits, but rather were liqueurs made by soaking the fruit in sake, brewed from rice, or in *shôchû,* a distilled spirit. In China and Korea as well as Japan, there are no historical documents that refer to the making of authentic fruit wine, sap wine, or mead. This would suggest that in Jômon times alcoholic drinks either did not exist, or at best were of low alcohol and high acidity. The general pattern throughout the world is that brewing techniques develop in agricultural societies but are lacking in hunter-gatherer societies, and this too casts doubt on the existence of alcohol in Jômon society.

To make liquor from grain or other starchy foods, the enzyme action of a substance such as malt or saliva must be used to change starch to sugar. When a very starchy food is chewed, either raw or after heating, diastatic enzymes in the saliva break down the starch into sugar. In this most primitive style of making alcohol from starch, the chewed mash is then spit out together with saliva, put in a container and fermented through the action of wild yeast. Liquor was made from chewed mash in Central and South America, including chicha beer made from maize or manioc, and in East and Southeast Asia. According to Chinese historical chronicles, liquor was made from chewed rice during the seventh century by the people of Primorsky Krai (the Siberian coastal region nearest to Korea and Japan), during the tenth century by minority groups of southern China, and during the Ming era (1368–1644) in Cambodia. Chewed-mash liquor survived up to the early twentieth century in Taiwan, where it was made by aboriginal peoples from their staple millet as well as from rice, and in the nearby mainland Chinese province of Fujian [Katô 1987:14–17].

One of the oldest cultural geographies (*fûdoki*) of Japan, compiled in the early part of the eighth century, tells us that at the southern end of Kyushu: 'Water and rice are prepared at one house in the village, the entire village is notified, and men and women gather there to chew the rice and spit it into a container for making liquor, and then return home. When it starts to smell like alcohol, they gather there again to drink it.' We know that in Taiwan the ingredients were chewed raw and accumulated in a container to which water was added for fermentation, and as water is mentioned in the above account, it is reasonable to guess that the process was similar. In Japan, the custom of producing chewed-mash liquor survived until relatively recently in southern Kyushu and also existed in the Okinawa islands and among the Ainu of Hokkaido. The Ainu and Okinawans prepared chewed-mash liquor for special festival ceremonies, and only women chewed the rice.

Malt is the agent that is typically used in Europe and Africa to convert starch to sugar in making alcohol, as in beer brewing. What is generally used in East Asia is a fermentation starter that is made by placing spores of *kôji* mould on a grain base. The mould propagates throughout the mash in the same way that leavening yeast permeates bread dough, working best when kept at certain temperature and humidity levels as it saccharifies the starch. Techniques of *kôji* fermentation evolved in the damp climate of monsoon Asia where moulds grow easily, and are found from Assam eastward. They are particularly well developed in China, Korea and Japan, where *kôji* is used to brew not only alcohol but also the ubiquitous soy sauce and miso (fermented soy paste), the essential flavourings of Japanese cuisine.

There is a record of a fifth-century immigrant from southern Korea named Susukori who knew how to brew alcohol and presented drink to the Japanese emperor. It has been said that the Japanese made only chewed-mash alcohol until Susukori introduced *kôji* fermentation, but this is an erroneous interpretation. Alcohol was being brewed with *kôji* in China around the time that rice cultivation was brought to Japan. It is only natural to conclude that brewed sake, which stands with the staple of boiled rice as one of the main forms of processed rice, was introduced to our country along with wet rice cultivation, and that *kôji* was used to brew alcohol during the Yayoi period. There are many methods of brewing alcohol with *kôji*, and some 15 types of sake were made at the Japanese court in the tenth century [Katô 1987:96–103]. What Susukori brought from Korea was one variation of the technique of *kôji* brewing.

When *kôji* is grown on a starchy substance, the type of molded mash that is created varies according to the type and form of the base substance, the presence or absence of heat, and the environmental conditions. In China and Korea, *Rhizopus* or *Mucor* spores are placed on the outer surface of loaves of wheat flour that have been soaked in water before being kneaded. In Japan *Aspergillus* mould is cultivated on steamed rice, being placed on the surface of each individual grain.

The technique of cultivating *kôji* mould on wheat is believed to have originated in the second century BCE in northern China and to have spread from there to Korea. Wheat had been introduced from Central Asia to northern China, the centre of ancient East Asian civilization, where at that time it was widely grown and customarily eaten as flour. *Kôji* rice mash does exist in southern China and Korea where, due to the influence of a flour-based diet, the mould is grown on lumps of rice flour. In Japan, where the eating of powdered grains did not catch on, *kôji* mash was and still is made with grains of rice, as will be described below. Although no documentation is available, it is logical to assume that prior to the transmission of *kôji* wheat mash from northern China, the rice-growing areas of China used the same sort of *kôji* mash that is found in Japan, and that this ancient technique was introduced to Japan along with wet rice cultivation.

As the base ingredient for liquor, glutinous rice is often used in China, while in ancient times the staple crop millet was used in northern China, and later after kaoliang was introduced it was adopted throughout China. Chinese liquor is often made from a combination of two or more grains. In Korea drinks with rice as the main ingredient are the mainstream, although they are made with wheat *kôji*. Thus completely pure rice liquor, made from rice using rice *kôji*, is made only in Japan. The sweet potato, introduced to Japan in the seventeenth century, has also been used to make distilled spirits in areas where it is widely cultivated. Previously, with the rare exception of drink made from millet, virtually all Japanese alcoholic beverages were made from rice.

2.5 Fermented Fish and Flavourings

Shiokara is fish, shellfish, squid or (rarely) meat that has been pickled in salt amounting to 25 or 30 per cent of its volume. The mixture is left for a long period in a watertight container, and the salt acts to prevent decay while proteolytic enzymes, which are present in the flesh and organs that make up the bulk of the food, act to produce amino acids. The result is a preserved paste with a distinctive and very salty flavour. It is also slimy and stinky, and some people find it disgusting. Westerners tend to label it 'rotten raw fish' and give it a wide berth, and some Japanese dislike it as well.

Although nowadays the *shiokara* fish paste of Japan is eaten mainly as an hors-d'oeuvre while drinking sake, until recently it was eaten by many as a side dish with rice at daily meals. It can be served with no trouble as it is normally taken straight from the pickling jar to the table, and a tiny bit of the very salty paste goes down very well with a large bowl of rice. Formerly, fish paste was also used as a flavouring in stock for boiling vegetables or as a sauce for dipping.

A type of fish paste was eaten in China from ancient times until the Ming era, but it gradually disappeared as the Chinese shifted away from eating uncooked foods, and now remains only in one area of the Shandong Peninsula. In Korea the same type of paste that is found in Japan is widely eaten and is used as an ingredient for some forms of *kimchee*, the spicy pickles that are the trademark of the national cuisine. A similar paste made from freshwater fish is the main preserved food among the farmers of Indochina. In Indonesia and West Malaysia a shrimp paste is made from planktonic shrimp.

Fish sauce is made by leaving the fish and salt unopened for a longer time, until the flesh and organs decompose completely into a liquid form, which is then strained. The *nuoc mam* of Vietnam is the best known version, and fish sauce is also used in Cambodia, Thailand, Laos, Burma, West Malaysia and the main Philippine island of Luzon, as well as in the maritime districts of Guangdong, Fujian and Shandong provinces in China, and along the southwest Korean coast. In Japan, fish sauce was formerly made in many areas, but today it remains only in Akita and Ishikawa Prefectures as a flavouring for local dishes. Fish sauce also existed in the Roman empire, where it was called *garum* or *liquamen*, and while it was apparently similar to its counterparts in Asia, the two regions probably had no contact and developed them independently.

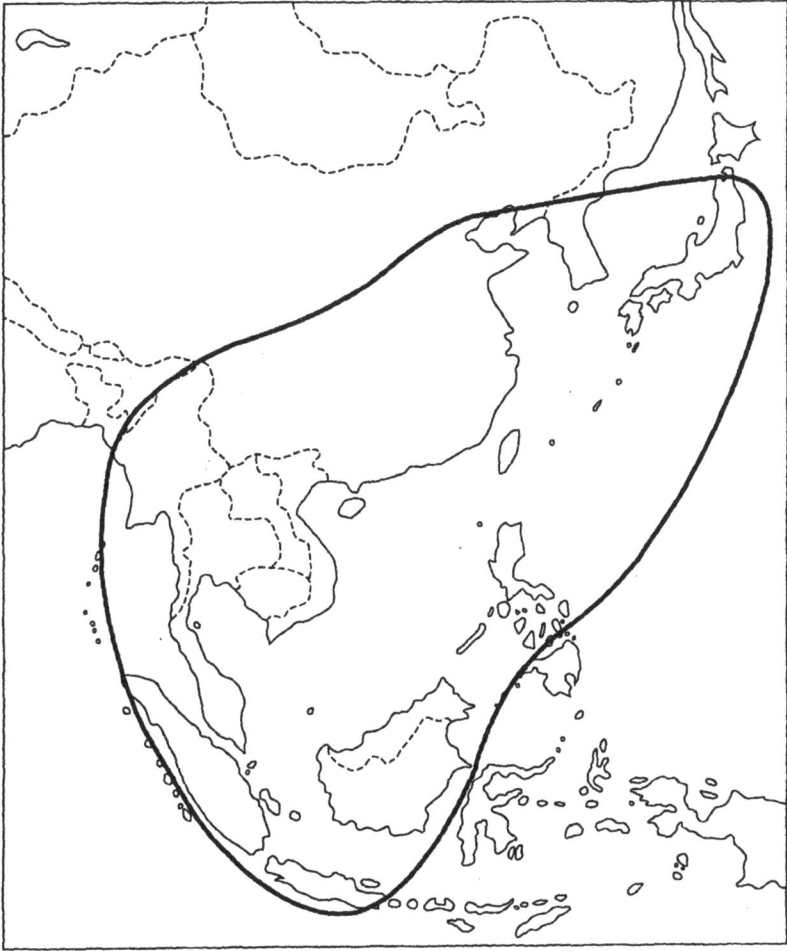

Figure 1   Sphere of fermented fish cuisine

The author has done field research on fish paste and fish sauce in 13 Asian countries and determined that there is a very strong correlation between fish paste production and paddy farming. Specifically, the areas where these flavourings were traditionally made and the traditional areas of wet rice cultivation are virtually coextensive (see Figure 1). Fish paste is found in areas of Southeast Asia where wet rice has been cultivated since the fifteenth century or earlier, but not in areas that have depended mainly on dry-field crops or on hunting and gathering. The island of Hokkaido, where the Ainu inhabitants did not practise wet rice cultivation, lies outside the fish paste range. The presence today of fish paste in a zone of dry-field farming that extends across the northern and eastern parts of the Korean Peninsula and into northeastern China is exceptional, but may be explained by the fact that this zone historically comprised a kingdom where the diets of wet rice and dry-field farming were intermingled.

A rice field can serve as a fish habitat at the same time that rice is being grown, and the custom of cultivating freshwater fish on a small scale in paddies and irrigation channels evolved hand in hand with wet rice cultivation. Rice-field fishery does not require specialist fish breeders, but rather is carried out by the farming family as a supplemental activity to provide enough fish or crustaceans for their own table. Unlike commercial fishery, the self-sufficiency operations carried out on a very small scale by farm families lies outside the market economy, and hence very little statistical data exists. As almost all of the historical information on Japanese fishery pertains to commercial ocean activities, and there are virtually no written records of the diet of agricultural areas, rice-field fishery remains largely unresearched.

During the rainy season in the monsoon zone, as the rivers flood and merge with the paddy fields, river fish swim into the fields and spawn. If traps are set, fish can be caught in great numbers when the waters recede at the end of the rains, and this marks the height of the paddy fishing season. However, since this is the time just after spawning, much of the catch is small fry with too low a proportion of flesh to bones to be worth cooking. The best thing to do with the small fish is to make them into fish paste, and moreover the best thing to do with the huge quantity of fish caught all at once is to preserve them as fish paste so they may last through the year.

In present-day Japan, Korea and the Philippines, fish paste is usually made with marine fish. It seems that this food originated as a way to process freshwater fish from the paddies, but in areas with lengthy coastlines and large marine catches, the procedure was adopted for marine fish. In Indochina and China, where freshwater-fish paste is a staple food, marine fish are often used to make fish sauce, a situation that has arisen through the commercialization of the fish sauce industry and its reliance on large-scale ocean fishery to obtain ingredients in great quantity.

Excavations at the site of Fujiwarakyo, the capital of Japan from 694 to 710, have yielded a set of wooden labels that were attached to goods received from the provinces as tax, and one of them reads 'carp *shiokara*'. This is the oldest record of fish paste in Japan. Since this food can easily be made with only salt, fish and a jar, surely it was eaten in Japan long before it was documented in writing, and from its close association with rice-field fishery, we may infer the possibility that fish paste was eaten as early as the Yayoi period.

In Chinese, the general term for fermented flavourings is *jiàng*. Records from the court of the Zhou dynasty (1050?–256BCE) refer to various types of *jiàng* sauces for use with various dishes, and professional *jiàng* brewers who served the court. Zhou-era *jiàng* was a paste made from meat or fish with alcohol and mould mixed in. In the Han era (206BCE–CE 220), *jiàng* was also made with cooked grain or beans, especially soybeans, as the basic ingredient. Those vegetable substances also generate amino acids when broken down through the action of rice mould. Thus vegetable *jiàng* and fish paste have in common their high content of both salt and flavourful amino acids.

Vegetable *jiàng* fermented with salt and mould eventually came to be used for flavouring in Korea and Japan. The most typical forms are miso and soy sauce, which contain large amounts of glutamic acid. The flavour-enhancing nature of that amino acid is confirmed today by its widespread use in the industrially processed form of monosodium glutamate (MSG). Analyses of fish paste and fish sauce which the author collected from many areas have shown that in glutamic acid content, those fermented fish products are on a par with miso and soy sauce [Mizutani et al. 1987].

Vegetable and fish *jiàng* were simultaneously in wide use in China for a time, then from about the fifth century the vegetable flavourings became the mainstream. In Japan, where soybeans have been found at relatively few Yayoi period sites, it seems likely that vegetable *jiàng* was introduced no earlier than the Kofun period. Later, fermented soy flavourings would become indispensable to the daily diet of the Japanese.

A comparison of the sources of salt in the daily diets of Japan and the United Kingdom is presented in Figure 2. In the UK much salt is supplied by meat and dairy products, foods which traditionally were not eaten in Japan, where instead a substantial amount of salt is taken from preserved fish products. The greatest difference is in the role of crystal salt which, used in cooking or at table, supplies 32 per cent of the average UK intake and just 13 per cent for the Japanese. In contrast, the Japanese on average ingest 45 per cent of their salt from flavourings, with miso and soy sauce accounting for 43 per cent of that amount. The same pattern is found in China and Korea. Fermented soy foods are the leading source of salt in East Asia because, rather than preparing a different, salted sauce for each specific dish as is the rule in Western cooking, these ready-made products which are on hand in every kitchen are used in almost all cooking as a sort of universal flavouring. For Southeast Asia, we may expect that in areas where fish paste is widely used, it serves as the main source for salt in the same way that fermented soy flavourings do in East Asia. In the absence of reliable statistics for the region, the author has observed a family living in the suburbs of Rangoon and calculated the average daily intake of salt from fish paste as 6.3 grams per person. Among contemporary Japanese, the corresponding figure for miso and soy sauce is 5.6 grams. Despite the difference of vegetable versus animal ingredients, in terms of the use of fermented flavourings as agents of salt and taste, the East and Southeast Asian regions have much in common [Ishige and Ruddle 1990:187, 347–350].

Another type of fermented fish is *narezushi*, which is made by packing salted fish and boiled rice in a sealed jar for a long period

Japan (1980)

13 grams/day

Flavourings 45%

Seasonings 2

Soya sauce 27

Miso 16

Cooking salt / table salt 13

Other foods 16

Pickles 12

Foods 42

Wheat products 7

Marine products 7

Source: Ministry of Health and Welfare

United Kingdom (1978)

9.8 grams/day

Vegetable products 5%

Marine products 1

Cheese, cream, fats 11

Cooking salt / table salt 32

Milk 5

Meat, eggs 19

Grain products 27

Source: Bull and Buss

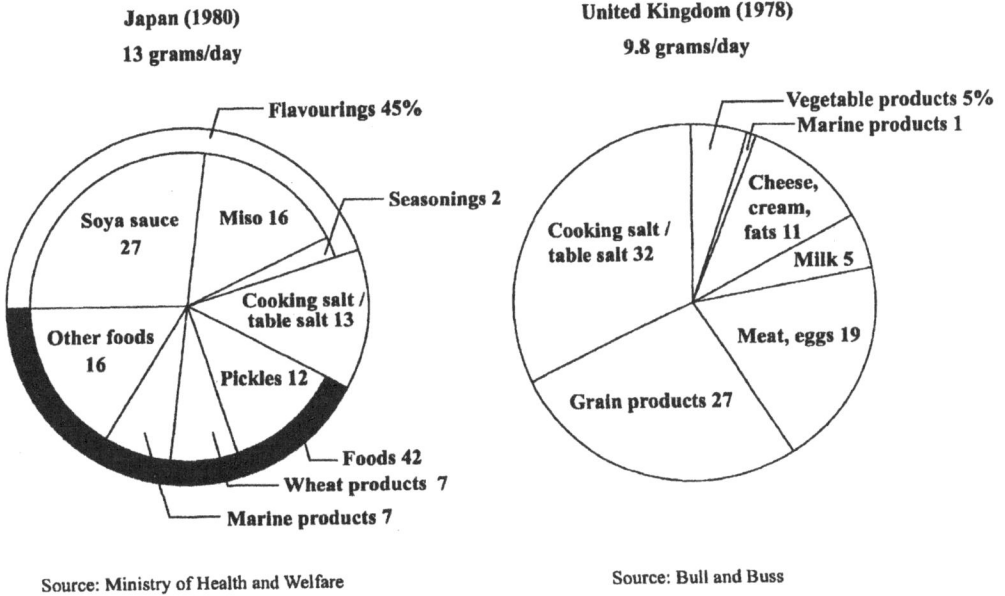

Figure 2   Sources of salt in the diets of Japan and the UK

which forms as the rice ferments. Unlike *shiokara* in which the fish parts are decomposed to a paste, in *narezushi* the fish can be kept whole for a year or more. The pasty remains of the rice are discarded and the fish, which has an odour comparable to a pungent cheese, is sliced and eaten without cooking, as a savoury food rather than a flavouring. *Narezushi* is believed to have been eaten in the past throughout Japan, except Hokkaido and the Ryukyus, but today it is found only in the district around Lake Biwa.

The word 'sushi' originally referred to that long-fermented type of fish. From the latter part of the fifteenth century, variations appeared which were prepared in shorter periods, and to distinguish the original style it came to be known as *narezushi* ('matured sushi'). The sushi of today is not a preserved food at all, for it can be promptly prepared by placing a slice of raw fish on top of a bite-sized portion of boiled, vinegared rice. Nonetheless, the vinegar that is always added to sushi rice provides an acidic tinge, and although lactic and acetic acids impart somewhat different tastes, some vestige of the original food is retained. Indeed, the word 'sushi' is said to derive from a similar-sounding archaic form of the word for acidity or tartness.

The salted, fermented fish known in Japan as *narezushi* is thought to have originated in ancient times in the Mekong River basin of Indochina and thence to have been transmitted to China, from where it was introduced to Japan [Ishige 1993]. This method of preserving fish is apparently also related to rice-field fishery, as the range in which it is found in Southeast Asia coincides closely with the traditional wet rice farming zones. Whole fermented fish was eaten in China from Han through Ming times, but as the Han Chinese moved away from eating uncooked fish, it disappeared along with fish sauce from the mainstream diet, and is found today only among hill tribes in the southwest.

From various Japanese records dating as far back as the early eighth century, it is known that up to the tenth century *narezushi* was made much more often with freshwater fish than with marine fish. It seems fair to conclude that *narezushi* carries rather strong traces of rice-field fishery (See Figure 3).

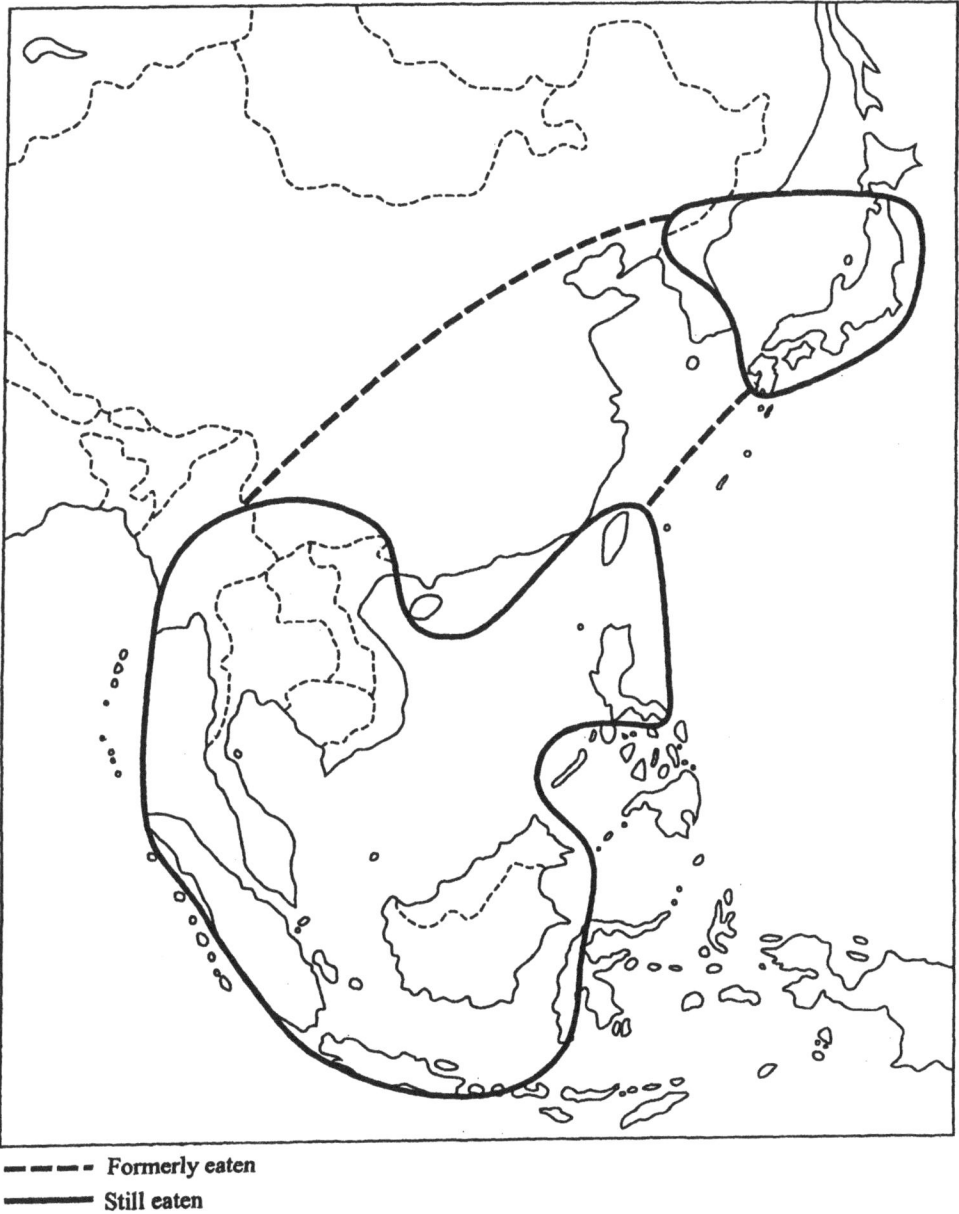

- - - - - Formerly eaten
————— Still eaten

Figure 3   Sphere of *narezushi* in the nineteenth century.
(Dotted lines mark the area where it is presumed to have existed
previously.)

CHAPTER 3

THE FORMATIVE PERIOD OF JAPANESE DIETARY CULTURE

3.1 Historical Setting

While earlier, prehistoric periods must be studied mainly through archaeological materials, the later Kofun period is the dawn of Japan's historical epoch. Records written within the country provide detailed knowledge about the Japanese from the latter part of the sixth century, near the beginning of the ancient age. Historians have divided Japanese history into four great ages: ancient, medieval, early modern and modern (see Table 1, page 4).

The ancient age was marked by a centralized system of national government controlled by the emperor and the aristocracy who comprised the imperial court. From the late seventh century the court governed on the basis of a comprehensive legal code derived from a Chinese model. The historical part of the Ancient Age spans the Asuka and Hakuhô periods (593–710) when the court was moved to a new location in the Yamato Basin (now Nara Prefecture) by each empress or emperor; the Nara period (710–94) when the capital was fixed at the city now called Nara; and the Heian period (794–1192) named for the capital at Heiankyo (later Kyoto).

In the medieval age the nobility were displaced from power by the new class of samurai or provincial warriors, and the regional military leaders built up landholdings and became daimyo (feudal

45

lords). At the apex of the decentralized polity was the shogun, the head of the national military government. The medieval shogunates were headquartered first at Kamakura (in modern Kanagawa Prefecture near Tokyo) and later in the Muromachi district of Kyoto. The medieval age is hence divided into the Kamakura period (1192–1336) and the Muromachi period (1392–1568). During the intervening period of the Northern and Southern Courts (1336–92), a conflict between rival lines of the imperial family generated military disturbances. The medieval emperors were no more than nominal sovereigns, for the imperial court functioned only as the venue of official ceremonies while actual power was wielded by the shogun and local lords.

In this history of dietary culture, we shall largely ignore that conventional periodization which is based on political structures, and instead treat the first millennium of historical Japan – from the sixth century until the end of the fifteenth century – as a single epoch. This was the 'Formative Period' when Japan absorbed aspects of Chinese civilization relating to dietary culture and transformed them into indigenous patterns that became the basis of Japan's own distinctive dietary culture. If we were to venture to subdivide this basic period of Japanese dietary culture, a line could be drawn after the start of the tenth century to distinguish an early and a later phase. Until the tenth century Japan borrowed foods and eating habits from China and Korea and concentrated on imitating them. Then, during the next few centuries, the foreign influences were assimilated and reorganized according to the preferences and native customs of the Japanese to form the national diet and cuisine of Japan which have been handed down to the present.

Up to the time of contact with the West in the sixteenth century, the civilization that furnished the model for Japan was that of China. The same was true for other countries in the vicinity, notably Korea and Vietnam, but they are contiguous with China and were thus able easily to conduct interchange with the centre of civilization, and moreover had historical experience of direct subjugation by China. Ancient Japan, which was geographically isolated by seas and never brought under the suzerainty of a Chinese emperor (or any foreign power), accepted Chinese civilization through a different historical process. Because of its distance from the centre, in most cases the influences that reached Japan came not directly from China but indirectly through intermediary nations, usually through Korea. Also, since the Japanese never came under direct Chinese rule, they were not forcibly compelled to accept Chinese civilization, and hence did not adopt it in a wholesale fashion but rather were able to pick and choose among the constituent elements of the civilization according to their own preferences. In other words, the Japanese could select elements of the Chinese cultural vocabulary out of context and situate them within their own native context. Thus, even as Japan borrowed heavily from Chinese civilization, a 'Japanliness' developed because the borrowings were removed from Chinese context.

Broadly speaking, during the Kofun period civilization came to Japan from Korea. For much of that period the Korean Peninsula was divided into the competing kingdoms of Paekche, Silla and Koguryo. During the fifth century the Japanese court concluded an alliance with Paekche and provided military assistance, and in the sixth century a Japanese military colony was established on the southern part of the peninsula. Silla, in alliance with Tang China, defeated the other two kingdoms and brought the whole peninsula under unified control in the middle of the seventh century. Japan had sent a substantial force to aid Paekche, and after sharing in the crushing defeat at the hands of Silla and China, withdrew from the peninsula in 663. Those circumstances brought the Korean Peninsula entirely under the influence of Chinese civilization. To Japan, where immigrants were already flourishing on the basis of technological leadership, came a new wave of refugees from defeated Paekche and Koguryo bearing additional elements of continental civilization. Buddhism (associated with the taboo on meat, see Section 3.2) was one of the cultural influences that reached Japan via Korea during the Kofun period. Another was *sue* ware, the Japanese name for a type of unglazed grey earthenware fired stone-hard at high temperatures, which was developed in Korea from earlier Chinese techniques. *Sue* ware was manufactured in Japan from the mid-fifth century for use in cooking and eating, and later gave birth to other wares that were widely used in medieval times.

THE FORMATIVE PERIOD

From the end of the sixth century, Japan pursued the policy of obtaining Chinese civilization directly from the source. China was reunified under the Sui dynasty in 581, ending nearly four centuries of fragmentation that followed the collapse of the Han dynasty. The succeeding Tang dynasty (618–907) established an enormous empire, larger than any previous Chinese state, and China became the centre of the most advanced civilization of the contemporary world. Nearby nations moved eagerly to 'modernize' by adopting Tang institutions and culture, and Japan was no exception. The first of 17 Japanese embassies to Sui and Tang China was dispatched in 600, and the last left for the Chinese capital in 834. Part of the purpose of those missions was to keep political relations with China on a favourable footing, but from the Japanese viewpoint their significance was primarily cultural and their most vital tasks were to promote trade and the study of Chinese civilization. Each mission was made up of between 250 and 500 persons, including many scholars and monks who would reside for some years in China. They undertook thorough studies of government and administration, law, science, literature, medicine and pharmacology, art, Buddhism and technology and amassed collections of documents before returning to Japan, thereby fulfilling the diplomatic goal of acquiring civilization.

As it was the state which undertook the import of civilization, the fruits were enjoyed first at court and in Buddhist monasteries. At banquets of the court nobility, such delicacies as savoury 'Chinese cakes' (tôgashi) and dairy products were served, the tables were set with luxurious glass and metal ware produced in Japan by using Tang models and techniques, and chopsticks and spoons were used. Buddhism was the state religion during the Nara period, and monks and priests received state subsidies to study Buddhist doctrine, speeding the adoption of Chinese dietary culture in the monasteries. The earliest date when tea is known to have been drunk in Japan is 815, when it was served to the emperor during a visit to the Sôfukuji temple near Lake Biwa, by a prelate named Eichû. He had studied in China for 30 years during the period when tea drinking achieved its initial popularity there.

In 894 an embassy to Tang China was cancelled shortly before it was scheduled to depart, and the government decreed that no further official missions would be sent. Among the reasons were the decline of Tang power and a series of internal disturbances in China, and the risks of the sea journey (previous missions had been savaged by typhoons). Also, Chinese merchants had by that time begun moving to Japan where they were assisted by huge investments of state funds, making continuation of official contact with the mainland less vital.

So began the era when Japanese culture moved beyond imitating China and began to display originality. As an example that may elucidate that process of cultural development, let us turn briefly to the area of writing. Just as Latin was long used for official records throughout western Europe, in the orbit of Chinese civilization it was the Chinese writing system, specifically classical Chinese prose, that was regarded as the civilized and expected form for official records. In Korea, although the indigenous Hangul alphabet was devised in 1443, it was long scorned as writing for the unlettered masses, and did not come into general use until the twentieth century. Traditional Korean literature meanwhile took the forms of classical Chinese poetry and prose, which inevitably tended to reflect the Chinese concepts that underlie the ideographs, and were ill–suited to portraying the subtleties of a vernacular which sprang from a different linguistic family. Furthermore, full literacy was limited to the intellectuals who could read thousands of Chinese characters. In Vietnam, the Chu Nôm characters devised in the early fourteenth century for writing Vietnamese are a modified form of Chinese script which never came into universal use for writing, and classical Chinese remained in official use until the beginning of the twentieth century. The general population of Vietnam could not read and write their own language until the diffusion in the twentieth century of an adaptation of the Latin alphabet, devised by a Western missionary.

In Japan's case, while records were kept in classical Chinese, experiments in transcribing the native tongue began early on. In Chinese, each character has a fixed pronunciation, and moreover is an ideograph with a fixed meaning. Yet the *Man'yôshû*, an eighth-century collection of 4,500 poems by Japanese ranging from nobles to peasants, consists entirely of Chinese characters which were used only as phonetic symbols to transcribe Japanese pronunciation, with no reference to the Chinese meanings. Later, a proper Japanese syllabary (kana) was devised by simplifying the forms of certain Chinese characters, enabling free expression in prose of the vernacular culture. Official documents and some other writings were made only with Chinese characters (used for their meanings) up to early modern times. A mixture of kana with characters eventually became the popular style, and is now the rule for modern Japanese. Most of the ideographic characters that are interspersed among the phonetic kana syllables are based on things or concepts of Chinese origin. Yet their readings have been altered from the Chinese pronunciations, often beyond all recognition, to match the phonemic structure of Japanese, thereby forming a Japanese vocabulary that corresponds to Chinese ideographs. Thus in modern writing we find that a selection of ideographs which the Japanese have taken from within the Chinese language, and which have been modified so as to be Japanese, lie within a context of the Japanese language as expressed in kana.

Much of the early poetry in Japan was written by educated intellectuals in classical Chinese. The spread of kana script led to a new genre of verse in the vernacular, called *waka*. Apart from being accessible to the common people, *waka* also supplanted Chinese poetry to become the favourite literary pastime of the refined nobility of the Heian court. As a legacy of that era, the imperial family still cultivate the art of *waka*, and one of the court events at the New Year is a nationwide *waka* contest on a theme set by the emperor. In prose, kana script gave rise to a narrative literature that began in the later ninth century and flourished for several centuries thereafter. One example is *The Tale of Genji*, the oldest novel in the world, written at the beginning of the eleventh century.

The developments in literature are symbolic of the trend throughout Japanese culture from the tenth century, of moving beyond imitation of China and forming original Japanese conventions. Trade with China and the Korean Peninsula continued, but was no longer associated with the impulse to run Japan on the basis of models taken from outside civilizations. Until the nineteenth century, when a movement emerged to take Western civilization as the model for reorganizing and modernizing the country, Japan operated under systems that were generated through the historical process within its borders.

During the late tenth and early eleventh centuries the court-centred culture of the Heian nobility was in its golden age at the capital, but in the countryside there were already signs of the martial order of the medieval age. Displaying more enthusiasm for the elaborate court culture than for affairs of state, the nobility lost the capacity to govern the provinces and authority began to pass into the hands of local samurai. The men who guarded the landed estates of the nobility banded together, large warrior groups developed and intervened in the political affairs of the court, and finally in 1192 a national military government was established at Kamakura. That was the end of the system of centralized government under the imperial court which had been patterned after a Chinese model.

In most countries during premodern times it was the court that fostered the development of refined cooking and dining etiquette, and ancient Japan was no exception. Produce sent as tax from all areas of the country was collected at the court and prepared by a corps of professional cooks, and there were also imperial offices in charge of brewing various types of sake. The Heian nobility, who held government posts commensurate with their ranks, gathered frequently for court banquets which were conducted as ceremonial events, often to confer various levels of official and social status. Thus eating and drinking was actually a political affair at the court during its heyday. After the warrior class took power, however, the court was in straitened circumstances and lost its role as the centre of cuisine. Thereafter, the emphasis in court meals was on ceremonial and official aspects, and nutritional substance and flavour became irrelevant. In medieval and modern times the imperial court has had virtually no influence on the dining habits of the Japanese.

Most of the samurai who rose to power were men of peasant origins who themselves operated estates and were involved in agricultural production. They tended to subscribe to an ethic of austerity, holding self-sufficiency in high regard, preferring meals that were simple and substantial, and taking pride in the avoidance of refinement, ceremony and luxury. The samurai retained that character through the Edo period as the steadfast upholders of stoicism in Japanese society, in counterpoint to the epicureanism practised by the premodern nobility and later by wealthy merchants. Under samurai rule, which continued until the mid-nineteenth century, their austere lifestyle was the moral standard for public life.

A trend in Japanese culture which became pronounced at the end of the Heian period and continued during medieval times was the fusion of Chinese-style civilization as adopted by the upper class and the traditional folk culture of the masses. Traditions based on the refined fashions of the Heian court survive today, not in their original forms but with changes and Japanization, including the elimination of elements that did not suit the lives of the common people. In clothing, for example, while the court adopted a decorative dress style known as 'Chinese clothing', the clothes of the common people were plain, being functionally designed for labour. Over time these two different lines of clothing influenced each other and the changes led, by the end of the medieval age, to the prototype of the kimono worn in modern Japan. A similar process of change occurred in the area of food, to the specifics of which we now return.

3.2   The Taboo on Meat Eating

One of the basic precepts that Gautama, the founder of Buddhism, taught his followers was to refrain from killing animals. The orthodox Buddhist might therefore be expected to live as a complete vegetarian, eating neither meat nor fish. In actuality, however, the number of Buddhists who eliminate all forms of animal protein from their diet has always been very small. Among the Theravada Buddhists of Southeast Asia, lay people eat fish and meat freely and even professional monks and nuns are permitted to consume flesh as long as the animal is not killed by them, killed within their sight, or known to have been killed on their account. With the Mahayana Buddhists of China, Korea and Japan the principle is more strictly maintained as a total prohibition of fish and meat, but it is only the clergy who obey it.

A sixth-century Chinese emperor decreed that bonzes who disobeyed the Buddhist prohibition of meat were to be executed, from which we may infer that at the time there were some who ate meat. Thereafter the clergy did not eat meat or fish, but lay people continued to consume them as part of their daily meals. In China today there are devout Buddhists who follow a vegetarian diet only on certain days, especially on the first and fifteenth days of the month and on anniversaries of the deaths of close relatives.

On the Korean Peninsula in the sixth century the kings of Silla and Paekche issued Buddhist-inspired decrees against the killing of animals, but meat eating was not strictly prohibited. Under the unified Silla dynasty (676–918) killing was prohibited during the animal breeding season in the spring and summer, and the killing and eating of animals was prohibited on six days of every month. When Buddhism reached its zenith on the peninsula under the Koryo dynasty (918–1392), the general populace tended to avoid meat or fish, and slaughtering was not skillfully performed. A member of a Chinese delegation that visited Korea in 1123 recorded the following observations on the slaughter of a sheep or pig: 'The four legs are tied together and it is laid on the fire, and if it comes back to life it is beaten with a sharp-cornered pole until dead, then the stomach and entrails are ripped open and the excreta washed away. Meat thus cooked has a stink and is quite inedible.'

During the thirteenth century Korea was invaded by the Mongols and made a part of their Yuan empire, and the occupation forces established stock farms and began rearing horses and cattle in great numbers. Local people took up butchery, using mallets for slaughter in the manner of the Mongols, and later the profession they founded was treated as an outcast group. Under Mongol rule, meat cooking was resurrected in Korea and recipes used by the Mongols and the Mongol-dominated Chinese were introduced. This is thought to be the origin of the Korean barbecue that is popular today in Japan [Lee 1980:217–219].

The first prohibition of meat eating in Japan was promulgated by Emperor Temmu in 675. The main provisions of his law were an outright ban on hunting and fishing traps designed to catch indiscriminately, and prohibition during the fourth through ninth months of the eating of beef, horse, dog, monkey and chicken as well as the use of certain fishing traps, all on pain of execution. That decree has usually been interpreted as having sprung from the Buddhist precept against the taking of life. Yet it did not ban the eating of deer or wild boar, the most important animals in the Japanese diet at the time. The fact that the ban was limited in scope to certain animals and seasons suggests that it reflected something other than Buddhist morality [Harada 1985:503–508].

Dog meat was commonly eaten in Southeast Asia, Oceania, China and Korea. In those regions, where neither stock breeding nor hunting developed, people likewise developed no particular fondness for dogs, and are apt to view the propensity of Westerners to treat sheepdogs or hunting dogs as constant companions as a sort of fetishism. The inclusion of dogs in the imperial decree confirms that they were domesticated in Japan, but they were used mainly for hunting and guarding and were not raised for food.

Monkey was eaten in Japan from the Jômon period but was not widely hunted. Its resemblance to humans gave the monkey a special position in Japanese folk customs, and in some areas it was regarded as a messenger of the deities. In later times hunters avoided killing monkeys. When monkey meat was eaten it was taken not merely as food, but in the belief that it had medicinal effect for curing illness. In that light it is hard to believe that monkey meat was a popular foodstuff even at the time of the decree in the seventh century.

Chickens were brought to Japan in the Yayoi period. In the legends of ancient times they held an important place as messengers of the deities. They were often considered taboo as food, and we may therefore suppose that they were not raised as poultry. The Japanese have a long tradition of viewing chickens as pets with a sacred nature, and of appreciating cocks for their dawn crowing and as fighting birds.

Cattle and horses were introduced and bred domestically during the Yayoi period, but as late as the seventh century they were relatively rare and precious animals. In battles of that time horses were ridden only by commanding officers, who led not cavalry but infantry forces. Most of the peasantry did not possess cattle or hitch them to ploughs, but farmed entirely with human labour.

Agricultural rituals in ancient Japan did include the sacrifice and eating of a cow or horse on the day that cultivation began in the paddies. Such rituals were introduced from China or Korea.

Meanwhile, there are records of other ancient traditions which claim that agricultural rituals involving meat eating would lead to crop damage by drought or insects. There are very few records of ritual sacrifice of animals in Japan from the Yayoi period on. The custom was introduced by immigrant groups from China and Korea and was practised for a time during the ancient age, but is entirely unknown in the Shinto ceremonies of later times. The tension between the foreign rituals and the Japanese custom of not performing animal sacrifice is illustrated by the following. A decree issued in 642 prohibited the sacrifice of cattle or horses during rain-prayer ceremonies, and during a famine in 706, instead of sacrificing a living cow, a 'cow' made of earth was used in a ritual prayer for an abundant harvest.

In light of the above, it is possible to view the prohibition decree of 675 as a policy which was prompted by the spread of what had once been a purely ritual practice of eating cattle and horse meat into the sphere of private enjoyment among the peasantry; and which was motivated by fear of a decline in the already sparse number of animals. As noted above, the dogs, monkeys and chickens which were also protected by the ban were animals with which the Japanese had special relationships or which probably would not have been killed in great numbers even without express protection. The main purposes of the ban were to prohibit the eating of beef and horse meat and protect the livestock population, as well as to prevent drought, insect damage and famine. Moreover, it was limited to the spring and summer months which constitute the paddy farming season. The additional provisions against indiscriminate trapping of animals and fish may be interpreted as reflecting the Buddhist principle of preventing needless bloodshed.

In the Nara period (710–794) a system of government based on Buddhist ideology was instituted, and the state built and administered temples and monasteries throughout the country. The operative political conception was that of a union of church and state, through which the diffusion of the Buddhist spirit of compassion was equivalent to the nationwide extension of the benevolence of the sovereign. Emperors and empresses in this period frequently issued decrees banning all killing of animals. In a proclamation that appears to have been connected with celebrations of the completion of the Great Buddha of Nara (even today the largest bronze Buddha image in the world) as the centrepiece of the national network of temples and monasteries, Empress Kôken ordered that no animal was to be killed anywhere in Japan throughout the year 752, and promised adequate rice supplies to support the fisherfolk whose livelihoods were to be suspended.

Numerous other decrees prohibiting the killing of animals were issued up to the twelfth century, underscoring the great difficulty of convincing people to forget the taste of meat. A compendium of laws from 833 records that monks or nuns who ate meat, or violated the Buddhist precept against drinking alcohol, or ate one of five odoriferous vegetables (garlic and green onions) forbidden for the clergy were to be punished with 30 days of hard labour, although a monk or nun was allowed to eat meat for the treatment of illness for a period of days specified by a supervisor. Thus we learn that meat was eaten on the quiet in temples and monasteries during the ninth century. By the tenth century the eating of animal flesh was widely regarded as a sin among the Buddhist clergy, the nobility and city dwellers. Later, as Buddhism penetrated the rural population, the Buddhist concept of the transmigration of souls and the taboo on mammal meat became linked, and the belief spread that a person who ate the flesh of a four-legged animal would after death be reincarnated as a four-legged animal.

According to the *Engi shiki*, a collection of government regulations completed in 927, any government official or other member of the nobility who ate animal flesh was deemed for the next three days to be unclean and thereby disqualified from participating in the Shinto observances held at the imperial court. This shows that there were still some who ate meat among the upper class, and also indicates that meat eating had come to be seen as taboo in the Shinto religion. In later times the Shinto prohibition was strengthened. Regulations set out in 1318 for the Ise Shrine, the most important of all Shinto shrines and the place where the guardian deities of the imperial family are worshipped, stipulated that the eating of wild boar or deer flesh would bring on a hundred-day period of defilement during which it was forbidden to visit the shrine.

In Shinto, much importance is attached to the state of defilement or ritual impurity (*kegare*), which is most acute for matters concerning death or bloodshed. Formerly, when a close relative died, a person would become contaminated by the defilement of death, and would have to remain isolated from social activities for a certain period in order to avoid passing the defilement on to others. The defilement of blood obligated one to avoid contaminating the sanctity of the family hearth. Since childbirth and menstruation involve bleeding, women were isolated at those times. In some districts it remained customary as late as the twentieth century for a woman to stay in a different building from her family and to prepare her meals on a different hearth during lying-in or menstruation. Avoidance of the discharge of blood explains the absence of sacrifice in Shinto rituals. Along with the sanctity of the hearth, the defilement associated with blood may well have been the reason for placing meat eating in the category of ritual impurity. The Buddhist injunction against killing any living creature, strictly applied, prohibits the killing or eating of fish and shellfish, whereas in Shinto there is no mention of the blood of marine animals, and both fish and shellfish are regarded so highly as to be worthy for votive offerings.

With not only Buddhism but also the indigenous Shinto religion discouraging them from eating meat, a substantial portion of the Japanese came to avoid it. Yet in Buddhism generally it was only the clergy who actually were forbidden to eat any living creature. In Jôdo Shinshû, a sect which was founded in the thirteenth century on the basis of indigenous Japanese Buddhist ideas, the clergy are permitted to eat seafood and also to marry. Excepting professional hunters, the people generally did not eat the flesh of mammals, but neither fowl (other than chicken) nor fish were particularly avoided, except during certain periods of Buddhist observance or on the annual or monthly death day of a close relative. Yet game fowl were eaten only on rare occasions, and dairy products were not a customary part of the diet (as explained below), leaving seafood as virtually the only source of animal protein. Consequently, fish is the traditional festive dish for the Japanese and occupies the place of honour in Japanese cuisine.

THE FORMATIVE PERIOD

As for mammals, the largest of the class, the whale, has traditionally been thought to be a fish and hence unquestionably a foodstuff. The samurai who rose swiftly to power, especially in eastern Japan, often held military drills cum grand hunts in which they caught and ate deer and wild boar. The flesh of mammals was also eaten as a means for strengthening a delicate constitution. Eating meat for the purpose of curing an illness, known as 'medicine eating' (*kusurigui*), was permitted, and was sometimes used as an excuse for indulgence by healthy people who simply liked meat.

Along with the general avoidance of eating mammal flesh, people engaged in the slaughter and skinning of animals or the manufacture of leather products came to suffer social discrimination. As their work involved dismembering cattle, horses and deer and they also ate the flesh, their jobs were repulsive under the Buddhist precept of taking no life, while from the Shinto viewpoint they were heavily defiled. When the meat taboo spread among the common people during the Kamakura period (1192–1336), systematic discrimination began against those tradespeople as a group and they were isolated from society. As discrimination intensified in later times they became a caste, and traces of this social problem have persisted in Japan up to the present.

3.3   The Lack of Dairy Industry

The spread of Buddhist and Shinto ideology alone is insufficient to explain how meat could disappear from the tables of the general populace. The key factor in the background is the fact that traditional Japanese agriculture did not include the systematic raising of livestock for meat and milk.

In central China, Korea and Southeast Asia, cattle and horses were bred domestically at the rate of only one or a few per household. Large herds of livestock were kept in Central Asia, where dairying held strong cultural importance. In Southeast Asia, south and east of the Arakan Yoma Mountains that divide Burma from Bangladesh, the custom was entirely lacking (See Figure 4). In China, generally speaking, milking was done in regions north of the Great Wall but not to the south. Indeed, the Great Wall was

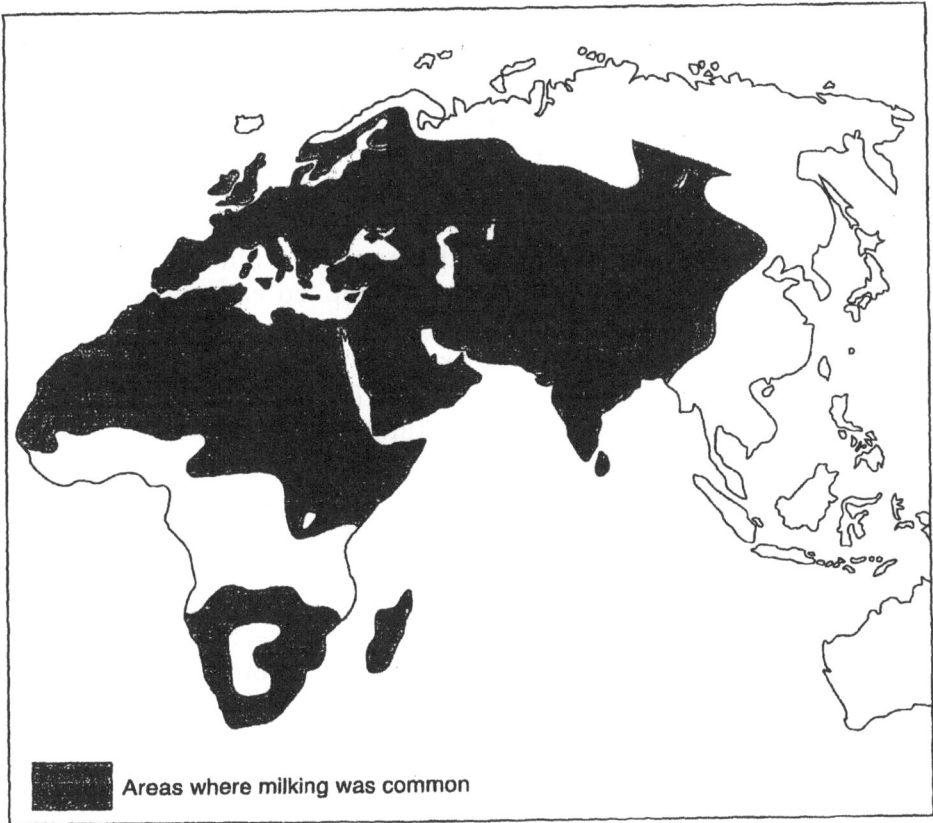

Figure 4   Areas where milking was common in the fifteenth century

originally built for the purpose of preventing the nomadic groups whose economic base was livestock breeding from penetrating southward into the territory of the agricultural Han. Milk was utilized in certain areas south of the Great Wall, by the Tibetans to the southwest of China and by non-Han minorities in the Chinese heartland.

The domestic animals raised for food in ancient China were mostly pigs and chickens. Sheep, kept in herds, were also raised in the north for meat rather than for milk, while ducks were kept in the south. It was the farmers who undertook the raising of stock animals or fowl. The rice-based agricultural complex that was transmitted to Japan during the Yayoi period did include pigs and chickens, but not sheep or ducks. Yet chickens, as stated above, were not commonly eaten, and archaeological discoveries of pigs are few, especially in comparison to the numerous finds of wild boar. The *Nihon shoki* historical chronicle, compiled early in the eighth century, informs us that from the fifth century until that time there were specialized groups of pig breeders attached to the imperial court. Yet it seems that few farmers were engaged in pig breeding.

A densely populated agricultural society in which meat is generally eaten on a daily basis requires a social system for the production of domestic stock and fowl. The agricultural society of ancient Japan, where such a system was not established, relied almost exclusively on hunting as the source for meat. During that period the population of Japan grew continuously, and the consequent expansion of cultivated lands drove wild game from the plains, limiting their range to the forest lands of the mountains. Thus the people grew accustomed to a diet in which meat was not consumed on a daily basis. This background situation may be the reason why the religious prohibition of meat eating could catch on.

Milking was not generally practised in East Asia and dairy products played an extremely small role in the daily diet, but dairying was nevertheless not entirely unknown. A sixth-century treatise on agriculture and food processing techniques written for the Han people of what is now Shandong province (*Qi min yao shu*) describes methods for producing five types of dairy products. Dairy products were consumed as exceedingly rare luxury or medicinal items by the Han upper class until the Ming dynasty (1368–1644).

In a Korean history written during the Three Kingdoms period (the Kofun period in Japan), there is a legend of a dragon that took the form of a cowherd and consecrated dairy products to a monarch. Milk in Korea was taken mainly as medicine, either in a condensed curdled form (known in Japan as *so*) or boiled with rice as a gruel [Lee 1990:48–54].

The oldest record of milk in Japan is connected with Zenna, a person of Chinese descent who in the mid-eighth century came to Japan from the Korean Peninsula, presented milk to the empress, and became a medical officer of the court with the title Yamato no Kusuri no Omi. The first mention of a processed dairy product is a record of *so* being prepared on imperial order in 700. In order to supply that drink to the court, during the eighth century the Palace Medical Office recruited farmers to raise milk cows. The number of cattle raised for milk was nonetheless quite small; calculations based on data in the *Engi shiki* suggest that in the early tenth century no more than 1,500 cattle were bred for *so* production in all Japan, an average of one animal for about 4,000 persons. By comparison, in 1975 there was one milk cow per 50 persons in Japan, and substantial amounts of dairy products were imported as well. This provides further evidence that dairy products were largely absent from the diet of the ancient Japanese [Adachi 1980:197–234].

So was the only dairy product in use in ancient Japan. The *Engi shiki* records that, 'So is made by boiling milk down to one-tenth the volume'. It is also known that *so* was transported in baskets, indicating that it had a solid form. Since the solid content of milk is at least 12 per cent, simply boiling off the water content of milk will yield a residue in excess of one-tenth the original volume. There are various theories as to the actual nature of *so*. The most plausible, proposed by Wani, is that *so* was the skin formed on the surface of milk kept at a gentle boil, and that it was accumulated by repeated skimming. The identical process is used today in Mongolia to make *ulm*. Although *so* was not churned in Japan, the sixth-century *Qi min yao shu* uses the Chinese version of the same word (*sû*) to describe a type of butter obtained by churning milk skin with boiling water [Wani 1987:31–4].

Milk and *so* were consumed only by the court nobility, an extremely tiny segment of the population, and after the collapse of the court culture in the twelfth century, *so* disappeared as a foodstuff. Not until the seventeenth century was the high nutritional value of dairy products rediscovered in Japan, by scholars reading Dutch scientific and medical treatises. In 1727 the shogun imported three milk cows, which were probably of Occidental origin, through Dutch traders, and a herd was bred from them at a ranch on the shogunal lands. Milk from that herd was mixed with sugar and gently boiled while being stirred to obtain a solid food called *hakugyûraku* ('white butter') which was produced in very small quantities and consumed by the shogun and his closest retainers as a nutritional health tonic. Milk and dairy products were not part of the daily diet of the general population of Japan until the twentieth century.

3.4 Annual Observances and Rites of Passage

Ethnologists distinguish two sorts of time in the life of a traditional Japanese community: ordinary periods of everyday activity (*ke*) and extraordinary sacred days (*hare*) which have special significance for the community or certain individuals. *Hare* brought on a different frame of mind which was reflected in many ways. Work was suspended to allow participation in a ceremony or festival, special clothes were worn, and special treats were eaten, for the meals on *hare* occasions included dishes which were too labour-intensive or expensive to be served routinely.

   Mochi, or cakes of pounded glutinous rice, is the most typical of the foods eaten on *hare* days. *Mochi* is characteristically associated with sacred occasions, and moreover, due to the time and considerable labour involved in its preparation, it could be made only on extraordinary days. The latter was also true for noodles and tofu, which in former times were customarily eaten on festive days in most farming villages. Before the appearance of waterwheels and animal-powered mills, villagers ground flour by hand with millstones. The first step in cooking noodles was grinding wheat or buckwheat, and the making of tofu began with grinding soybeans. Unlike city dwellers, who could buy noodles or tofu from tradespeople who made and sold them for a living, villagers lived in a self-sufficiency economy and hence could have them only on special occasions.

Even impoverished peasants, whose rice pots were usually topped up by mixing in barley or millet before boiling, ate unadulterated white rice on festival days. Those whose rice was normally served only with side dishes of vegetables, or at best dried fish, would splurge on fresh fish. The exceptions were Buddhist-related observances, during which fish eating was prohibited. To mark the end of that taboo and the return to the normal diet, a point was made of serving a meal that included fish.

It was mandatory for portions at a festive meal to be so generous that they could not be finished, and that usually applied to sake as well. Sake brewed in homes was intended mainly for drinking on festival days. Sake drinking during the extraordinary *hare* interval was expected to be done to the point of intoxication and forgetting oneself, so as to enter further into an extraordinary psychological state. At the least, etiquette demanded that one feign drunkenness. Prior to the modern era, the routine life of the Japanese was punctuated each year by 20 to 30 days of *hare* (schedules differed according to social class, occupation and region).

One measure of the range of a civilization is the spread of a common calendar. Europe adopted the Gregorian calendar, and North Africa and West Asia adopted the Islamic calendar, so that the same religious holidays fell on the same days throughout the respective cultural spheres. Likewise in East Asia, calendars based on the same fundamental principles were adopted in Japan, China, Korea and northern Vietnam, thus defining a single sphere of civilization. In 553 the Yamato court requested the Paekche kingdom to send calendrical experts and in the following year they came, bringing to Japan the calendrical system that had been established in China. From then until the late seventeenth century, when the shogunate promulgated a new calendar drawn up by its astronomers and more precise even than that of China, Japan used the ancient Chinese lunar–solar calendar.

Adopted along with the calendar were annual observances, as well as the associated ceremonial foods, which were of Chinese origin. As a result, many of the foods that are customarily eaten today during certain festivals in Korea and Japan derive from

Chinese customs [Tanaka and Ôta 1981:220–3]. Most of the Chinese-style ceremonial meals that were adopted while intercourse between China and the Japanese court flourished, up to the early tenth century, are believed to have spread to the general populace. Buddhist observances initially were performed only at court, in the homes of the nobility, and in temples and monasteries, but later spread as the religion took hold among the masses. Most of the many older, seasonal observances that have survived to the present day are connected to agricultural ceremonies, and they usually involve the participation of Shinto shrines. As the planting, reaping and other agricultural activities connected to these observances occur at slightly different times in each area, the festivals do not occur on the same day throughout the country. There are also regional differences in the varieties of food associated with the events.

Here we shall briefly survey the foods and beverages associated with a few of the most important of the numerous annual festivals held throughout Japan. The dates given are those of the solar (Gregorian) calendar adopted by government decree in 1872, and hence the events tend to fall about a month earlier than in the traditional calendar, which counted from the lunar or Chinese New Year.

1 January: The most important of the festival days and the first day of the calendar, the New Year is a time of prayer for a year of happiness and ceremonies in anticipation of an abundant rice crop. Homes are made ready for the visit of the deity of the incoming year (*toshigami*), which may be understood in anthropological terms as a rice spirit. Large *kagamimochi* rice cakes which symbolize the deity are popularly displayed. New Year observances and the eating of *mochi* continue until 7 January.

Zôni, a soup containing *mochi* and other ingredients such as leafy greens and fish, is traditionally the main dish of the morning meal on the first three days of the year. Similar dishes are customary at the New Year in southern China and in Korea. Before eating *zôni* on the first day, sake laced with medicinal herbs (*toso*) is drunk, another practice that was introduced from China, where it has now died out.

7 January: Seven Herb Festival. On this day, which is important in the Chinese calendar, the Japanese eat a rice gruel containing seven herbs, which is derived from a similar Chinese soup.

3 March: Doll Festival (Hina Matsuri). Each of the days numbered with a repeated odd digit (e.g. the third day of the third month) held special significance in the traditional Chinese calendar. On this date in Heian Japan, courtiers would stroke themselves with paper dolls and then float them down a river, in the belief that they were purifying themselves by transferring and setting adrift the evil spirits that dwelled in their bodies. *Mochi* containing mugwort has been eaten on this day since about the ninth century, and later came to be called *hishimochi* after its diamond shape. The character of the festival changed during the seventeenth century, and now instead of floating dolls away, a set of elaborate dolls is displayed in a cheerful festival for girls. Various delicacies are consumed, including sweet white sake, and young women are permitted to drink openly.

21 March (approximate): Higan, a seven-day Buddhist memorial observance during which family graves are visited, centres on the vernal (and also the autumnal) equinox. There is some regional variation in ceremonial foods, but a type of *mochi* called *botamochi* or *ohagi* is popular nationwide. This is a dumpling made by boiling a mixture of glutinous and non-glutinous rice, pounding it lightly, moulding it into balls and coating them with sweetened adzuki bean paste. Sweets and green tea tend to be the foods of choice. Fish and sake are avoided in keeping with the Buddhist nature of Higan.

5 May: Children's Day is celebrated especially by families with sons. Colourful carp streamers (symbolizing success) are flown outside the house and warrior dolls and miniature weaponry are displayed inside. The main festive foods are *chimaki*, a sweet *mochi* steamed in bamboo or water oat leaves, and *kashiwa-mochi* cakes which are filled with sweet bean paste and wrapped in oak leaves. The custom of eating *chimaki* on this date originated in China and was introduced to Japan in ancient times.

7 July: Celebrations of the Tanabata Festival involve the display of bamboo branches carrying strips of coloured paper inscribed with wishes and romantic aspirations. Typical foods include melon and *sômen* (very thin wheat noodles). The custom of eating *sômen* on this date is originally Chinese, and may also reflect an amalgamation of wheat harvesting ceremonies held during the same season.

15 August: Held for several days around this date, the Bon Festival is the second most important event of the traditional calendar, after the New Year. It honours ancestral spirits, who are believed to visit the homes of their descendants at this time, and is a conjunction of ancient Japanese ceremonies and Chinese Buddhist observances. A special altar is erected in the home to welcome the spirits, and offerings are made of vegetables, fruits, *sômen* , *mochi* and *dango* (small rice flower dumplings). Vegetarian fare is the rule during this period of Buddhist observance, and fisherfolk traditionally refrain from work to respect the injunction against killing animals.

Full Moons of September and October: Observances at these times centre on votive offerings of food – *satoimo* (a type of taro) in September and green soybeans in October. The harvest festivals for these crops were combined with full moon rituals of Chinese origin, resulting in the present ceremonies.

Apart from festivals that are widely observed in each household, typical examples of which were presented above, there are a great many seasonal festivals that are observed by the entire community at the local Shinto shrine. These tend to be associated with rice cultivation, specifically with planting in spring, protection from insects during the summer, and reaping in the autumn. The characteristic foods and cooking vary by region.

Rites of passage in the life of the individual are also marked by festive days. They include birth, attainment of adulthood, marriage, the sixtieth birthday (regarded as the start of a new life cycle in accordance with the sexagenary cycle of the East Asian calendar) and death. Funerals are usually conducted according to Buddhist rites and hence involve vegetarian meals. Although the foods associated with celebrations of the other rites of passage and with community festivals vary greatly from area to area, some foods are common to certain festivals throughout Japan. Along with *mochi*, *sekihan* (steamed glutinous rice with adzuki beans) is a mark of festivity. The beans turn the rice red, which in Japan is the colour that symbolizes the driving out of evil spirits and strengthening of life force. Seafood is indispensable at most festivals, the preferred species being sea bream and spiny lobster, which redden when cooked. *Sashimi* (sliced raw fish filets), a popular and pricey favourite of the Japanese, often appears on the festival table, in line with the tradition for *hare* days of serving choice foods that are not normally eaten.

3.5   Place Settings and Table Settings

Chopsticks originated in ancient China, spreading from the Yellow River basin, which was then the centre of Chinese civilization, to surrounding regions from about the fifth century BCE. Chopsticks and spoons have been found in graves of Chinese settlers of Han – dynasty colonies in Korea which were established at the end of the first century BCE. On the Korean Peninsula chopsticks and spoons have been unearthed from the grave of a Paekche king who died in CE 523, indicating that they were in use by that time.

In Japan the earliest evidence of the use of chopsticks is their discovery in great numbers in excavations of the Heijokyo capital (at present-day Nara) which was built from 710, although they could have been used previously by the imperial family and the nobility. The Heijokyo finds have been almost entirely limited to the area where the palace and government offices were located, rather than the residential areas for officials and commoners. This pattern suggests that while chopsticks were used for banquets at the court and government offices and for meals served to government officials while they were working, most people ate with their hands at home. Yet excavations of Nagaokakyo, the capital from 784 to 794, show that by then chopsticks had spread to the living quarters of the general population [Sahara 1991]. From the traditional Chinese viewpoint, which equates chopsticks with civilization and regards eating with the hands as barbarian, civilized dining in Japan appears to date from the eighth century.

Eating with chopsticks and a spoon was the rule in ancient China and Korea. Rice began to be eaten with chopsticks throughout China under the Ming dynasty (1368–1644) and the spoon came to be used only for soup, whereas previously it had been customary to eat rice and other grains with a spoon [Aoki 1970:482–9]. That had been practical because the staple grains of northern China, which for many centuries was the centre of the civilization, were millet and non–sticky *indica* rice. The founders of the Ming dynasty came from the lower Yangtze River basin where the staple was rice of the stickier *japonica* type which can easily be picked up with chopsticks, and their rise to power was the impetus for the wider use of chopsticks. As chopsticks came into general use for rice, it became common to eat *indica* rice by holding the edge of the rice bowl up to the mouth and shoveling the rice into the mouth with the sticks.

The older Chinese custom survives on the Korean Peninsula, where rice, soups and those pickles which are served in sauce are eaten with a spoon while other dishes are eaten with chopsticks. In Korean dining etiquette, as in Europe, the plates are not lifted to the mouth but remain on the table at all times, and food is carried to the mouth with a spoon and chopsticks. Koreans are apt to scorn the Japanese custom of holding bowls of rice and soup up off the table while eating from them as 'beggar's manners' (beggars of ancient times ate as they walked). The Japanese, meanwhile, believing that chopsticks are properly used to grasp mouthfuls of rice and lift them to the mouth, tend to look upon the Chinese custom of shoveling rice from a bowl held to the mouth as coarse behaviour.

In Japan during the eighth and ninth centuries, the court nobility took their cues from Chinese culture and used chopsticks and metal spoons at official banquets. The spoon never caught on among the common people, probably because metal spoons were expensive and were not necessary, given the Japanese custom of swallowing soup directly from a bowl held to the mouth. The masses used only chopsticks, and with the waning of Chinese influence after diplomatic relations ceased in 894, the nobility too gradually abandoned the spoon, leaving chopsticks as the sole dining utensil for all.

Where food is eaten only with a spoon and/or chopsticks – rather than using a knife at the table to cut food into bits, or serving hunks of meat on the bone to be picked up and gnawed – it must be prepared in pieces small enough to pick up and put in the mouth with those utensils. Dicing ingredients at the start of the cooking process is thus a primary characteristic of East Asian cuisine, and there is no kitchen without a chopping board. When chopsticks are used, it is also easier to eat out of a small bowl than from a plate, and this is especially true for rice. Small bowls are therefore preferred in cultures where rice is eaten with chopsticks. Although the Chinese customarily serve the other dishes of the meal on platters or in large bowls which the whole table shares, at traditional meals in Korea and Japan the food is eaten almost entirely from small bowls.

The archaeological evidence suggests that Jômon households ate with their hands from a common plate on which all the food was heaped. In the remains of some Yayoi homes from the late second and third centuries, four or five pieces of unglazed ceramic tableware of similar size and shape have been found at the same place, indicating that separate portions were served to individual family members. At Heijokyo in the eighth century, government offices served lunches to employees during working hours, and a number of the bowls which are thought to have been used for those meals are inscribed with a person's name and a message prohibiting use by others. Out of many similarly shaped bowls, an individual would designate one for exclusive personal use [Sahara 1992].

It is the rule in Japanese homes today that ceramic rice bowls and tea cups, and lacquered soup bowls and chopsticks are reserved for particular individuals and are not to be used even by other members of the same family. Until quite recently, when food was placed on the table on a large platter, it was the general custom for individual servings to be taken not with chopsticks that had touched one's mouth, but with special serving chopsticks. These practices make clear that the Japanese believe that food or drink which has come in contact with someone else's mouth should not be taken into one's own body. Rather than a hygienic notion of physical purity, it seems likely that what lies beneath the mentality of avoiding contact with another's mouth is the Shintoist avoidance of personal defilement in the mystical sense. Common use of tableware is avoided to prevent the ritual pollution of one user from contaminating the next.

In apparent contradiction to that theory stand ceremonial drinking customs that involve passing the cup. There is a Japanese tradition when drinking sake for a person of lower rank to take the cup of a person of higher rank, drink from it, and refill it. In the tea ceremony, the same cup is used to brew tea for each person in succession. This is purposefully unconventional behaviour which is intended to forge solidarity by transmitting the mana of the higher-ranking person in anticipation of a mystical effect of personal activation, or by creating a sense of communion among all present.

Let us turn now to table setting. In present-day China chairs, tables and beds are used as they are in the West, but in former times mats were spread on earthen floors for sitting, and bedding was spread out on top of the mats. In those days, an individual meal would be served in the kitchen and carried out and placed before the diner, either on a place mat or on a small, portable, personal dining table, with or without legs. Sometimes, when a table was used, the diner sat not on the earthen floor but on a long, low bench. Chairs and tables were later introduced from Central Asia, and came into general use in Tang dynasty China (618–907). With several persons sitting on chairs around a single table, the method of service changed. Rather than serving a single portion of each dish, only rice and soup were placed in bowls as single portions while the other dishes were placed on platters or in large bowls from which individuals would serve themselves with their own chopsticks. At a typical meal in China today, all of the food is laid out before the meal, but in upper-class homes with servants, and in restaurants, the meal is served as a succession of separate courses so that the food is always hot. Serving in courses probably grew out of the custom of sitting in chairs to eat. In contrast to Western practice, even when the next course has been brought out, the previous course is left on the table until it is finished.

Due to the Confucian emphasis on differentiation of men and women, until 1949 in most Chinese households the males would eat as a group first, and the females would eat together afterward. In traditional Korean households the meal service is more strongly influenced by Confucianism and meals are segregated by generation as well as by gender, so that in an upper-class home separate meals are served successively, on differing types of tables, to the grandparents, the head of the household, the sons, the daughters, and finally the wife. Low tables are generally used, with sizes varying for individual or group use, and the diners sit on the floor. Although each person has a private set of chopsticks, spoon, rice bowl and soup bowl, when several people sit around one table the other dishes are placed on common platters and food is taken from them with the personal chopsticks, rather than with serving chopsticks. All dishes are placed on the table before the meal [Ishige and Inoue 1991:11–16].

The Japanese probably began using dining tables at about the time chopsticks were introduced. Commoners used a legless rectangular tray called an *oshiki* and the upper class used a small, lacquered, portable table with legs called a *zen*, and the diner sat on the floor in either case. Food service was thoroughly individualized, with a separate table for each person, on which a single meal was arrayed. For an elaborate meal in which many different foods were served, two or more *zen* would be placed before each person. The grandeur of a banquet was judged by the number of tables involved; in the Edo period a five-table dinner was considered first rate. Confucianism in Japan amounted to little more than a philosophy for intellectuals and did not influence the lives of the common people as it did in China and Korea. It was generally the custom for the whole family to eat together, but their places were carefully determined. The head of the house had the seat of honour, the employees sat at the opposite end, and other members of the family occupied the intermediate places with males and older persons closer to the head.

3.6   Cooking and Banquet Styles

All of the basic cooking techniques of the traditional Japanese cuisine that has been handed down to the present day were already in place by about the ninth century. To wit, there are written records indicating that the following types of dishes had become popular: grilled fish and meat (*yakimono*); simmered foods (*nimono*); steamed foods (*mushimono*); soups of chopped vegetables, fish or meat (*atsumono*); jellied fish (*nikogori*), prepared by simmering with seasonings; sliced raw fish served in vinegar-based sauce (*namasu*);

vegetables, seaweed or fish in strong dressing (*aemono*); and pickled vegetables (*tsukemono*), cured in salt to cause lactic fermentation.

Figure 5   An upper-class family meal in the Edo period. The parents have higher meal stands than the children. From a book of "Everyday Knowledge" (1838).

Virtually no cooking was done with oil or fat. Since meat was not commonly eaten and butter was not produced, cooking with animal fats was unknown. Sesame was cultivated and pressed, but the oil was very costly. Sesame was used mainly in roasted form as a seasoning, usually either sprinkled over rice or ground to a paste and mixed with other seasonings in a dressing. A rare example of a recipe that called for sesame oil is the *tôgashi* (Chinese cakes) that were eaten as a dessert at banquets of the nobility. They were made in various shapes, using a dough of wheat, rice, soy or adzuki flour which was deep-fried in sesame oil and occasionally sweetened (with the likes of *amazura* syrup from ivy sap, or the grated skin of dried persimmons).

The Chinese practice of sautéing was not imported to Japan in the ancient age, for it developed in Sung China after Japan had suspended contact. The absence of oil and fat became one of the distinctive characteristics of traditional Japanese cooking. In a nation grown accustomed to such cooking, the taste of oil or fat was considered 'cloying' and 'unrefined'. When Western and Chinese cooking were introduced in the late nineteenth century, the stereotypical first impression was, 'It's so oily, so heavy'. Tempura, the deep–frying technique that is so popular today, was introduced in the sixteenth century. When it first became popular in the late eighteenth century, it was served at roadside stalls and regarded as vulgar fare.

Records of the banquets held by the Heian court and nobility indicate that fish and wild fowl were the main fare, and few vegetables were served. This is likely because vegetables were held in lower regard than fish and fowl.

At banquets of the Heian nobility the guest of honour was served at a private table some one metre square while the other guests sat together around a table two metres square or larger. These were placed on mats which covered the floor. There were two forms of seating, either directly on the floor mats or on stools that stood a fair height from the floor. Even when several persons shared a table, all of the food was served in individual portions and arrayed on the table before the meal. Silver tableware was used at the most sumptuous dinners.

Placed directly in front of the diner were rice and soup, chopsticks and spoon, and four small plates of seasonings. These were salt, vinegar, and *hishio* (a fermented mixture of soybeans, rice, wheat, sake and salt; an early form of soy sauce). An empty plate was placed next to the seasonings so that each diner could mix them to taste, to make a sauce in which bites of food would be dipped. This practice suggests that most of the food was cooked either plain or with simple flavouring.

The banquet meal consisted of four types of food: *himono* (dried food), *namamono* (fresh food), *kubotsuki* (fermented or dressed food), and *kashi* (desserts). Dried fish and fowl, such as salted salmon or pheasant, steamed and dried abalone, or dried and grilled octopus, were served thinly sliced. Fresh fish, shellfish or fowl were either sliced raw and served in a vinegar dressing, or grilled; carp, sea bream, salmon, trout and pheasant were typically eaten. The *kubotsuki* foods ranged from small balls of salt-fermented sea squirt, fish or giblets (the type of food later called *shiokara*), to jellyfish or fish *aemono*. Desserts included the Chinese cakes described above as well as nuts and fruits, such as pine nuts, dried chestnuts, acorns, jujube, pomegranate, peach, apricot, persimmon, and a type of citrus fruit. Counting the desserts, which were placed furthest back on the table, an elaborate banquet consisted of an assortment of 28 types of food. We may note from the above that the cooking was generally simple, with preserved foods taking up much of the menu, and that little of the food was served hot, since everything was set out on the table before the meal.

The formal meal took a long time, and after it was finished sake was served. Official banquets of the Heian court consisted of two parts, the ceremonial meal and a drinking party. Eight to ten different foods were served in the course of the drinking party, including such filling dishes as a hot soup and a noodle soup called *konton*, and the elaborate *tsutsumiyaki* ('stuffed grill'), a fish which was stuffed with nuts and seaweed and sewn up, and then grilled, sometimes after boiling. For entertainment, the cook might bring in a pheasant or other fowl tied to a tree branch and cook it before the eyes of the guests. Shows of singing and dancing were also held. The party would begin with the ceremonial drinking of three rounds, after which everyone drank as much as they pleased. On these occasions it was permitted to behave in a free and easy manner without regard to the hierarchy of court ranks. The pattern of rigid formality during the first half of a banquet followed by an informal, relaxed atmosphere in the second half has continued to the present day, which is to say that the basic format of the Japanese banquet was established in Heian times.

Toward the end of the Heian period, the formal banquet meal began to be served on small, portable tables, several of which would be arrayed before each individual. This was a harbinger of *honzen ryōri* service, which is described in Section 4.4.

The meals of the warriors who wrested power from the nobility in the late twelfth century were plain and simple. The first shogun, Minamoto Yoritomo, punished samurai who affected the showy style of the nobility, and his successors maintained a similar policy through the Kamakura period (1192–1336). The banquet style of the early shoguns, exemplified by the New Year dinner which was attended by military leaders from the provinces, is called ôban. Ôban originally referred to a luncheon held on festival days at the imperial court in the late Heian period for the provincial soldiers who served as guards, a meal of rather higher quality than their daily fare. The ôban menu of the early thirteenth century was limited to slices of dried abalone, jellyfish aemono, pickled apricot, salt and vinegar for seasoning, and rice. The pickled Japanese apricot (umeboshi), with its strong salty-sour taste, developed in Zen monasteries before spreading to the samurai class, and is a popular part of the Japanese diet today.

As the warrior class established feudal domains and solidified its economic base, samurai meals were embellished by imitating the cuisine and table manners of the nobility. It was later, during the Muromachi period (1392–1568), that the samurai exerted real influence on culinary culture, in the form of the honzen ryôri banquet.

3.7 The Role of the Monasteries

While the official banquet cuisine of the Heian nobility had consisted mostly of cold food, in medieval times hot food became more common. This reflected the shift from grilling to stewing as the basic cooking technique. From the Kamakura period onward, most of the menus that have been documented include boiled fish and vegetables, and the method of cooking the staple rice changed from steaming to boiling. Iron pots, including the deep kama used to boil rice, came into use, and fragile unglazed pottery was replaced by ceramic ware fired to hardness at high temperatures. These changes in the kitchen, especially the adoption of iron pots, facilitated the spread of boiling and simmering techniques.

Another factor in the spread of boiling was the development in Buddhist monasteries of the vegetarian cooking known as shôjin ryôri. Meat and fish were easily prepared on the grill, but so long as the Japanese were unfamiliar with the technique of sautéing in oil or fat, vegetarians could cook their vegetables and seaweed only by boiling. The practice of adding miso when simmering such foods

75

probably developed first in the monasteries. Miso, made by fermenting soybeans in salt, is a rich source of various amino acids, including glutamic acid which is widely recognized as a taste enhancer. Hence other foods absorb a rich, salty flavour when they are boiled in water containing dissolved miso. Miso has a somewhat granular texture and although it was formerly eaten plain as a side dish, it is now ground to a paste and dissolved in water as a flavouring. The earthenware mortar (*suribachi*) that came into general use during the Kamakura period was used for that purpose, as well as to make sesame or walnut paste for dressings, and hence promoted the popularity of dishes of stewed vegetables in dressing. Another technique that developed in the monasteries was the boiling of kelp, which is also rich in glutamic acid, to make a broth for stewing vegetables.

During the medieval age it was the priests and monks of the Zen school of Buddhism, which blossomed in Japan during the twelfth and thirteenth centuries, who served as agents for the transmission of Chinese civilization to Japan. In the course of their religious training at monasteries in China, they absorbed knowledge of culture, technology and the arts, including many new foods and cooking methods. Zen attracted many followers among the samurai class, and they brought the foods and cooking of the Zen temples into their strata of society. The influence was clearly visible in the formal meals that later developed among the samurai lords.

The first written record of tofu (bean curd) in Japan is from 1183. Tofu is made by soaking soybeans in water, mashing and straining them to obtain soy milk, and adding a coagulant to form curds. If the soy milk is instead heated in a shallow pan, a protein-rich film forms on the surface which is skimmed off to make *yuba*, which may be eaten either plain or dried as a preserved food. The method for making *yuba* is thought to have been brought from China by Zen monks during the Kamakura period. Another type of food that came from China during that era and spread from the monasteries to the masses is *fu* or wheat-gluten cakes. Wheat dough is wrapped in cloth, immersed in water and kneaded to dissolve the starch, leaving the protein as a lump of sticky gluten which is steamed, boiled or baked into *fu*. The monks who were prohibited from eating animal products must have known from experience the importance of tofu, *yuba* and *fu* as protein sources. The methods for making these foods developed at temples and monasteries, and they gradually entered the popular diet as specialized producers appeared among the lay population (see Sections 9.5 and 9.6).

The medieval monasteries also originated the custom of eating a *tenshin* or midday snack. To tide them over between their morning and evening meals, monks ate a variety of foods that were common in Chinese monasteries, such as steamed wheat buns with fillings of sweet bean paste or salty vegetable paste (called *manjû* in Japan), or noodles, as well as traditional Japanese foods such as *mochi*. Tea drinking was another custom that spread in Japan from the Zen temples, where tea was commonly taken with a light snack of fruit or sweets, later known as *chanoko* or *chagashi* (tea cakes). Tea cakes and the *tenshin* snack were formative elements of the tea ceremony and *kaiseki* cuisine which evolved somewhat later (see Section 4.4).

3.8   The Popularization of Noodles

Noodles came to be widely eaten in China during the Tang dynasty (618–907). For Japan, there is evidence of a food of Chinese origin called *sakubei* or *muginawa* that was eaten from the eighth century until the medieval age. Although some think it was a confection, the records of the ingredients and tools used to make *sakubei* have led me to believe it was a predecessor of the very thin wheat noodles called *sômen*. Experiments have proven that *sômen* can be made with those ingredients and tools [Ishige 1991:78–92]. *Sakubei* was made by kneading five parts wheat flour and two parts rice flour with salt water to make a dough, forming it into long strings, attaching the ends to two sticks of bamboo, pulling on the sticks to stretch the dough into fine threads, and drying. *Sakubei* was boiled or steamed and either eaten in a hot miso-flavoured soup, or dipped in a sauce of cold miso soup with vinegar, mustard and black pepper.

About the mid-fifteenth century *sakubei* came to be called *sômen* (from the Chinese *suomien*). The traditional method for making *sômen* is basically the same as for *sakubei*, except rice flour is not used and the dough is coated with vegetable oil before it is attached to the sticks. The oil allows the noodles to be stretched more thinly. A recipe calling for vegetable oil appears in a thirteenth-century Chinese cookbook, but it is not known when that modification was introduced in Japan. Since expertise is required, the noodles must have been made either by specialists or by farmers who took it up as specialized work during the slow season. Among today's master *sômen* makers who work without machinery, the standard extra-fine product is a bundle of about 4,000 noodles cut to a length of 20 centimetres, with a dry weight of 100 grams. Such very thin noodles dry completely almost as soon as they are made, and hence will keep for a long time without spoiling and can be shipped over long distances. The nobility and the major temples and shrines had *sômen* made at their provincial estates and delivered to their headquarters. It was also sold commercially in towns. But because of the difficulty involved in making *sômen* , the farmers who lived in a self-sufficiency economy could not eat fine wheat noodles even if they grew wheat.

Nowadays, *sômen* is especially popular in summer. After boiling, it is commonly served in ice water, in a glass bowl to impart a visual sense of coolness, with a separate cold dipping sauce consisting of soy sauce and other flavourings and a garnish of grated ginger, wasabi horseradish or chopped scallion.

To make *udon* noodles a wheat dough is rolled out flat, folded repeatedly, and cut into strips with a knife. As a high degree of skill is not required, *udon* can be made in an ordinary kitchen. The technique was developed in Tang China but in Japan the earliest documented menu including what appears to be *udon* is from the mid-fourteenth century, and it became popular from the fifteenth century. Its popularization was probably connected with woodworking technology, because a large, flat surface is necessary to roll out the dough. Italian pasta is rolled out on a marble table, but in Japan it was not customary to have a stone table in the kitchen. When the plane came into general use during the fifteenth century, the boards required for making *udon* became easily available.

Soba or buckwheat noodles are made in the same way as *udon*. The debut of *soba* in the historical record was in 1574. Previously, buckwheat had been boiled whole to make a gruel, or ground up and kneaded with hot water to a texture resembling polenta. As the technique of rolling out dough became popular, *udon* and *soba* became the two main types of noodles. *Soba* is traditionally more popular in eastern Japan, where dry field cultivation is more common, while *udon* tends to be preferred in western Japan, where the warmer climate allows the cultivation of wheat as a second crop after rice is harvested from the paddies. Both types reached a height of popularity as snack foods in the urban noodle shops of the Edo period, described in Chapter 5.

Figure 6   Traditional production of *sômen* noodles. The cut and ripened noodles are stretched with sticks hung outdoors to dry. This illustration, from a guide to local specialties published in 1754, shows the technique at Miwa in Nara Prefecture, where *sômen* is still made in the same way.

CHAPTER 4

THE AGE OF CHANGE

4.1   Historical Setting

We turn now to the age of upheaval and change spanning the sixteenth and the first half of the seventeenth centuries. In historians' parlance, this age runs from the late Muromachi period into the beginning of the Edo period. During this time the medieval order collapsed, a century of provincial wars ensued, and finally the feudal system was reorganized.

The central military government which was established in 1392, known as the Muromachi shogunate, effected control over the regions by appointing influential samurai as provincial lords. Those lords, however, gradually consolidated their grip on their respective domains and grew less inclined to submit to the control of the shogunate. By the mid-fifteenth century the shogun ruled in name only, and real power was held by the autonomous local lords, who were called daimyo. In 1467 the most powerful daimyo split into two factions and began fighting the first of a series of provincial wars, in a protracted military race to determine who could set up a government that would unify all Japan.

The historical backdrop to the taking of de facto power by the provincial daimyo includes important economic developments and the attendant growth of regional cities. We may glimpse the farming economy of the fifteenth century through the words of a Korean envoy who visited the area around Osaka in 1420:

> The farmers of Japan sow barley and wheat in the autumn, harvest it in the early summer of the following year, and then plant rice seedlings which they harvest in the early autumn, and they also sow buckwheat for harvest in the early winter. The means which enable them to harvest three crops from a single plot of arable land involve damming rivers and irrigating to make paddies, and then releasing the water to make dry fields [Zokugun 1993:103].

During the fifteenth century, horse-drawn iron ploughs became widespread, as did the use of wood ash and animal or human wastes for fertilizer, and improved crop varieties were disseminated throughout the country. In addition to such improvements in farming technology, daimyo who wanted to bolster the economic power of their fiefdoms promoted the cultivation of new land and actively undertook irrigation and riparian works to increase agricultural productivity.

The merchants and artisans of medieval times worked largely under the patronage of major shrines and temples, and were organized in guilds called *za* to which they contributed a portion of their profits in exchange for protection of their monopolies. This system was threatened as military disturbances spread and some shrines and temples came under attack. The daimyo tended to dislike the *za*, which they saw as exclusive groups whose loyalties often lay outside their domains. They encouraged merchants and artisans to trade independently, and free markets were established near the castles that served as the headquarters of the daimyo . As merchants and artisans congregated near these citadels, towns and cities took shape and became the centres of their regional economies. Distribution networks linking the regional centres were established, the transport of goods in large quantities was undertaken nationwide, and accounts came to be settled with money orders rather than in heavy coin. Although it was a time of continual warfare, it was also an age of social and economic reforms, and substantial progress was made in agriculture, commerce and manufacturing.

In 1543 a Chinese junk washed up on the small island of Tanegashima south of Kyushu. From a Portuguese passenger on the boat, who exacted a very high price, the lord of the island obtained two guns. This was the first time a European is known to have visited Japan, and the first introduction of firearms. Using those two guns as models, local blacksmiths were able to begin domestic production, and guns spread rapidly through the competitive demands of the ambitious daimyo who hoped to prevail and found a national government. With the introduction of firearms, military campaigns moved away from cavalry battles toward strategies based on infantry corps, and castle design was also modified. Oda Nobunaga, the daimyo who most effectively utilized the tactics of firepower, emerged victorious from the struggle among the various warlords, but he was assassinated just as he was about to assume formal power in 1582, and it was his successor Toyotomi Hideyoshi who completed the national unification. After Hideyoshi's death the Toyotomi government was toppled by an allied daimyo, Tokugawa Ieyasu. He became shogun in 1603 and set up his government at Edo (present-day Tokyo), inaugurating the Tokugawa shogunate which ruled until 1868.

Contact with Europeans brought various cultural influences besides firearms. Saint Francis Xavier was the first to bring the Christian gospel to Japan, in 1549, and with the subsequent arrival of Jesuit missionaries who actively propagated the faith, some 150,000 persons were recorded as Catholic adherents by 1582. There were converts among the daimyo of western Japan, but their motives were not limited to the purely religious. Trade was closely associated with proselytization, and thus the advantage of steering commercial profits to their own domains would have entered into a daimyo's calculations in building rapport with missionaries.

The Muromachi shogunate shifted its official trade with China to Portuguese ships, which had larger cargo capacities than the East Asian vessels of the time. The Portuguese ships arrived carrying guns and gunpowder, as well as spices and medicines from tropical Asia, and raw and woven silk from Ming China. They plied in stages on the return voyage as well, typically stopping in China to deliver Japanese silver, which was exhaustively mined at the time, and then taking on Chinese wares and proceeding to Goa.

Stimulated by Portuguese trade, the daimyo and wealthy merchants of western Japan began to dispatch ships of their own to trade with China and Southeast Asia, and established resident colonies in various countries. It has been reckoned that at least 100,000 Japanese left the country during the first three decades of the seventeenth century, before the Tokugawa shogunate completely implemented its policy of national seclusion. To Korea, meanwhile, Hideyoshi twice dispatched large invading armies, and twice they were beaten back by combined Korean and Ming forces. Historically speaking, the Japanese ventured further overseas during this period than ever before.

Foreign contact during this era influenced the diet in various ways. Plants which originated in the New World, including the pumpkin, the sweet potato, cayenne pepper and tobacco, were brought to Japan and cultivated. Sugar had been imported from China since ancient times, but it had been a precious item used more as a medicament than as a flavouring. As trade flourished with Southeast Asia, sugar began to be imported in large quantities and confectionery began to be made. Although some traditional savoury delicacies were sweetened, many new recipes for sweet cakes and candies were brought in from Europe and, as we will see below, some have remained to this day with local modifications. Technology for distilling spirits was introduced from Thailand to the Ryukyu kingdom (now Okinawa), where it was applied to produce *awamori* rice liquor, which is still made today. The taste of grape wine from Europe became known in Japan. European cooking techniques were circulated, and some Christian converts ate beef. Later when Christianity was suppressed, the preparation of meat dishes was prohibited and the recipes were substantially modified through the substitution of ingredients such as tofu. Yet some traces of the European dishes that were introduced in the sixteenth century still remain today. The armies sent by Hideyoshi to Korea forcibly brought skilled artisans back with them, including potters who constructed kilns and practised sophisticated techniques in various locations. This is the origin of the continuing Japanese manufacture of beautiful ceramic tableware.

Continuous warfare did not bring on an interlude of cultural sterility. Indeed, the period of provincial wars, from the late fifteenth to the late sixteenth century, occupies an important place in Japan's cultural history. During this time both farmers and townspeople tended to resist the feudal lords and a role reversal took place, not in the sense that vassals became lords, but rather in that the people became charged with energy. It was a dynamic, creative period during which an old order collapsed and new movements were born. Important arts were born which survive today with rich traditions, including the *Nô* drama, *kyôgen* farce, *kabuki*, and *ikebana* (flower arrangement). In painting and architecture an original and arguably the most creative Japanese aesthetic sensibility, that of *wabi*, took form. Amid this burst of cultural innovation, the salient development in dietary culture was the establishment of *chanoyu*, the tea ceremony. The menu, the order of service, the aesthetics of food arrangement and tableware, and the dining etiquette that were formulated for the meals which evolved along with the tea ceremony in this period have survived up to the present.

The end of this era, which stands as the most vital in Japanese history before the present century, is marked by the shogunal decree of national isolation. Christianity had at first been tolerated by the Edo government, but once trade was initiated with the Protestant nations of Holland and England, it was no longer necessary to accept Christ for the sake of commercial gain. Otherwise, the Establishment had no particular liking for this religion which did not hesitate to deny the absolute authority of the shogun, and there was even some concern that missionaries could be the vanguard for eventual colonization. Restrictions were placed on the number of overseas departures and arrivals of foreign ships. Then in 1639, shortly after a rebellion of Christians was put down at Shimabara in Kyushu, Portuguese ships were forbidden to call at Japanese ports. Finally in 1641, with the transfer to Nagasaki of the trading offices of the sole permitted European nationality, the Dutch, foreign trade came under strict government control and the Tokugawa policy of national isolation was complete. Thereafter in diet and cuisine, as in other areas of culture, the process of change via external stimulus virtually ceased, and Japan entered a phase of seeking refinement and maturity within itself which was to last for some 200 years.

4.2   The Diffusion of Tea

The earliest record of *cha*, or tea, in Japan is from 815 when, as mentioned earlier, it was served to Emperor Saga at a Buddhist temple. The abbot of that temple had studied in China, and it is believed that he brought back some tea seeds and planted them in the temple grounds. Emperor Saga ordered that tea be grown in provinces near Kyoto so it could be presented to him each year, and he also established a plantation in the capital itself. Tea soon became familiar in the salons of the nobility as well as among the Buddhist clergy, but during the ninth century it probably remained limited to a niche as a fashionable beverage among those who were fervent admirers of Tang culture. There are fewer records of tea from the tenth century, after the sending of embassies to China had been suspended, and it seems it was not at all common, as mention is limited mainly to its consumption at special temple rituals or as a medicine among the nobility. The tea which was then used was brick tea which was subject to a fermentation process that gave it a distinctive smell. It has been suggested that tea drinking did not take root during Heian times because that smell did not suit Japanese taste [Kumakura 1990:30-7].

Tea reappeared on the scene after an interruption of some three centuries. The Zen priest Eisai, who had studied in China and founded a temple at Kamakura whose parishioners included the shogun and his family, returned from a second Chinese sojourn with tea seeds or seedlings which he cultivated. In 1214 he was called to attend the shogun Sanetomo as a faith healer, for in those days the supplication of a high priest was regarded as the most effective form of medical treatment. The shogun had drunk too much at a banquet the day before and was hung over. Instead of offering the usual incantations, Eisai prescribed tea, and the tremendous effect of the caffeine induced a prompt recovery. Afterward Eisai wrote 'A Treatise on the Preservation of Health through the Drinking of Tea' (*Kissa yôjôki*) and presented it to the shogun.

What Eisai transmitted was the method of tea preparation of Sung dynasty China. The tea leaves are steamed soon after being picked, and after the leaves are dried they are ground with a mortar and pestle to produce *matcha*, or powdered green tea. This is placed in a bowl, hot water is added, and after stirring, the mixture is drunk as a single portion, just as in the present-day tea ceremony. The fragrance evidently suited the local palate. During the thirteenth century, the custom of drinking *matcha* first penetrated the temples and the upper level of samurai society, and then spread to the common people. In the process, tea changed from a medicinal concoction to a drink enjoyed for its taste.

Parties based on a tea-drinking game called *tôcha* were common in the fourteenth and fifteenth centuries. *Tôcha* was a guessing game in which teas from several districts were served and a prize was awarded to the player who could correctly identify the most varieties. According to a fourteenth-century document entitled 'Conventions of Tea Drinking' (*Kissa ôrai*), a *tôcha* party began with three rounds of sake, followed by a dish of noodles with a cup of tea, a main course of various delicacies, and a dessert of fruits. After a recess in the garden, the guests reassembled in a special tea drinking room on the upper floor, sweets were served, and the *tôcha* game was held. Then the tea utensils were put away and rounds of sake drinking ensued with entertainments of song, music and dance. Thus the format of the *tôcha* party corresponds to that of the previously described drinking party of the Heian-period nobility, with tea drinking added on as the main event. The nouveaux riches daimyo were fond of *tôcha* parties, and the typical banquet room was lavishly and competitively decorated with magnificent art works imported from China, as if a feast were being held in an art gallery.

In opposition to the *tôcha* party with its boasting anddazzling splendor, a movement that was intended to bring a more inward, spiritual aesthetic to the tea drinking venue began in the late fifteenth century. Known as *wabicha*, it matured during the sixteenth century through the support of wealthy citizens in the international port city of Sakai, near Osaka. *Wabi* is a frame of mind which is marked by composure and applied to savouring a life of simplicity in retirement from worldly affairs. It eschews anything splendid, boisterous or shocking. It is oriented toward appreciation of the refined beauty which lies within the simplicity that remains after everything unnecessary has been stripped away. *Wabi* corresponds to the state of mind that is cultivated in Zen Buddhism, and the influence of Zen can be seen in the culture that supported *wabicha*, for example in the preference for calligraphy by Zen masters over conventional paintings as decorations for the tearoom. *Wabicha* was consummated by Sen no Rikyû (1522–1591), the founder of a tea-ceremony school to which several present-day schools trace their lineage.

The *wabicha* teahouse was meant to be 'a humble country hut in the middle of the city'. In contrast to the sumptuous mansions in which they lived, the merchants of Sakai who sustained the initial vogue for *wabicha* built small, rustic teahouses which appeared shabby at first glance, but were actually made from materials and designs that had been selected with great care. In this tradition, the garden attached to the teahouse is a stylized portrayal of a distant mountain scene. The effect is to orchestrate the site for the tea ceremony as a world apart, separate from the secular space where everyday life takes place. The custom of washing the hands and rinsing out the mouth before entering the teahouse is similar to rituals of purification that are carried out when worshipping at a shrine or temple. Thus the tea party is symbolically a sacred gathering, imitating religious ceremony. Accordingly, entry into the teahouse eliminated the mundane status distinctions between lord and vassal or rich and poor, as all participants are equal amid the intimacy of the small space. The energetic devotee of the tea ceremony adopts a *nom de thé*, and in the teahouse is addressed by that name rather than one's official name, thus abandoning the status and occupation of daily life to take on a special persona in the tea setting. Talk of worldly affairs such as politics, religion, business or family quarrels is taboo. After retiring to that sacred space for a few hours and refreshing the spirit, one then reenters the world of everyday life [Kumakura 1990:143–4].

Broadly speaking, the tea party as it was crystallized by Sen no Rikyû has two parts. The first part centres around a meal of *kaiseki ryôri*. *Kaiseki* is written with ideographs that mean 'pocket' and 'stone', deriving from the Zen practitioner's custom of wrapping a heated stone in cloth and placing it in the clothing while performing austerities. The *kaiseki* food of the tea ceremony is meant to be a light meal which similarly warms the body. Taking a limited amount of food into the body serves to moderate the stimulus of the rich, strong tea which will be drunk afterward.

Rikyû was firmly against the serving of extravagant meals, and accordingly the menu of the tea gathering was strikingly simple in comparison to the conventional dinner parties of his time. It consisted ideally of *ichijû-sansai*, or one soup and three small side dishes (plus rice). That pattern was later standardized as the four dishes of *shiru*, miso soup; *mukôzuke*, raw fish or vinegared vegetables; *nimono*, vegetables simmered with fish or fowl; and *yakimono*, grilled fish. These are arrayed for each person on a legless tray called a *kaiseki zen*.

Such is the basic *kaiseki* menu, but since Rikyû's time elements have been variously added and today this style of cooking is not always so modest. In principle it is to be prepared personally by the host, who likewise is expected to serve the food and prepare the tea with his or her own hands. Sake may be served with the meal, and there is a prescribed etiquette for its drinking, though it is an informal style in comparison to the ritual surrounding the initial drink at a medieval banquet.

The meal is followed by a dessert of sweets, after which the guests take a recess in the garden. This gives the host time to clean up after the meal, and to provide a new stage setting by changing the brushwork scroll which is displayed behind the flowers in the tearoom. When preparations are complete the guests re–enter the tearoom for the second and main part of the ceremony, the drinking of *matcha* tea. First a very rich, pasty mixture called *koicha* is prepared for each guest in succession, the same bowl being cleaned and reused. The etiquette for preparing and for receiving the tea is quite complicated, and one is expected to follow the established forms in a polished manner. Each of the teamaking utensils and tea bowls as well as the decorations in the tea room are carefully selected and coordinated in keeping with *wabi* aesthetics, and some appreciative comment on these items is considered mandatory. The tea ceremony concludes with the drinking of *usucha*, a foamy infusion with a smaller amount of *matcha*. We may observe that Rikyû's pattern for the tea party is an abbreviation of the *tôcha* party, with the initial, formal sake service as well as the final round of drinking eliminated. In later times, however, a tea party would sometimes end with adjournment to another room for sake.

The new tea ceremony style that was elaborated especially by Rikyû both synthesized the existing elements of classical culture and provided an atmosphere that offered opportunity for various new developments. The teahouse gave birth to the architectural style called *sukiya-zukuri*. The formal tea garden has strongly influenced landscape design down to the present time. The hanging scrolls which were painted or brush-written for the tearoom affected the formats of the fine arts, and tea-ceremony floral decoration led to the major schools of flower arrangement. The fashioning of utensils for making and drinking tea stimulated various developments in the metalworking, lacquerware and pottery industries.

Major influences from the tea ceremony may likewise be recognized in dietary culture. One of them is the importance which Japanese cuisine gives to conveying a sense of the season, including prominent placement on the table of certain seasonal foods. The subtle changes of the seasons are so thoroughly reflected in the aesthetics of tea that a tea ceremony held in January requires a different interior design than one in February or December, and is performed with a different combination of teamaking utensils, bowls and plates. The same symbolic effect was sought in the food which accompanied the tea, and it spread to all refined cooking. Another influence on cuisine stemmed from the tea ceremony's Zen-style philosophy. Disavowing anything that is excessively artificial or perfect, avoiding design with symmetry that does not occur naturally, this approach discovers the beauty of the incomplete and the balance of the uneven. Zen painting leaves blank white spaces where one may look on to an emptiness which is unpaintable, unlike the Western tradition in which the entire canvas is painted over. The plates at a medieval dinner party were entirely covered with food, piled high and symmetrically, but with the advent of *kaiseki ryôri*, symmetry was avoided and the food was arrayed with an awareness of the beauty of empty space, a principle which survives today as the aesthetic basis of Japanese cuisine. Also, the decorum of the tea ceremony has had a substantial influence on dining etiquette.

4.3   The Impact of the 'Southern Barbarians'

In the traditional mindset of China, the area to the south of the Chinese sphere of civilization was a barbarian world. Japan had inherited that concept, and so the Portuguese and Spaniards who arrived there by sailing around India, Southeast Asia and southern China were referred to as *nanban*, or 'southern barbarians'. The term was benignly applied to the cooking they brought with them, *nanban ryôri*, as well as to confections made from European recipes, *nanban gashi*. The Dutch and English arrived some time later, and those Protestant northwest Europeans were called *kômôjin*, 'redheads', to distinguish them from Iberians. During the period when the country was closed, *kômôjin* was synonymous with the Dutch, who were the only Europeans allowed.

The first Japanese Christians were converted in Malacca by Saint Francis Xavier, and some of them guided him to their homeland in 1549. They advised him not to eat meat so as not to offend the local sensibilities, and he complied although there was evident amazement at the idea of meatless meals. The sense of desperation was recorded by one member of his retinue:

> Usually we ate no meat or fish. That was undeniably no small penance. Although Father would have spent the whole day walking about in the severe cold and snow, what was served us at the inn was a small portion of rice cooked in nothing but water and a tiny bit of salted fish, or occasionally boiled or grilled fish, all of it badly flavoured, along with a bowl of foul-smelling vegetable soup. Father would leave his fish, and since there was nothing else, he ate only the small portion of rice and the soup [Frois 1982:94–5].

It is likely that the fare at their inn, including what was probably miso soup, was typical of the common people's food at the time.

Missionaries nevertheless persevered with some success, and as converts to Catholicism were freed from taboos observed in Buddhism and Shinto, they began to join the Jesuits in eating meat. A priest recorded that on the day after Easter in 1557, in the town that is now Oita, the fathers bought a cow and cooked it with rice and served it to some 400 local Christians, who were greatly satisfied with the meal. In the Kyushu cities of Nagasaki and Hirado, where *nanban* ships frequently docked, not only Christians but also the general populace began eating beef. We know of a sudden jump in the price of beef in Nagasaki. There are also records of pigs being reared for food in those areas, but that may well have been connected to the fact that Chinese ships also called frequently at the two ports [Etchû 1982:18-21].

Bread, indispensable for celebrating mass, was made for the Europeans in Nagasaki and Hirado by local bakers. It made little headway as a foodstuff; according to one European's report, some Japanese were eating it between meals as if it were a type of fruit [Etchû 1982:29-35].

Christianity was prohibited by the Tokugawa shogunate in 1612, some years before the closing of the country. As a first step toward eradicating Christian-style customs among the populace, the government banned the eating of beef and bread at the same time. In contrast, the Chinese colony in Nagasaki, which had grown up around the substantial Chinese ship traffic there, were not targeted, for the meats which they enjoyed – pork, chicken and duck – were not subject to the ban.

After the decrees that closed the country, the Dutch traders who were the only remaining Europeans were isolated on a tiny island in Nagasaki harbour and barred from contact with ordinary citizens. Hence their culinary customs had virtually no impact during the two hundred-odd years of the Edo period. In contrast, the earlier *nanban* influences brought by Iberians were substantial even though the interval of contact was relatively brief, and many examples of their cooking methods were adapted to Japanese tastes and transmitted to the present day. The process is illustrated by a 'Nanban Cookbook' which appears to have been written about the time the country was shut, although the surviving manuscript is from the end of the Edo period [Okada 1979]. It provides recipes for forty different dishes and sweets. A few of them seem to have originated in China or Japan, but most are of Portuguese provenance. Some of the recipes had already been altered, as in the omission of milk or cream from dishes that would have included them in Portugal, or the substitution of powdered glutinous rice for wheat flour. Instead of yeast, bread dough is to be leavened with *amazake*, a very sweet rice wine with extremely low alcohol content which contains a yeast fungus that will ferment and make the dough rise.

A number of *nanban* recipes survived through the Edo period in the home cooking of Nagasaki, but most that are extant today have been substantially altered and, apart from their names, can barely be recognized as Western in origin. The degree of local adaptation may be seen in dishes where the main ingredient has changed from meat to fish, or dairy products are conspicuously absent, or seasonings such as miso or soy sauce are used. Still, it should be of interest to survey some of these Japanized *nanban* foods.

The Nagasaki dish called *hikado* is made by dicing tuna, *daikon* radish, carrots and sweet potatoes and simmering them with a seasoning of soy sauce. The name comes from the Portuguese *picado* ('mince'), and in the original recipe the beef was sautéed in oil before boiling. Here a red fish took the place of beef, and since cooking with oil was quite unusual in the Japanese kitchen, the recipe was abridged to just boiling.

Patties made of crushed tofu with bits of vegetable and fried in oil are called *ganmodoki* in the east of Japan, and *hirôsu* or *hiryôzu* in the west. The name derives from a type of pancake fried in oil and eaten with a topping such as honey, called *filhos* in Portuguese or *fillos* in Spanish. In a 1784 book entitled *Takushi shiki, hiryôzu* is described as a dough made from egg and powdered glutinous rice, fried in oil and topped with sugar syrup. The usage of the word *hiryôzu* probably changed first to include not just pancakes but anything cooked in oil, and later to the name of one type of tofu dish.

Tempura, today one of the most typical foods of Japanese cuisine, was probably originally based on Portuguese cooking. The earliest written mention, as *tempôra*, is from the end of the sixteenth century, but is not accompanied by a description. There are several theories of the etymology from Portuguese. One points to the word *tempero*, 'to season'. Another cites the religious term *tempora*, which signified certain days on which fish was to be eaten instead of meat (namely the first Wednesday, Friday and Saturday of March, June,

September and December), and states that the Japanese, having seen how the missionaries cooked on those days, first adopted the word to denote fish fried in oil. There is no conclusive evidence, and some say that both the food and its name have Chinese roots.

A recipe for *nanban* cooking is found in the oldest known Japanese collection of recipes, a book entitled *Ryôri monogatari* that appears to have been compiled at the beginning of the seventeenth century. It calls for boiling a chicken with a *daikon*, boning it and returning it to the pot, seasoning with sake and salt or miso, and adding garlic, scallions, mushrooms and the like. That recipe spread from Nagasaki to Fukuoka and after further modification became the present-day Fukuoka speciality known as *niwatori no mizutaki*.

A type of pickles known today as *acharazuke* consists of vegetables such as *daikon*, turnip and lotus root, finely chopped and marinated in a mixture of red pepper, vinegar, sugar and salt or soy sauce. The name may derive from Portuguese, which borrowed it from the Persian *achar*. However, there are similar pickles today on the Malay peninsula called *acar*, and both the food and the name came to that area via India. Hence it is possible that this food arrived not with Portuguese visitors, but rather with Japanese returning from Southeast Asia in the early seventeenth century.

Compared to *nanban* cooking with its then-unusual ingredients of meats, oils and spices, *nanban* confectionery was more popularly received in Japan, a pattern that still holds true today. Since the kitchens lacked ovens, the baking of cake or bread was accomplished by placing a large iron pot on coals and also covering the lid with coals, so as to apply heat from both sides. *Kasutera* is a sweet sponge cake made with eggs and based on *bolo de Castela*, Castilian cake. It was originally a Nagasaki speciality but is now made throughout the country. Other cakes with names deriving directly from Portuguese were the Hirado speciality *kasudosu* (*castela doce*) and the *taruto* of Ehime (*taruta*). Some other confections which have been handed down to the present also have Portuguese names, including *konpeitô*, *aruheitô*, and *karumera* (*confeito*, *alfeloa*, *caramelo*). Handmade cakes with egg yolk as a main ingredient were called *fios de ovos* (egg threads) in Portuguese; they spread from Nagasaki to Fukuoka where they are familiarly known today by the Japanese name *tamago sômen* (egg vermicelli).

Far more important in the history of food than *nanban* cooking and confection, in terms of socioeconomic impact, were the cultivable vegetables of New World origin which arrived during this period. Spaniards and Portuguese brought the new crops to Southeast Asia and China, and they reached Japan through the efforts not only of Europeans but also Chinese traders, as well as Okinawans and Japanese who did business in various parts of Asia.

The sweet potato was the most influential of the new crops. Having been introduced by Spaniards to Luzon in the Philippines, it spread to the Chinese province of Fujian in 1593. Potted seedlings were taken from there to the Ryukyu kingdom (now Okinawa) in 1605 by a returning envoy, and it was soon put in cultivation all over the Ryukyu Islands. The first cultivation of the sweet potato on the main islands of Japan was in a field planted by Richard Cocks, the manager of the East India Company office in Hirado, who brought it from the Ryukyus. Thereafter it was widely cultivated in the warm and dry maritime districts of western Japan, and was steamed, boiled or grilled for daily consumption. It became very important as a staple food, particularly in areas geographically unsuitable for the establishment of paddy fields: Okinawa, southern Kyushu, the Bungo Channel coasts of Kyushu and Shikoku, Tsushima Island, and the islands of the Inland Sea. In some places sweet potatoes became the source for at least 60 per cent of the food energy intake of the local population [Koyama and Gotô 1985: 492–6]. In locales where rice production was low and habitation was sparse, there was perceptible population growth following the introduction of the sweet potato.

Two types of pumpkin squash had long been well established in Japan before new strains were introduced from the USA in the late nineteenth century. One group of varieties was called *bobura*, from the Portuguese word for pumpkin, *abobora*; the other was called *nankin* pumpkins after an improved strain that had been bred near Nanjing in China. The usual word for pumpkin is *kabocha*, based on the name of the country from which it first arrived, Cambodia. In certain areas it is called *tônasu*, which means 'Chinese aubergine'. Miso soup with pumpkin and pumpkin boiled with miso or soy sauce flavouring are extremely popular dishes during the summer in farming communities, where they considered toothsome as well as filling.

Cayenne pepper is said to have been introduced by Portuguese in 1542. It gradually replaced black pepper as the powdered seasoning customarily sprinkled over noodle dishes. In later times it was blended into the mix known as seven-flavour cayenne (*shichimi tôgarashi* or *nanairo tôgarashi*), which also includes Japanese pepper (*Zanthoxylum piperitum*) and powdered tangerine peel. This is used today as a tabletop spice, much as Westerners use black pepper. Cayenne was rarely used in other ways because the Japanese, who generally did not eat meats or fats, found it much too spicy for their liking. In recent years the consumption of cayenne has grown in step with the increase in meat consumption. But it is Japan's neighbours who really know how to cook with cayenne pepper. Hideyoshi's soldiers introduced it to Korea, and nowadays the average Korean cannot get through a day without tasting it.

The kidney bean is often found in Japanese food. Originating in South America, it was brought to Japan from China in 1654 by a Zen monk named Ingen, and is therefore called the *ingen mame*. The peanut, also of South American origin, was introduced from China during the eighteenth century and was traditionally called the *nankin mame* (Nanjing bean).

4.4   Formation of a New Style

In a picture scroll from the end of the twelfth century called *Yamai no sôshi* (The Book of Illnesses), there are scenes in which ordinary meals are shown in great detail. In one of them a meal for a man suffering from pyorrhea is laid out before him on a wooden tray about 30 cm square called an *oshiki*. The dishes appear to be either wooden or simple unglazed pottery. The meal consists of a bowl of rice, a bowl of soup, and three small side dishes: one consists of very small fish, and the other two are not clearly identifiable but may be pickles and dried fish. While the side dishes are quite small in quantity, the rice is heaped well above the top of its bowl, for during this period it was customary to dish out all of the rice to be taken at a meal as a single serving (see Figure 7). By the fourteenth century the procedure changed to serving a small amount of rice and then providing second and third helpings as the diner's bowl was emptied. Also in later times, in place of the *oshiki* tray, a small portable meal table with legs called a *zen* came into general use for individual meal service. Apart from those two differences, the dining scene in the painted scroll is a good depiction of the basic meal among the ordinary people of Japan up through the nineteenth century.

Figure 7   A meal of the Heian period. (From the *Yamai no sôshi* picture scroll.)

That pattern for the daily meal, still common today in traditional cooking, is regarded in terms of three categories of foods: rice, soup, and side dishes. The number of dishes – not counting rice and pickles, which are in any case indispensable – determines how substantial and impressive a meal is. The one in the picture scroll, consisting of one soup and three side dishes, is the same in format, if not necessarily in quality, as the *ichijû-sansai* pattern that Sen no Rikyû established as the basic *kaiseki* meal. The combination found in a typical daily meal was one soup with two side dishes. In other situations the pattern may range from *ichijû-issai*, a humble meal of one soup and one side dish, to *nijû-nanasai*, a banquet of two soups and seven side dishes.

A banquet-style meal with a large number of dishes will not fit on a single small *zen* table. In such a situation each guest is furnished with two or more tables, and the sumptuousness of a dining party is indicated by that number. The largest feast on record is a seven-*zen* banquet which included service of eight soups and 24 side dishes.

The banquet meal individually served on a set of *zen* tables is known as *honzen ryôri*. It appeared around the thirteenth century, and reached its full form as the official banquet style during the Muromachi period (1392–1568). It then spread among the general populace, and up through the first half of the twentieth century *honzen ryôri* was always served at formal dinner parties. A wedding banquet, for example, would be a simplified form of *honzen ryôri*. The table service as a rule is lacquerware, and it is mandatory to furnish each guest with a set of variously shaped *zen* and a number of different lacquer-coated bowls and plates. Until about fifty years ago, the storehouse of an urban merchant or a rural landlord would be stocked with dozens of sets of lacquered dinner service. These were not for the exclusive use of the household, but would also be loaned to relatives who could not afford such tableware to enable them to hold formal dinners.

Honzen ryôri was institutionalized as the banquet fare of the upper-class samurai and the nobility. Schools of cooking were established by professional chefs of the Muromachi period, notably the Shijô school for the nobility and the Ôkusa school for the samurai, and to emphasize their authority they developed a great many detailed rules for cooking and serving. At the extreme there were numerous intricate rules of etiquette for the shogun's palace or the imperial court, so that a *honzen ryôri* meal in high society became a complicated and endlessly formalized affair. For example, the questions of what shapes a large fish should be cut into and what sorts of dishes were suitable for serving the differently shaped pieces were discussed in theoretical terms based on Taoist philosophy, and complex sets of dos and don'ts evolved for the use of chopsticks. As *honzen* cuisine underwent such formalization, becoming gradually more extravagant and wondrous to the eye, it became far removed from the primary culinary quest for taste and satisfaction. It was against this background that *kaiseki* cuisine was born.

Four types of banquets were noted by a Western observer at the dawn of the seventeenth century [Rodrigues 1967:547–553]. There was the three-table dinner, the five-table dinner, and 'the most impressive of them all, a far more solemn party, at which seven dining tables were placed before each guest. This was naturally an affair held by the very high-ranking nobility, on occasions when similarly high-ranking guests were invited, and it served to express a cordial welcome and deep respect for them.' Of course that is a description of *honzen ryôri*, but the author goes on to report an important change in dining which had come about just before he wrote. This was the *chanoyu* dinner:

> The fourth type of banquet, which was first held during the time of Nobunaga and Hideyoshi, is presently spreading through the entire kingdom as the most fashionable style. Many things have been improved since that time, elements which are surplus or cumbersome have been dropped, and along with the changes from the old procedures the banquet and even the ordinary meal have been greatly reformed.... The cooking has eliminated those things which were presented merely to be seen as decoration, as well as cold items, and in their place hot food which has been sufficiently cooked is placed on the dining table at the appropriate time, and as with their tea ceremony, the contents are selected for their quality.

This *kaiseki ryôri*, which had begun in opposition to *honzen ryôri*, ultimately influenced its form and made the meals of the formal banquet style more substantial. *Kaiseki* also served as the motive force in the development of the informal banquet cuisine of the ensuing Edo period [Kumakura 1976].

It was only after the appearance of *kaiseki ryôri* that ceramic tableware came into wide use. During medieval times most tableware was wooden. The crudest bowls and plates were unlacquered, but the common people often used roughly lacquered wooden ware, coated simply in a subdued red or black colour without pictures or patterns. Also in common use was simple pottery, fired to firmness without any glaze. The sake cups, plates and bowls used at official dinners were soft reddish-brown earthenware which had been fired at low temperature. This earthenware tended to be of the crudest and cheapest sort, and would be thrown away after a single use. That custom was adopted from the procedures of Shinto festival rites, where all vessels used are freshly made for the occasion and discarded afterward. In Shinto observance the practice serves to avoid contamination by evil spirits and to ensure that only pure objects are used by the gods. However, the earthenware used at the time by the nobility for top-class dinner parties was nicely finished and would generally be kept for long service. As a result, the cheaper earthenware gradually came to be kept as well.

Ceramic ware imported from China had been used at table by a portion of the population since the thirteenth century. During the two invasions of Korea conducted by Hideyoshi at the end of the sixteenth century, participating daimyo took skilled Korean potters captive and brought them to Japan to construct kilns in their realms. Thus began the domestic production of technically sophisticated ceramics. The new product was actively patronized by practitioners of the tea ceremony, who adopted it as tableware and often placed orders for custom designs and for specific inscribed or painted decorations. Tea bowls in particular were esteemed by those aficionados as the most precious works of art. As a result of the fine aesthetic discernment of its patrons, Japanese ceramic tableware reached a high level of artistry within a short time, and soon a large variety of designs were being produced and exports to Europe were begun.

Kaiseki cuisine devoted a great deal of energy to the challenge of how most elegantly to fill with food these dishes which were painted with brilliantly coloured designs or shone with a pure whiteness. The lacquerware which had been the mainstream of tableware until then was shaped on lathes and hence limited in form to bowls and small round plates, while the colours tended to be dull and monotonous, offering little potential for creative design in arranging food. When ceramics that could be freely crafted with different shapes and colours and patterns became locally available, the potters were asked to produce pieces with particular shapes and decorations, often for the purpose of serving particular foods. In this way Japanese tableware came to possess the world's largest variety of designs, and the cuisine came to place considerable emphasis on the manner in which food is presented.

4.5 Change in the Frequency of Meals

Daily life at the imperial court in Heiankyo (Kyoto) at the close of the tenth century was vividly described by Sei Shônagon, a lady-in-waiting whose writings are among the most important in Japanese literary history. She once observed some carpenters who were remodelling a wing of the palace as they took a meal during the day, and had this to say:

> The way in which carpenters eat is really odd... The moment the food was brought, they fell on the soup bowls and gulped down the contents. Then they pushed the bowls aside and finished off all the vegetables. I wondered whether they were going to leave their rice; a moment later there wasn't a grain left in the bowls. They all behaved in exactly the same way, so I suppose this must be the custom of carpenters... [Sei 1967: 255].

The author evidently thought the correct way to eat a meal was gradually and alternately to take the three types of food – rice, soup, and the side dish of vegetables – rather than eating all of one thing and then going on to the next. Furthermore, only two daily meals were eaten at the court of that time, and she may have found it strange to see a meal in the middle of the day. The official meals consisted of breakfast at about ten in the morning and dinner at about five in the afternoon, but there was some variation according to occupation and social class. Commoners engaged in physical labour would eat after dawn and before sunset, and carpenters, soldiers and others doing especially heavy work would receive one or more simple meals during the day to supplement the regular two.

A document from the year 1221 describing customs at court, the *Kinpishô*, refers to the Emperor taking three meals per day whereas in former times it was only two, and we may thus surmise that by that point the nobility too were eating three meals. The custom in Zen monasteries of eating snacks (called *tenshin*) or tea cakes between the two main meals was adopted by other Buddhist sects, and in the temples of the sixteenth century the snack had been elevated to the position of a substantial noontime meal. Three meals per day was also normal among the populace of Kyoto in the sixteenth century. On the other hand, there are records indicating that in the late sixteenth and early seventeenth centuries, two meals per day was the rule among provincial samurai. By the end of the seventeenth century virtually the entire country was eating three meals. These data show that the shift from two to three daily meals proceeded with considerable variation by occupation, social class and region, and remind us that the era surveyed in this chapter was indeed a time of remarkable change.

It was during this era that lamps which burned vegetable oil became popular in the homes of the common people, and the production of candles began. It may be that as evening activities were extended, especially in the cities, two meals became insufficient and so a third was added to the day. But a case can also be made that the third meal resulted from a lengthened workday. This was the time when the self-sufficiency economy was beginning to break down and cash-based commodity trading spread through the country. As manufacturing systems were introduced and new lands were put under cultivation, productivity increased in comparison to medieval times. Commercial activities also developed rapidly. Since all this occurred well before the industrial revolution, the incremental growth in production was founded largely upon humanpower. Thus the people of this time worked more than their forebears, or were more likely to be workers. Long labour schedules, which delayed the day's final meal so that it was no longer unusual to eat after sunset, probably led to the universal insertion of the noontime meal between breakfast and supper.

CHAPTER 5

THE MATURING OF TRADITIONAL JAPANESE CUISINE

5.1   Historical Setting

Japan was almost entirely sealed off from the outside world from
1639, when the policy of national seclusion came into full force,
until the Tokugawa shogunate collapsed in 1868. Although very
little dietary culture was introduced from abroad, those elements
that were already well established were consolidated and
systematized. This period saw the formulation of what the Japanese
today regard as their 'traditional' culinary values, cooking and eating
habits. Afterward, during the age of modernization which began in
1868, a great deal of energy was devoted to the importation of new
foods and recipes but very little effort was made towards the further
refinement or alteration of traditional foods, which anyway had
reached such a degree of perfection that further change was difficult.
The majority of the traditional dishes eaten today date from the
220-year period of seclusion which is the scope of this chapter.

Society during this time operated as a feudal system. The
Tokugawa shoguns, with headquarters at Edo (now Tokyo), had
their own lands and their own bands of loyal retainers, but most of
Japan was divided into the domains of more than 200 daimyo who
were invested by the shogun. Under the Pax Tokugawana the

105

obligations of a daimyo included furnishing soldiers and going into battle at the shogun's demand; sponsoring the construction of public works as directed by the shogun; and maintaining a residence at Edo where his wife stayed as a hostage and he resided in alternate years. A castle was built in each domain to serve as the headquarters and stronghold of the daimyo, and towns grew up around the castles to house their samurai vassals as well as merchants and artisans.

The shogunate surveyed the agricultural lands of the entire country and appraised each area in terms of rice productivity. For example the Kaga domain (now Ishikawa Prefecture) had an estimated capacity of about one million *koku* of rice (a *koku* is about 180 litres). Rice was the monetary unit for the ruling samurai class: the daimyo collected tax in kind from the peasants and also provided their vassals with stipends denominated in *koku* of rice. To obtain cash, the samurai who were paid in rice sold it to merchants. Thus the national economy rested on the foundation of rice growing and rice distribution. Daimyo sought to increase their rice supplies by building riparian works and opening new land to paddy cultivation, and by squeezing higher in-kind levies out of the peasants. It was common for rice-growing peasants to deliver so much of their crops as tax that they did not have enough rice for their families to eat, and were thus forced to mix vegetables into their rice, or to make millet or sweet potatoes their staple food. The Edo period (1600–1868) is the only time in Japanese history when farmers who harvested rice could not eat it. In the towns, meanwhile, a cash economy existed and rice was sold in the markets, so even the poorest townspeople were able to eat rice as their staple.

Edo-period society was rigidly divided into classes, mainly the samurai, peasants, artisans and merchants. At the top of the official hierarchy were the ruling samurai. Next stood the peasants who comprised about 80 per cent of the population, followed by the artisans, while the merchants who were not engaged in productive work occupied the lowest rank. However, as peaceful conditions continued, towns and cities developed and the demand for consumer goods increased, and the merchants who purveyed them gradually acquired higher status. As they accumulated capital they were able to invest in manufacturing which yielded further profits, and wealth came to be concentrated in the merchant class.

By the eighteenth century the motive power of the Japanese economy clearly had passed from the samurai class, whose activities were centred on the old-fashioned rice economy, to the merchants who propelled the monetary economy. The daimyo began borrowing money from powerful merchant-financiers, using the rice produced in their domains as security.

The peasantry were the object of exploitation for rice tax. Improvement in their living standards would have meant conversion of some of their crops to cash, and the lessening of the portion taken by the feudal lords. The samurai therefore made every effort to keep the peasants in a self-sufficient economy, and enacted laws prohibiting them from indulging in the slightest luxury. In their own lives the samurai adhered to ascetic moral standards, and it was considered 'un-samurai-like' to eat extravagantly or to grumble about food.

Hence it was neither the samurai nor the peasants, but rather the urban merchants and artisans who were the chief bearers of dietary culture during the Edo period. Restaurants and snack shops appeared about the middle of the eighteenth century in the main cities of Edo, Kyoto and Osaka. Wealthy merchants were the main customers of the restaurants, while the snack shops were patronized largely by artisans, who were wage-earning labourers. These dining establishments proliferated rapidly, and at the end of the eighteenth century Edo probably had a higher density of restaurants than any other city in the world. With freewheeling competition among a tremendous number of restaurants, a great many new foods and styles of service were born. Many of them were subsequently adopted by the samurai and peasant classes, and also spread to the regional towns and cities.

In most countries, refined fashions in cuisine and couture originate at court or among the aristocracy, and gradually filter down to the lower-ranking levels of society. That general trend does not apply to Japan during the Edo period. Not only foods, but also kimono fashions and hairstyles originated mainly among stage actors and the high-class prostitutes of the licensed quarters in the major cities, and only occasionally among the samurai, the nobility or the peasantry. Merchants and artisans were the main patrons of the licensed quarters. As no popular revolution occurred, the samurai who were institutionalized as the privileged class continued to rule. Yet in actual fact during the eighteenth century a popular society was established in the major cities by the merchant bourgeoisie and the artisans, who constituted an urban proletariat at the base of the monetary economy.

Along with the development of manufacturing and commerce, extensive market networks were established across Japan, with Edo and Osaka as the main centres. Kyoto, although it had the majesty of the imperial court, was only the nominal capital with little real political influence. While it remained a centre of culture, art and craft, it declined in economic importance.

Osaka was the city where Toyotomi Hideyoshi had built his castle during his campaign of national unification in the late sixteenth century, but the seat of government soon moved east to Edo, and thereafter Osaka developed exclusively as an economic centre. While its location made it the natural distribution centre for western Japan, Osaka was also a hub for marine transport from the northern regions of Hokkaido and the upper Japan Sea coast, even though they were geographically closer to Edo, because the Japan and Inland Seas were safer for navigation than the Pacific Ocean. As a result, foodstuffs from all over Japan were collected in Osaka for distribution through much of the country. Rice remained the cornerstone of the national economy in that its price was the main determinant of the prices of all other goods. The daimyo converted substantial portions of their rice tribute to cash by shipping it to the markets of Edo and Osaka for sale to wholesale merchants. Osaka had the larger rice market and thus wielded considerable economic influence over the entire country. With its trade ranging from kelp gathered by the Ainu of Hokkaido to sugar from the cane fields of the Ryukyus, Osaka was known as 'the nation's kitchen'.

The new and burgeoning city of Edo initially relied on Osaka for supplies of consumer goods and of foods other than the basics of rice, vegetables and fish. Most of the soy sauce and sake in Edo were Kansai products, shipped by sea from Osaka, which were regarded as being of higher quality than products of the Kanto region. Later, soy sauce with a distinctive flavour that suited the taste of Edoites began to be produced nearby and largely displaced the Kansai product in the local market. For sake, however,

Edo/Tokyo has generally preferred Kansai brews up to the present day.

Edo tended to feel inferior to the Kansai region, which had a much longer history as the centre of government and culture. But with the stable stimulus of the Tokugawa government, Edo eventually grew into one of the largest cities of the world, with a population of about one million, and began to compete with Kansai in the cultural sphere as well. In cooking it developed an original style called *Edomae*, based largely around fresh fish. It was the people of Edo who nurtured such typical elements of modern Japanese cuisine as sushi, *soba* and tempura. Whereas previously only Kansai food had been thought of as refined, from the later part of the eighteenth century Edo became a second centre of culinary culture. Even today Japanese food preferences are often discussed in terms of two main styles of taste, that of western Japan centred around Kansai and that of eastern Japan influenced by Tokyo.

5.2 City and Country

In 1641–2, crop failures throughout the country caused by abnormal weather brought on the worst famine yet faced by the Tokugawa administration. Although there are no official statistics, it is believed that between fifty and a hundred thousand persons starved to death. Great numbers of starving peasants left their villages in search of food and flowed into the castle towns of the daimyo, other towns along the main roads, and the cities of Edo, Osaka and Kyoto, where most of them became beggars. The shogunate took various emergency steps to cope with the crisis, including providing foodstuffs to the starving, repatriating urban beggars to the countryside, and limiting the production of grain-wasting sake brewing and noodle making. The famine also induced the shogunate to decree several long-term policies, including programmes for riparian works to improve agricultural productivity, regulations governing the work and lives of the peasantry, and a permanent prohibition of the buying or selling of farmland. The official rationale for the land freeze, as proclaimed in the edict, was to prevent 'rich farmers growing richer and richer by buying and accumulating farmland, and poor farmers growing poorer and poorer by selling off farmland.' Yet the measure was clearly motivated by fears that the economic base which sustained the feudal system would be weakened by an increase in the number of farmers who were landless and hence incapable of paying taxes. Under that law it became difficult for those born as peasants to escape from the farming villages, and this led to a marked difference between the consumerist lifestyle of the townspeople and the agricultural lifestyle of the villagers.

The regulations for peasant life promulgated by the shogunate in 1643 included the following provisions regarding food:

- Cereals other than rice were to be used as the daily staple, and rice was not to be eaten without special reason.
- Foods requiring large amounts of grain or beans, such as *manjū* (bean-jam buns) and tofu, were deemed luxuries which could not be sold in farm villages.
- The brewing and sale of sake were prohibited in farm villages.
- Traveling to markets or towns in order to drink sake was prohibited.

The lives of the peasantry were regulated in numerous ways. Only cotton was to be used for clothing. The growing of tobacco was prohibited. Rice consumption in peasant households was limited to small quantities, and goods could not be sold for cash in farm villages. By prohibiting luxury and assuring that peasant living standards remained low, the ruling class sought to guarantee that sufficient amounts of tax – mainly rice – cold be squeezed from the peasants.

The peasants themselves also tended to restrict their consumption of rice, because whatever rice remained after taxes was their only means for obtaining cash. For daily meals it was therefore common to mix barley, millet or *hie* (Japanese barnyard millet) with the rice, and to add the leaves of vegetables such as the *daikon* radish to the rice pot. Yet complete substitution of other grains for rice was unusual. At least a tiny amount of rice would be included, and for wealthier farmers the major portion of the grain might be rice. There were even some areas where it was customary to cook rice only, with no other grains or vegetables added as filler.

Among historians and anthropologists dealing with the peasantry of the Edo period, a convention has developed of stressing the image of rice producers who were themselves unable to eat rice in their daily life. Yet there is some doubt as to whether or not that was actually the case [Ishige 1986]. Metrical analysis of statistics for Hida (now Gifu Prefecture) in 1873 proves that even in a mountainous region that is ill–suited to rice growing, where there was a relatively high number of poor peasants, rice was by far the main foodstuff consumed. Since those statistics are based on a survey taken immediately after the close of the Edo period, they may be assumed to reflect conditions which had existed with no change through most of those two centuries (see Section 2.1). Statistics from 1840 for Chôshû (now Yamaguchi Prefecture) show that among the non-samurai population (mostly peasants) rice constituted some 60 per cent of the staple foods. A similar proportion has been calculated as the national average for that time, a situation which is likely to have continued without change from the mid-eighteenth century [Kitô 1983:43–9]. The records of peasant life in the Edo period include many writings by urban intellectuals, who always ate unadulterated rice, which emphasize the meagreness of peasant meals. Their descriptions of conditions in particular regions were used as historical data and it was inferred that the same was true nationwide, and so the stories of peasants who could not eat rice came to be exaggerated.

The intentions of the ruling elite notwithstanding, it was impossible to prevent the peasants from being caught up in the cash economy. There was increased cultivation of commodity crops such as tea, tobacco, rapeseed (used for lamp oil) and cotton, and many kinds of vegetables were grown for shipment to markets on the outskirts of the major cities. During the slack season more and more peasants went to the cities to work. As a means of getting around the prohibition against selling land, moneylenders would loan cash to farmers with the land as security. When the loans were not repaid they would seize the mortgaged land, and thus in actual practice land was bought and accumulated. Hence the peasantry gradually became involved in cash-based economic activity, and the edicts forbidding peasants to have noodles, sake or tofu were relegated to nominal status. Such products were available in farm villages that lay near cities, but in outlying villages there were no shops that sold noodles or tofu until the late nineteenth century. In remote areas, noodles and tofu had to be made from scratch at home, and thus were too troublesome to be served as everyday meals and were reserved as festive foods for annual events and for entertaining guests. In records of feasts in farm villages we find that the menus often matched sake which was purchased elsewhere with tofu and noodles which were made in the homes.

The samurai, forbidden to engage in agriculture, were city-dwelling consumers who produced no food apart from limited amounts of vegetable and fruits cultivated around their homes for personal use. The samurai who served as retainers to the shogun maintained homes in Edo even when they were assigned to temporary posts in distant shogunal domains. Ordinary samurai resided in regional towns around the castles of the daimyo. From their lords they received salaries of rice and other foodstuffs, and they were able to obtain cash by selling what rice they did not need for their own households. Although there was variation according to rank, many of the samurai in regional towns were in the habit of mixing small amounts of barley with their rice, and flavourings such as miso and soy sauce were commonly made at their homes. In general the meals of the samurai were plain in comparison to those of the wealthy merchants. As the rice-based economic system of the samurai broke down and the cash economy spawned by industry and commerce became the driving force of society, the samurai were gradually impoverished. During the nineteenth century many samurai were forced to take side jobs or pawn their possessions in order to survive [Watanabe 1964:241-2].

Meanwhile in the large cities of Edo, Osaka and Kyoto even people of the lowest economic class ate daily meals of unadulterated rice. Beriberi became common in the major cities from the eighteenth century. As explained in Chapter 2, this 'Edo sickness' was contracted only by townspeople, for it was caused by a deficiency of vitamin B1, which traditionally was obtained from the outer layer of the rice grain. Beriberi was cured by leaving the city, where even servants ate highly polished rice, for a spell in the countryside.

The controls exerted by the samurai administration over the merchants and artisans who lived in the cities were lenient compared to those for peasants. Urban householders of the Edo period relied entirely on the cash economy and consumed freely according to their means, in contrast to the samurai who were constrained by the morality of thriftiness and moreover were gradually falling into economic straits. The urban population, which held the freest position in Edo society, did away with old-fashioned patterns and cooked meals that were substantial and delicious. Some urbanites acquired considerable refinement in the area of food, and there emerged gourmets and epicures who made a hobby of eating delicacies. Ultimately among certain people in the major cities food became a thing for display, an item of fashion or sport. It became a point of pride and fashion to pay a premium price for the earliest available specimens of a vegetable or fish, in order to be able to serve foods fresh before they were thought to be in season. The byword was, 'Eat the season's first produce, live 75 days longer.' A carpenter or other artisan who was not particularly affluent might proudly pay the equivalent of ten days' wages for a bonito that would sell for a tenth the price ten days later, and eat it sliced raw. In the late eighteenth and nineteenth centuries, contests to see who could eat and drink the most were popular in Edo; eating was becoming a sport.

The meals of the commoners in the cities, however, were plain. Most Edoites had a breakfast of rice, miso soup and pickles, and their lunch and dinner menus were similar, with the addition of one side dish of simmered vegetables or tofu, or simmered or grilled fish.

5.3   The Spread of Soy Sauce

Soy sauce and miso paste are both made by mixing soybeans with salt and a fermenting agent called *kôji*, as described in Section 2.4. Prototypes of these fermented soy foods were probably developed in China during the Han dynasty (c.200 BCE –CE 200), and eventually spread to Korea and Japan. The earliest record of their use in Japan is the Taihô Code of 701. The fermented soy foods mentioned in those laws are miso; *kuki,* similar to the present-day Daitokuji and *hama* varieties of *nattô,* in which the beans retain their shape and solidity in the end product; and *hishio,* a semi-liquid paste or gruel fermented from a mixture of soybeans, grain and sake.

At least 90 per cent of the miso consumed in today's Japanese households is used to prepare miso soup, which most people eat once a day. The soup is made by simmering fish or vegetables in *dashi* stock (see Chapter 1), and then dissolving miso into it. It is known to have existed as early as the tenth century, when miso was mentioned as a soup ingredient in the *Engi shiki,* but during medieval times it was not part of the meals of the common people. This may well have been because miso was considered a luxury and hence not made in quantities sufficient for daily cooking. Instead, small amounts were typically consumed by eating a side dish of miso or of vegetables pickled with miso.

Miso was also important as a flavouring. Small amounts were added for taste when simmering fish or vegetables, and miso was dissolved in vinegar as a sauce. There are many regional varieties with colour ranging from light yellow when rice is used as the main ingredient, to reddish brown when only soybeans are used. Food steeped in miso takes on the colour as well as the rich texture and flavour of the legume and grain constituents. In order to improve the outward appearance of the food or impart a lighter flavour, miso and water (or a cooked mixture of miso and water) would be placed in a cloth bag and the liquid that trickled out would be collected. This refined miso solution was used in preparing elegant meals for the upper class, and later was replaced by soy sauce.

Miso and soy sauce are made in very similar ways, the main difference being that miso is a paste rather than a liquid. The prototype of soy sauce, the semi-liquid flavouring called *hishio,* may have been used in Japan as early as the eighth century [Fukuo 1979]. If indeed it was known so early, *hishio* was probably too expensive to come into general use, for it is harder to make than miso and has a more refined flavour.

Soy sauce is mentioned in several sixteenth-century documents. By the second half of the century factories had been established in the Kansai region, and some trading ships were used exclusively to distribute the product to other regions. It was as a factory-made product that soy sauce became popular, initially coming into use at daily meals among the townspeople whose lives depended on the commodity economy. As Edo grew into a major city, its residents consumed large quantities of Kansai soy sauce, but late in the seventeenth century soy sauce aimed at the Edo market began to be made locally, in the districts that are now called Chôshi and Noda in Chiba Prefecture. In contrast to the lighter-tasting (*usukuchi*) Kansai product, the Kanto factories used a larger proportion of wheat to produce a rich, fragrant *koikuchi* brew. This suited the Edoites well, and by the latter part of the eighteenth century the locally produced soy sauce had taken over the metropolitan market.

In the cities, by the eighteenth century soy sauce had become the principal seasoning for food and miso came to be used almost exclusively for soup. But in remote rural districts, miso remained in use as a seasoning for daily meals until the early twentieth century, while soy sauce, purchased in small quantities from local factories, was eaten only at festival meals or when serving special guests. Many farm families made their own miso until the 1950s, whereas those who made soy sauce were always a rarity. Nothing is wasted in making miso because all of the ingredients are turned into the paste which is eaten. Making soy sauce not only involves more work but also leaves a substantial amount of inedible lees after the liquid is strained. The lower rate of yield from the raw materials made soy sauce a luxury item which the peasantry could not easily produce at home, and so miso remained the everyday seasoning among the rural population. What soy sauce was used was factory made. Besides the local sake brewery, every area had a small soy sauce brewery until the early twentieth century, when major firms with large factories and national distribution networks created an oligopoly market for soy sauce and it came into regular use even in poor rural households. Thus the main flavouring of Japanese cooking shifted from miso to soy sauce over a period of more than two centuries, as urban taste gradually diffused through the countryside.

When trying a new type of food, the Japanese are apt to begin by seasoning it with soy sauce. It is the predominant and universal seasoning today. Japanese cooking is not possible without soy sauce, just as salt and pepper are indispensable to the Western kitchen and dining table. Soy sauce is used in preparing food in the kitchen and a small container of it is usually placed on the table for seasoning food after it is served. Direct use of salt is much less common in Japan than in the West, for much salt is ingested indirectly from soy sauce and miso. A 1980 survey by the Ministry of Health and Welfare determined that soy sauce and miso supplied 27 and 16 per cent, respectively, of the average daily salt intake, while salt sprinkled on food in the kitchen or at the table accounted for only 13 per cent. In addition to saltiness, of course soy sauce and miso add other flavour and fragrance to food. Their tastiness results notably from their high content of glutamic acid (discussed in Chapter 2), and their complex flavour structures contain tart and sweet elements as well as alcohol.

Soy sauce, being a liquid, is easier to use than miso. A dash can be instantly added to the pot. It is also commonly mixed with sake or sugar, or with grated *daikon* radish or ginger to make sauces for dipping. With its greater convenience and wider range of use, soy sauce largely replaced miso as a seasoning soon after it appeared, and new styles of cooking were designed based on its use.

The popularization of soy sauce was connected with a change in the style of eating raw fish. Since the Heian period, slices of raw fish had commonly been served in a dressing made mainly of vinegar or miso, somewhat like a salad. The fish was usually mixed with the dressing on a plate before it was served, and thus comparatively little attention was paid to the way the fish was sliced. This type of dish was called *namasu* or *sashimi*, but after the advent of soy sauce the word *sashimi* took on the different meaning that it has kept to the present. *Sashimi* now means fish that has been sliced and arranged on a plate and served with a smaller plate of soy sauce, so that the diner may pick up each piece with chopsticks and dip it in the sauce. With this style, skill at cutting and arranging the slices in a pleasing way becomes a point of pride for the chef. Besides *sashimi*, such popular and internationally known dishes as sushi (*nigiri-zushi*), tempura and teriyaki, which all developed during the Edo period, are also meant to be eaten with soy sauce.

Soy sauce is used without discrimination on most types of food including fish, meat, vegetables and seaweed, and in various

116

types of cooking including simmering, grilling and steaming. Due to excessive reliance on this handy flavouring, the cooks of the Edo period were not very eager to develop new tastes. Their culinary ideal was not to create artificial new tastes, but rather to present the natural taste of the food itself in as pure a way as possible. The taste of soy sauce, which was found to complement almost any dish, was regarded as an intermediary flavour that allowed the taste of the food itself to play the principal role. In order to bring out the natural flavour it was believed that complex flavourings were to be avoided, and this gave rise to a peculiar value standard for cooking which holds that, 'Not to cook is the ideal of cooking' (see Section 9.2). Cooking which concentrates on avoiding creativity and complexity in taste, and which seeks to select the finest ingredients and to slice and serve them with the most beautiful technique, is what developed among the chefs of the high-class restaurants during the Edo period.

5.4   The Emergence of the Restaurant

In China, restaurants and drinking establishments that served simple meals developed during ancient times, and by the tenth century dining establishments worthy of being called restaurants took form in the cities. In other parts of the world the restaurant, as a place where meals are served for enjoyment and social interaction may occur, did not develop until relatively recent times. Restaurants appeared during the eighteenth century in Europe and Japan, and spread around the world along with the expansion of European colonies. In Korea, it was during the years before and after 1900, when Japan had intervened and was forcibly speeding the country's modernization, that restaurants appeared. The first high-class restaurant in Seoul opened in 1887 and served Japanese cuisine.

Although restaurants in Japan came into existence during the period of national seclusion and developed without influence from China or Europe, there is nevertheless a strong historical parallel between Japanese and Western European dining establishments. In both regions, the maturing of civic society served as the foundation on which the restaurant business was built.

In Western Europe until about the eighteenth century, inns and taverns were the only facilities where meals were served outside the home. Inn and tavern were often combined as a single establishment, especially along the highways where they were most common. The meals served in these places were the typical fare of the masses and bore no relation to haute cuisine. Top-quality foods and the techniques of preparation, along with dining rooms and fancy tableware suitable for eating them, existed exclusively among the upper crust of society, at the royal court and in the chateaux of the nobility. After the French Revolution, the restaurant business was inaugurated by chefs who had lost their employers. Thus with the abolition of the absolute monarchy and the establishment of civic society, it became possible for any member of the public who had the requisite cash to enjoy a refined meal.

In Japan too, although there was no popular revolution, a bourgeoisie formed during the Edo period and took effective power in society, and it was they who sponsored the appearance of restaurants serving gourmet cuisine in the largest cities. These developments are best described by observing the case of Edo, the main city [Ishige 1990].

There were two types of inns in medieval Japan. One was the *kichin yado* ('firewood-fee inn'), where guests brought their own food and used the kitchen facilities to prepare it themselves. The other type, called *hatago*, provided meals as well as lodging; these were clustered along main roads and in certain quarters of the towns and cities during the sixteenth century. Edo was growing rapidly at that time and *hatago* inns were established to serve travellers from the provinces, furnishing meals which probably were quite plain. In the seventeenth century, after the age of warfare had given way to a protracted peace, great numbers of people began travelling for tourism. To make travel more enjoyable, innkeepers began serving the specialties of their regions, and thus cooking became a selling point for some inns. This type of establishment, which provides lodging and also serves customers who come only to dine, still flourishes today under the name *ryōri-ryokan* (restaurant-inn).

While inns were related to the rise of the restaurant, another type of dining establishment known as the *chaya* or *chamise* (teahouse) was more important in this regard. The development of the teahouse was linked to the increase in tourism and in the number of pilgrims visiting temples and shrines in the cities and their suburbs. A document from 1403 tells us that tradespeople were offering tea to thirsty pilgrims near the gate of the celebrated Toji temple in Kyoto, but they were peddlers who did not erect permanent shops. In the sixteenth century huts were built to serve tea at points along highways where travellers were likely to need a rest, especially between the post towns where *hatago* inns were clustered. Soon the teahouses advanced into the post towns and began serving light meals of *mochi* or sweets, or sake with drinking snacks, but they were prohibited from serving full meals or lodging travellers under a law designed to protect the inns.

By the seventeenth century, teahouses had also appeared in the cities and towns, near the gates of well-known temples and shrines. These establishments began hiring pretty women as waitresses to attract customers, and in time woodblock *ukiyoe* portraits of teahouse women came to be widely sold, much as photographs of actresses are circulated in modern times.

On the streets of Edo in the seventeenth and eighteenth centuries, the teahouse differentiated into various forms of business, some of which had little or nothing to do with tea. Patrons began to rent teahouses and use them to entertain guests. Renting private rooms, primarily for rendezvous between a man and a woman, became the main business of some establishments, which were known as assignation teahouses (*machiai-jaya* or *deai-jaya*). *Sumô* teahouses developed beside the wrestling rings and *shibai* (stage play) teahouses developed around the theatres, furnishing rooms for resting and eating after the performances.

Teahouses that specialized in light meals were called *niuri-jaya* ('teahouses selling simmered food'). These offered limited menus in table d'hôte style, in a large earthen-floored room where customers sat on benches next to strangers. They were patronized not by persons of rank but by labourers and travellers, having originated as canteens for the workers who gathered in Edo to rebuild the city after it was two-thirds destroyed by fire in 1657. As the *niuri* teahouses flourished, some of them made sake rather than food the basis of their trade, and these evolved into the *izakaya* (taverns) which are common today. Noodle shops which served *soba*, the Edo-style buckwheat noodles, also became common in the aftermath of the 1657 fire.

Documentary evidence suggests that dining establishments did not develop to any appreciable extent during the half century between the time when Edo became the seat of government and the great fire. When a teahouse specializing in a regional rice dish (Nara *chameshi*) opened in 1657 near the gate of a famous temple in Asakusa, townspeople flocked around it to watch the rare phenomenon of a meal served outside the home. It was Edo's first restaurant.

Prototypes of the cooking teahouses (*ryôri-jaya*) which were the first genuine restaurants in Japan seem to have developed in Kyoto and Osaka during the 1680s, although the historical record is unclear. Three such establishments are recorded as operating in the Ryogoku neighbourhood of Edo during the 1760s, which likely means that some number of others were operating elsewhere in the city [Hirata 1992: 72]. At a high-class *ryôri* teahouse the guests sat on tatami mats facing a Japanese garden, in an elegantly designed room decorated with a brushwork scroll, consuming foods that they had specifically ordered and which were prepared with refined techniques. The prices there were extremely high, beyond the reach of ordinary townspeople.

Before the appearance of *ryôri* teahouses, high-ranking samurai and wealthy merchants held banquets at their homes. The rooms and tableware in the houses of the very rich were more splendid than those at teahouses or inns, and their domestic help provided meticulous service. However, there is considerable room for doubt regarding the tastiness of the food itself. The *honzen ryôri* that was the dominant cuisine at banquets of the rich was designed primarily for show. There were more dishes than one could possibly consume, mostly served cold, and very complicated etiquette was observed while eating. The cooks who worked in the mansions of the elite had to know how to prepare a large variety of special meals for different events and ceremonies, but they tended strongly toward an anachronistic cuisine that emphasized forms from the past over actual taste.

Being commercial dining establishments, the *ryôri* teahouses had to serve meals that were not just aesthetically pleasing but also delicious to eat, or they would lose their customers. Their main class of guests were the bourgeoisie who had no interest in ceremony or official events, but rather sought to enjoy delicious meals in an informal atmosphere on no particular schedule. Here the cooks were directed not to follow the banquet forms of the past, but to make food that was truly good to eat. Due to these circumstances, the cooking techniques that originated in the *ryôri* teahouses gave rise to the Japanese gourmet cooking that has been passed down to the present. With teahouse chefs as the core, a guild of commercial cooks was formed outside the established schools of chefs who served the nobility and the top samurai. Over the years the new guild branched into a number of schools which exist today.

The *ryôri* teahouses were originally patronized by wealthy merchants, and they functioned not only as places for enjoying meals but also as sites for business meetings. Among the samurai class, who generally disliked dining out, the first to take meals at the Edo teahouses were the official resident representatives, or *rusui*, of the provincial daimyo . These high-ranking vassals used provincial funds to gather at the teahouses for meetings with colleagues from other provinces to discuss politics and diplomacy, or with wealthy merchants to arrange loans to cover the chronic deficits in provincial finances. As a result the high-class cooking establishments of Edo came to be called *rusui* teahouses. The well-known custom among today's Japanese businessmen and politicians of conducting negotiations in restaurants originated with the *rusui* teahouses of the eighteenth century. As the venue for protracted meetings, often with entertainments of song and dance by accomplished geisha performers, which in any case involved constant rounds of sake drinking, the cooking teahouses served dishes which were not so much meals as they were accompaniments for drink. The practice continues today in the high-class restaurants called *ryôtei*, where foreign guests are wont to complain that the food is 'nothing but an endless series of hors-d'oeuvres'.

By the early nineteenth century Edo had an immense number of *ryôri* teahouses. Some were high–class establishments but many were patronized by middle-class merchants and artisans. Those that were equipped with large rooms often served as venues for social and cultural events, including poetry readings, dance recitals and exhibits of calligraphy or painting, at which refreshments would be served. When the firemen of Edo gathered to resolve a dispute in 1818, the teahouse used for the assembly was able to accommodate 900 persons on two floors.

5.5   Snack Shops

A survey by the Edo city government in 1804 found 6,165 shops engaged in serving food. Using an estimate of the population at the time, that works out to one for every 170 townspeople. But the number of shops must have been larger because the survey did not cover the theatre district or the extensive Yoshiwara licensed quarter, where there were numerous food peddlers and dense concentrations of restaurants. In 1860 the question of raising *soba* prices due to an increase in the cost of buckwheat prompted a general meeting of the *soba* trade of Edo, with 3,726 shops represented. That number did not include the many peddlers who prepared and sold the noodles. During the first half of the nineteenth century, Edo may well have had the highest density of restaurants in the world.

The *ryôri* teahouses, being banquet venues serving full-course meals of various types of food, were just one of several kinds of restaurants that flourished in Edo. The majority of the city's restaurants served the common people on a daily basis, and specialized in serving one type of food as a light meal. Except for a few high-class establishments, these popular restaurants were inexpensive *soba*, sushi or tempura shops. Another favourite among Edoites was eel *kabayaki* (grilled on skewers with sweet sauce), but since it was somewhat expensive a trip to the eel shop was considered a treat. These foods all developed in Edo and are still popular specialties of Tokyo today, but over the years they have tended to become more refined dishes and, with the exception of *soba*, can no longer be regarded as inexpensive snacks.

Generally one *soba* shop could be found on each block of the Edo streets (usually about 120 metres long). In livelier neighbourhoods where many people were about in the evenings and snacks were in high demand, a single block might have three or four stalls and shops serving *soba*, sushi and tempura. In the busiest areas of the city, half the buildings fronting on to the street were eating establishments, and most served the typical snack foods.

Snack foods originally developed as items served at stalls. While some dining establishments originated as teahouses, there was another pattern of restaurateurs who began as mobile vendors, setting up a stall at a regular place by the side of a street to serve customers who ate standing up, and later obtained a space in a building for their business. Shops serving snacks generally were of this type. Stalls became numerous on the streets of Edo during the 1770s.

A feature of any urban centre is round-the-clock activity, with many places to obtain a light meal outside the normal eating schedules. In addition to that universal aspect of modern cities, Edo had the special characteristic of a large population of single men, and this was the stimulus for the development of snack foods. Most of the samurai who accompanied the daimyo to Edo for their obligatory period of residence during every second year came alone, leaving their families behind. The men who worked in large retail shops came from the provinces and were given board and lodging by their employers. Construction work was very common, not only because the city was steadily growing larger, but also because the dense conurbation of wooden structures was repeatedly struck by fire, and the labourers who were recruited from the provinces in great numbers to rebuild the city generally came alone. Surveys of the non-samurai population of Edo from the 1710s to the 1740s confirm that the gender ratio was extremely uneven, with 57 to 59 women per 100 men.

When store employees were not satiated by their board meals they went out for snacks. Labourers and artisans, who lived in very cramped quarters where only minimal cooking was possible, often purchased food from peddlers or went out for snacks. The wages of an artisan or labourer may have been low, but usually he was paid in cash each day, and since work could always be had in Edo, there was no great enthusiasm for saving money. On the contrary, under the prevailing ethos it was shameful to have money left over from the night before, and extravagance was not seen as a vice. Hence money would be used to dine out, and the numerous dining establishments prospered.

The common people's habit of dining out also influenced the upper class. Some restaurateurs opted to expand beyond their poorer clientele by erecting grander shops and charging higher prices for more elegant versions of the same snacks. Culinary styles diversified according to the class being served, and Edoites ate out frequently, regardless of social standing. From documentary evidence it is clear that in the mid-seventeenth century *soba* was a low-class food, but in the early eighteenth century splendidly equipped *soba* shops emerged where persons of rank would eat, and in the late eighteenth century senior samurai in attendance at the homes of daimyo discussed which *soba* or sushi shops were the tastiest.

Edo, Kyoto and Osaka had their respective social tempers. Writings from the mid-nineteenth century comparing the cities report that among Kyotoites it was expected that the box lunch carried on an excursion would contain home-cooked food, for it was vulgar to pack food purchased from a restaurant. In contrast, Edoites of any class were likely to set out empty-handed and eat at a snack shop, and a box lunch would be carried only by the poor. The convention in Osaka fell in between those of Edo and Kyoto: a box lunch was always to be carried, but it was expected to contain food from a restaurant, not from home [Hirata 1992:73].

5.6 Books on Cooking and Restaurants

Japan had the highest rate of literacy in the world during the Edo period. Many common people could read and write, and a print culture flourished as great numbers of books were printed by woodblock. Cookbooks were among them, and for the first time it became common for cooking techniques to spread by means other than word of mouth and actual example. Thus knowledge about refined cooking could spread beyond a particular region or class, and travel quickly to the countryside and the population at large. More than 120 different block-printed cookbooks from the Edo period, and more than twice that number of hand-copied cookbooks are extant [Hirata 1985:537].

A hand-copied work from the end of the thirteenth century, the *Chûji ruiki* (Kitchenry Cyclopedia), is the oldest known Japanese document recording practical cooking techniques. The ten or so chief surviving examples of cookbooks written between then and the seventeenth century detail the foods, serving etiquette and table manners of ceremonial banquets for the nobility and samurai. Their authors were either members or associates of the schools of cooks who served the court and the Muromachi shoguns, and the works are evidently intended for those who were qualified to attend such banquets and those who cooked for them. In short, the cookbooks of the medieval age had extremely limited circulation.

The first modern cookbook was titled *Ryôri monogatari* (Accounts of Cooking), and went through many editions. The oldest surviving specimen was printed in 1643, but it is very likely that it was originally published about 1600. Its unknown author wrote from an independent standpoint that was not allied with any particular cooking school. Eschewing the authoritarian, formalistic descriptions of trivial and antiquated procedures that had characterized previous cookbooks, the *Ryôri monogatari* presents practical knowledge in a thoroughly pragmatic spirit. It contains 20 sections which fall into two main parts, the first containing the names of many different dishes listed by ingredient, and the second providing general descriptions of the techniques for preparing stewed foods, grilled foods etc. along with recipes for typical dishes. Under that arrangement there are many dishes that are mentioned by name without instructions for their preparation, indicating that the book was not written with amateurs in mind, but rather for those with a fair degree of cooking knowledge, mainly professional cooks [Harada 1989: 17–29].

From the seventeenth century, books of practical explanations of cooking were published one after another. They are organized in various ways, by ingredient with lists of recipes; or by cooking technique with lists of ingredients; or by menu with instructions for preparing each item. What most of them have in common is that they are not mere collections of recipes, but attempts to explain cooking techniques in systematic fashion.

In addition to cookbooks, various scholarly works concerning foodstuffs were published. These were written mainly by specialists in the field of traditional Oriental natural science (*honzôgaku*), in which Chinese medicine and pharmacology played strong roles. They were concerned with the effects of different foods on the body and with the choice of foods for maintaining health and healing illness. The outstanding work of this genre is the *Honchô shokkan*, written by Hitomi Hitsudai and published posthumously in 1697. It is a 12-volume, illustrated encyclopaedia of a tremendous number of animal and plant substances, with explanations of processing methods, cooking techniques, pharmacological characteristics, and folklore.

The number of printed cookbooks increased from the 1760s, the same time that restaurants began to proliferate in the cities. Previous cookbooks had strong colouration as insider's manuals, written by cooks and aimed at readers who were cooks. From the latter part of the eighteenth century many works appeared which were aimed at a general audience, and a significant number were written not by specialists but by intellectuals with literary skill. This new genre went beyond the bounds of practical manuals. Conceived primarily as interesting reading matter, the books tended to be in literary prose style with quotations from other books or descriptions of strange foods, and were lavishly illustrated [Harada 1989:104–31]. These 'fun-to-read cookbooks' may well have circulated among the common folk via the lending libraries which developed during the period.

An influential example is *Tôfu hyakuchin* (A Hundred Tofu Curiosities), originally published in Osaka in 1782. It presents a hundred ways to prepare tofu along with illustrations, sketches of popular restaurants specializing in tofu cooking, relevant excerpts from Chinese and Japanese literary works, and citations concerning the history of tofu. The population was quite familiar with tofu, and this book allowed everyone to satisfy any intellectual interest they may have had in the food. The pseudonymous author is suspected to be a sinologist who was active in Osaka at the time. The book won enormous popularity and within the year a second volume presenting another hundred ways of preparing tofu was published and both volumes were available in Kyoto and Edo bookshops as well. This success promptly motivated a bookseller in Kyoto to issue a series of 'hundred recipes' books on such foods as eggs and porgy (in landlocked Kyoto, freshwater carp was long rated the tastiest fish, but saltwater porgy displaced it during the Edo period). Thus, cookbooks came to be designed by publishers as potential bestsellers.

Restaurant guides constituted another category of food-related publications. With the proliferation of restaurants in the three main cities, the need arose for information to help in selecting a place to eat. A variety of guides, aimed at the newly emergent wandering gourmet as well as the provincial traveller who was visiting the city, were published from the end of the eighteenth century. Many of them were broadsheets, typically with two columns listing the names and addresses of about 150 currently well-rated restaurants, in descending order and type size according to their ranking. These were imitations of the established format of the sumo standings, which ranked the wrestlers of the eastern league on the right and the western league on the left, with the names of the referee and promoter in a centre column. In the centre column of the restaurant list, in place of the referee, was the name of a very famous restaurant. The sheet could easily be carried as one walked around the city.

The fact that such restaurant guides were sold confirms that the number of restaurants had increased to the point where it was difficult to choose among them. It also suggests that the diversion of going out to eat in a fine restaurant was no longer limited to a certain set or class of people, but had spread to the population at large. There is no way of knowing how the restaurants were selected for the list, and there are some indications that the promotion of certain restaurants was intended. Even if they were not compiled through a strict judging system, the fact remains that guides were available to those who sought gourmet food in the main cities of Japan a century before the first *Guide Michelin* was published in France.

An example of a guide in booklet form is *Edo shuhan tebikikusa* (Pocket Guide to Eating and Drinking in Edo), published in 1848. It lists the names and addresses of 594 general-fare restaurants, *soba* shops, sushi shops and eel restaurants. As a hint of its editorial policy, we may note that out of the thousand or so eel restaurants that are known from other sources to have been operating in the city at the time, this guide selected only 90 for inclusion.

5.7   The Ainu

For well over a thousand years after the unification of Yamato Japan, the extent of the authority of the central government was the three large islands of Honshu, Shikoku and Kyushu and the small islands near their shores. Despite local variations in dialect and culture, these areas of traditional Japan shared a common history as a homogeneous society. Meanwhile, two other populations at the extremes of the Japanese archipelago – the indigenous Ainu of the large northern island of Ezo (later Hokkaido), and the people of the southern Ryukyu island group that is now Okinawa Prefecture – were not incorporated into the Japanese nation until they came under the rule of the Tokugawa shogunate from the seventeenth century. With their long independent traditions these two ethnic groups maintained distinct dietary cultures.

Hokkaido, the second largest Japanese island after Honshu, has a subarctic climate with predominantly conifer forests and landscapes resembling Europe north of the Alps. The people who have inhabited the island since ancient times are called the Ainu (from the word in their language meaning 'people'). They were formerly thought to be of Caucasoid origin, due to physical characteristics such as thick head and body hair and well-defined facial features, but recent research has discredited that theory and suggested origins in the same Mongoloid racial pool as the Japanese. Curiously, physical anthropologists have found many similarities between the Ainu in the far north and the Ryukyu islanders in the far south of Japan. This may be explained by the theory that in the Jômon (neolithic) period the entire area of present-day Japan was inhabited by Mongoloid groups with similar physiques, and a later influx of different groups changed the population in the central areas only. Indeed the Yayoi and Kofun periods (c. 400BCE - CE 700) saw the assimilation of large numbers of immigrants from China and the Korean Peninsula, who brought rice-growing culture with them. Thus the population of the central parts of the archipelago may represent a mix of Jômon and Chinese/Korean characteristics, while the Ainu and Ryukyuans may have remained relatively pure Jômon groups. At any rate, uninfluenced by the Yayoi culture which used metal tools and practised farming, especially paddy rice cultivation, both groups long remained reliant on hunting, gathering and fishing for their food.

Ainu history since the fifteenth century can be traced through records written in Japanese by visitors from Honshu, but the Ainu were a non-literate society and archaeological investigation is the only means of observing their history in earlier times. After the Jômon era drew to a close on the main island of Honshu around 400BCE, an extension of Jômon culture continued on the island of Ezo. The Satsumon culture that flourished there from the ninth through twelfth centuries brought in new influences from Honshu, evidenced by earthenware shapes and by Japanese inscriptions on some earthenware found at sites on the southern part of the island. Contemporaneous with Satsumon culture in eastern and southern Ezo was Okhotsk culture, which also existed along the lower and middle reaches of the Amur River in Siberia and on Sakhalin and the Kuril Islands, and presumably was carried south to Ezo by the Nivkhi (Gilyaks) who inhabited the lower Amur and Sakhalin. Ainu culture appears to have incorporated various Okhotsk elements, including wood-carving designs that are similar to those of some Siberian ethnic groups and the *i-omante* bear festival (described below). Metal tools came into use through intercourse with the Japanese and Okhotsk cultures, and short iron swords spread through Ezo during the thirteenth and fourteenth centuries. It was probably around that time that the small river-basin villages of Ainu society coalesced into groups under a chieftainship system. A national polity was never formed. During the seventeenth and eighteenth centuries, the Ainu were spread through the Kuril Islands and the southern half of Sakhalin, and they journeyed by dugout canoe to trade with the Tsugaru and Shimokita Peninsulas at the northern tip of Honshu, and the Amur valley of Siberia.

Relations between the Ainu and the people of Honshu, generally speaking, comprise a history of exploitation by the Japanese. Through coastal trade which developed from the thirteenth century, iron tools and rice were brought in from

Honshu and in return the Ainu supplied hides, hawk feathers for arrows, salmon, trout and kelp. The Japanese began to penetrate southern Ezo in the early fifteenth century and had built twelve forts along the coast by 1457, when the first full-scale fighting broke out with Ainu resisting Japanese rule. There were many other armed uprisings against the invading Japanese until 1789 but each ended in defeat as Ezo, as well as southern Sakhalin and the southern Kurils, came entirely under the military control of Japanese colonists.

The Tokugawa shogunate (1603–1867) granted a part of Ezo to the Matsumae family as a feudal domain and gradually brought Ainu lands throughout the island under central government administration. Under the *bakuhan* system of the Tokugawa, the domain (*han*) of a daimyo consisted of ownership and governing rights for a fixed area of land which was delineated mainly on the basis of its rice yield. As an exception, in Ezo where the climate made farming difficult, the Matsumae daimyo received not only their own land at the southern tip of what is now Hokkaido but also a monopoly on the trade of produce from the immense expanse of Ainu lands covering the rest of the island. At the start of this arrangement the Ainu were in the position of trading partners with the Matsumae family, but their position declined as merchant shipping between Ezo and Osaka expanded in the late seventeenth and early eighteenth centuries. The Kansai region was then agriculturally well developed and once the farmers began to use Ezo herring as fertilizer demand for this product grew to enormous levels. There was also increasing demand for Ezo kelp as a food product. The Matsumae contracted fishing grounds to commercial operators, and the portion they took of the proceeds from herring and kelp sales became an important source of revenue for the domain. Merchants came from Honshu to work in the Ezo trade, but it was Ainu labourers who made up the fishing proletariat, a situation which promoted the dissolution of traditional Ainu society.

With the Meiji Restoration, the renamed island of Hokkaido came to be regarded as the nation's internal frontier and was swept by waves of immigration. Japanese settlers had been confined to the southern edge, but after 1868 they soon spread to all parts of the island and succeeded in growing rice despite the cold climate. Government policy since that time has promoted assimilation, and through intermarriage the number of pure-blooded Ainu has become extremely small, while most of those with Ainu ancestry do not speak the Ainu language. As a result, the diet of the approximately 25,000 Ainu who live in Hokkaido today hardly differs from that of other Japanese.

There are various surveys of Ainu foods in the first half of the twentieth century [e.g. Haginaka et al. 1992] and later, but research on historical aspects of Ainu dietary culture is clearly insufficient, having been limited to reconstruction from fragmentary records of the Edo period (1600–1868). There was some small-scale cultivation of millet (*hie* and *awa*) during that time, but the traditional Ainu diet was not based on agriculture. Instead, they continued to rely as they had since Jômon times on hunting and gathering wild plants in inland areas, and fishery along the rivers and coasts. Hunting and fishing were men's work while the women gathered. From spring through autumn the main activities were catching salmon and trout as they came upstream to spawn, gathering wild berries and rhizomes and other plants, and preserving these foods for the winter season. During the winter deer and other game were hunted. Seals, including fur seals, were also hunted for food. In contrast to most areas of Japan, where carbohydrates made up a very large proportion of the diet, the major features of the Ainu diet were the large amounts of protein and fat ingested from fish and meat.

Salmon, the most important fish, became a staple in season and was sometimes called the 'divine fish'. It was roasted over an open fire or boiled, and salmon caught in late winter was left outdoors to freeze and then eaten raw in thin slices. The present-day custom of eating artificially frozen raw salmon with soy sauce and wasabi horseradish, which has its origin in the Ainu mode of eating raw fish, extends to some areas outside Hokkaido. There were many techniques of cooking salmon including recipes for the organs and head, and everything but the large bones was consumed, the cartilage being pulverized to make it edible. Salmon was mainly an autumn food while trout was a frequent food of the summer season. Both types of fish were also preserved by drying, smoking and freezing.

Deer ranked with salmon and trout as a key component of the diet. The word for deer in the Ainu language is also the generic word for game, and deer were formerly so plentiful on Hokkaido that it was said that one would put the pot on the fire and then go catch the deer. Being such common quarry, the deer, unlike the bear, was not deified. In the Ainu conception, the bear inhabits the world of deities located deep in the mountains where humans cannot go, but it sometimes likes to come and play in the world of humans, and on the visit carries meat as a gift and wears a pelt as an overcoat. Accordingly, the meat and fur are considered presents from the bear deity to the people, and when a bear is caught it is divided, according to rules of distribution, among everyone in the village. The *i-omante* ritual bear slaughter is the most magnificent of Ainu ceremonies. With great reverence, a bear that was caught as a cub and raised by the community for a period of one to two years is slaughtered, the meat is consumed at a feast, and votive offerings are made to the bear's soul as gifts to be carried on its return to the other world. This hunting rite, intended to support the reproduction of their food, celebrates the deity that incarnates as an animal and becomes hunting quarry in order to assist human beings, by offering hospitality to the incarnated soul and then releasing it to return to the other world. Similar rites are held in forested regions of Siberia and North America where bears live.

The most important vegetable food in the Ainu diet was the starchy bulb of the wild *ubayuri* (*Cardiocrinum cordatum*). Traditionally, the bulbs are crushed with a wooden mortar and pestle and soaked in water for a day and night, then the solution is filtered through a bamboo colander and left to sit, and the precipitated starch is dried and preserved to be eaten as boiled dumplings or gruel. The dregs left in the colander are fermented and preserved for eating.

Small-scale cultivation of Japanese barnyard millet (*hie*), foxtail millet (*awa*), and *kibi* millet (*Panicum milliaceum*) was practised by the Ainu during the Edo period, though it is impossible to determine when the crops were introduced. These foods were usually eaten as gruel but on ceremonial occasions they were boiled with rice or ground up and cooked as dumplings. The glutinous *kibi* was regarded as the finer cereal and was usually made into cakes for eating. But rather than staple foods, cereals were cultivated primarily as ingredients for alcoholic drink. Rice obtained through trade was also used for that purpose, as were *ubayuri* bulbs and water chestnuts. During the Edo period, rice-based *kôji* mould obtained from Japanese was preserved and used as a fermentation starter for brewing, while in earlier times liquor was probably made only by chewing and spitting out grain mash. To make rice wine, women would chew uncooked polished rice and spit it into a container where it was left to ferment, the enzymes in the saliva effecting the conversion to sugar.

Meals were usually taken twice a day, morning and evening. The typical main dish was a hearty soup called *ohau* containing pieces of game or fish and various wild plants, while side dishes might include a watery gruel of *hie* or *awa* millet, or grilled fish. Salt was not made by the Ainu, but they consumed salt obtained in trade and used sea water in their cooking along the coast. The fat of deer, bears, fish and sea mammals was boiled down and congealed to be used as flavourings in cooking, a technique also found among other subarctic peoples.

For cooking, the Ainu used iron pots obtained in trade or pots made of bark. During the Edo period plain wooden bowls, chopsticks and spoons were used for daily meals, and Japanese lacquered bowls and small *zen* tables were brought out for ceremonial occasions.

5.8   The Ryukyu Islanders

A chain of islands extends like steppingstones to the southwest between the tip of Kyushu and Taiwan. There are two relatively large islands, Amami Oshima and Okinawa, lying respectively about 300 and 500 kilometres from Kyushu. The islands to the north of Amami Oshima have historically shared the homogeneous culture of the main Japanese islands. Amami Oshima and the islands of the Ryukyu chain to its south, while basically constituting an element of the Japanese cultural sphere, are nevertheless a region of their own with a very distinctive character. For example, the Ryukyu dialects unmistakably share a common ancestor with the ancient Japanese language, yet they differ remarkably from other Japanese dialects. Okinawa Prefecture, as the Ryukyus are now officially known, comprises about a hundred small islands, of which 44 are settled and the others are small coral reefs. The climate is subtropical, and the Okinawans grow sugar cane and produce sugar and also grow pineapples, papayas and other tropical fruits. Other than tourism, industrial resources are scarce.

Palaeolithic human bones about 30,000 years old have been discovered on the island of Okinawa, but no specific evidence of the diet of those people has been found. Early Jômon-period remains in the Ryukyus show that in neolithic times they contained the same sort of culture as the main islands of Japan. Yet despite contacts during the Yayoi period with practitioners in southern Kyushu of the rice-growing culture that had recently reached the main islands, rice did not spread to the Ryukyus. A hunting and gathering economy continued for many centuries and the diet was centred on wild plants, boar, and fish and shellfish. In terms of cultural development it was an outlying, backward area, as metal tools arrived much later than on the main islands and stone tools remained in use until about the tenth century. Slash and burn farming of *awa* (foxtail) millet, taro and yams appears to have been practiced from about the third century. Barley cultivation was begun later and paddy farming was introduced in the eleventh century, though rice yields proved to be small.

Regional petty rulers gained ascendance during the twelfth century and constructed fortresses to struggle with one another. By the fourteenth century three of them had triumphed over their rivals and established small kingdoms, each based on part of the island of Okinawa. In 1372, soon after the establishment of the Ming dynasty, those monarchs began paying tribute to the Chinese court and came under the nominal protection of the empire. In 1429 the islands were unified as the Ryukyu Kingdom.

As one of the proximate satellite nations of China, Ryukyu for several centuries remained a tributary state and also received Chinese investiture missions to legitimize its royal successors. The tributary relationship formally consisted of the sending of missions to the Chinese court bearing ceremonial gifts, and the reciprocal bestowal of gifts by the emperor. In actuality, tribute was a euphemism for trade, as the Ming court prohibited Chinese citizens from journeying abroad and hence foreign trade officially did not exist (there were Chinese smugglers who travelled on junks). Ryukyu eagerly pursued the tribute trade, dispatching a total of 171 tribute missions during the 270 years of the Ming dynasty, far outstripping the 89 missions sent by the second most active tributary state, Annam. Lacking in resources, Ryukyu exploited its geographical position to pursue an entrepôt trade, exporting to China goods obtained from Japan, Korea, Siam, Malacca, Palembang (on Sumatra), Annam (in Vietnam) and Luzon (in the Philippines). From the fourteenth through sixteenth centuries when Ryukyu was a flourishing trading state, the cargoes of its merchant ships included silk and ceramic ware from China, swords and artworks from Japan, ginseng and tiger skins from Korea, and ivory, spices and dyestuffs from Southeast Asia.

In 1609, with the permission of the Tokugawa shogun, Ryukyu was conquered by the Shimazu domain which was headquartered at the southern end of Kyushu. Though the kingdom was nominally preserved, the Shimazu daimyo assumed the power to designate its rulers and top officials and levy substantial taxes, thus bringing the islands under Tokugawa control. Tributary relations with China remained in effect, leaving Ryukyu a doubly subjugated semi-autonomous kingdom. Foreign trade was permitted only with China, but this also came under the regulation of the Shimazu daimyo and the shogunate. Enduring a harsh head tax imposed by the Shimazu, the Ryukyuans lost the prosperity they had enjoyed as a mercantile state. As soon as the shogunate was replaced by the Meiji government, the formal ownership of the islands became an issue. The government wanted to abolish the kingdom and make it a prefecture in the new national administration, but the islanders were opposed and the Ch'ing court of China also asserted its interest. In 1879, using the threat of military action, the Japanese government effected the creation of Okinawa Prefecture.

Although the legacy of Chinese influence includes a perceptible strain of Taoism, the indigenous religion at the foundation of Ryukyu spiritual life is shamanistic. Buddhism did not penetrate the general population before the Meiji period, hence there was no taboo on meat eating. The raising of animals for food is nevertheless a relatively new practice, apparently started when pigs and goats were brought in through trade with China in the fourteenth or fifteenth century. According to the journal of a Korean who drifted onto the small island at the southwestern end of the archipelago in 1477: 'On Yonagunijima chickens are raised but the meat is not eaten. On Okinawa horses, sheep, cats, pigs, dogs, chickens and ducks are raised and beef, horse and chicken are eaten.' [Shimabukuro 1989:20]. We may assume the reported sheep were goats.

The pig was the most important domestic animal in the Ryukyu diet. Due to limited feed supplies, pork could not be eaten on a daily basis, but was instead a delicacy for religious and ceremonial occasions. Pork cooking was an indispensable part of the New Year festivities, and each household would slaughter a pig beforehand. Some of the meat was salted, and part of the salted meat was smoked over the oven for later use. Little was wasted as the fat, organs and blood were also used. Pig's ears and organs are even today notable delicacies of Okinawan cooking. This stands in sharp contrast to the main islands of Japan, where organs were generally not eaten even with the resumption of meat eating in the Meiji period, until Korean barbecue came into vogue after the Second World War, and even today blood is never used in cooking. While male pigs are castrated in Okinawa, a practice that probably came from China along with the introduction of pigs, castration was not practiced in the traditional animal husbandry of Japan, having been introduced for cattle and horses only in the twentieth century.

With much of the soil formed from uplifted coral reefs, Okinawa is not well suited to cultivation of rice or other cereals, and the many typhoons that pass through each year tend to destroy crops and have often led to famine. Hence the Japanese sago palm (sotetsu; Cycas revoluta, a cycad), with the substantial starch content of its trunk, marrow and seeds, is an important foodstuff. It also contains formaldehyde which makes it dangerous to consume unless processed with a large amount of water, and in former times many people died from eating sago palm during famines.

The notable exception to the agricultural handicap is the sweet potato which can be grown in large quantities throughout the year in the subtropical climate, and its introduction to the islands was a momentous event. Having been brought from the New World by way of Manila to southern China in 1592, the sweet potato was in cultivation in the Ryukyus by 1605. The kingdom's population at that time of about one hundred thousand had doubled by the middle of the eighteenth century, largely on account of the sweet potato. Into the twentieth century, the commoner's daily meal consisted of just two dishes, boiled or steamed sweet potato and a miso soup of fish, vegetables and seaweed, occasionally accompanied by a third dish of rice. Members of the upper class ate rice as a main dish three times a day. Small sweet potatoes, and tips and skins of sweet potatoes left over from meals were used for pig feed.

Sugar making was introduced to Amami Oshima from China in 1610 and by 1623 had spread to the Ryukyus. The subtropical climate was ideal for cultivating sugar cane and sugar became the chief product of the islands. Until its abolition in 1879, the monarchy controlled sugar production and the revenue from sugar exports to Japan was a mainstay of the kingdom's economy. The crude brown Ryukyu sugar was rich in minerals and vitamins B1 and B2 which contributed to the health of the island residents.

The most refined cooking of the Ryukyus was the court cuisine prepared for official functions, and this cuisine was strongly influenced by the political situation of the islands before and during the Edo period. The grandest court events were the welcoming ceremonies for the Chinese missions that brought imperial rescripts to invest new Ryukyu monarchs. An investiture mission comprised some four or five hundred people and stayed for half a year or more, and as the reception was a necessary point of honour for the kingdom, the costs were huge. It was recorded that the hosting of the investiture mission that arrived in 1533 involved the slaughter of 40 to 50 pigs per day, and a local shortage led to the procurement of pigs from remote villages and outlying islands. Imperial missions were entertained with Chinese cuisine, prepared at first by chefs invited from China and later by Ryukyu chefs who had been sent to China for training. From the other direction, in order to entertain high officials of the Shimazu domain when they visited Naha, the principal Ryukyu trading port and the headquarters of the Japanese, chefs were sent to Kagoshima for instruction. The court cuisine shaped by both Chinese and Japanese influence spread to the homes of the upper class and affluent merchants and became the haute cuisine of the islands.

Further important influence on the development of Ryukyu cooking came from the brothel quarter of Naha. In traditional Japan the government-licensed brothel quarter was a centre not only for prostitution but also for enjoyment of artistic singing and dancing performances, and for banquets to entertain special guests or socialize with friends. Shimazu retainers established a licensed quarter in Naha soon after the islands were conquered and some of its establishments doubled as restaurants, which the city otherwise lacked. The fine cuisine prepared by professional chefs and served in these establishments influenced Okinawan home cooking.

Thus the classic Okinawan cuisine formed during the Edo period and passed down to the present has an original style based on the local climate and produce as well as the influence of the two large neighbouring cultures. The courses and settings are patterned mainly on *honzen ryôri*, featuring individual lacquered *zen* tables set with Japanese lacquer and ceramic ware and chopsticks, usually without the Chinese spoon (see Section 4.4). As in *honzen ryôri*, the number of *zen* tables increases with the quantity of the food, and food is arranged attractively on the plates with great importance attached to the technique of slicing for visual appeal. But the use of pork as the *pièce de résistance* and the preference for thick sauces using lard show the strength of Chinese influence. Most of the names of the dishes and the cooking methods in Ryukyu cuisine were transmitted from China, but some influences appear to have entered via the busy Southeast Asian trade routes. For example, the long pepper (*Peper officiarum*) which originated in Java is cultivated in the southern Ryukyus where it is called *pipachi* or *pipazu*; the powdered seeds are used to spice pork dishes and the young leaves are chopped and used for their fragrance. A distinctive feature of the Okinawan diet is that tofu (soybean curd) is frequently eaten. The most common method of preparing tofu is to stir-fry it with chopped vegetables in lard. That dish is known as *champuru*, a word that may well derive from the Indonesian/Malaysian word *campur* (mixture) which is also used today in those countries as the name for dishes combining several ingredients.

Until the fifteenth century, the liquor–brewing methods used in Japan (see Section 2.4) were not practised in the Ryukyus, where drink was made only by chewing rice mash. Then distilling was introduced through trade with Siam, leading to the production of *awamori*, the liquor that today remains a well-known Okinawan product. *Awamori*, which for centuries continued to be made from imported Siamese rice, is fermented with a *kôji* mould (*Aspergillus awamori*, different than the *Aspergillus oryzae* used for sake) and after distillation is aged in special jars, which were at first brought from Siam and later came to be produced at local kilns.

The Japanese today have the longest life expectancy of all nations in the world, and within Japan Okinawa is renowned as the prefecture where people live the longest. Nutritionists have observed that in pre-modern times the Japanese diet was deficient in protein and oils and fats, whereas the Ryukyu islanders ingested much animal protein from pigs and fish, as well as large amounts of vegetable protein from tofu, and also fat from lard. Other factors contributing to long life included high consumption of sweet potatoes, seaweed, and the locally produced brown sugar.

Many kinds of seaweed are harvested along the Ryukyu shores and used in cooking, but one of the most commonly used kinds is kelp, which is not a local product. In fact, statistics show that Okinawans consume more kelp than other Japanese. Why should this be so when kelp is produced mainly in Hokkaido at the opposite end of the archipelago? The answer lies in the trading patterns of the Edo period. In Naha, where the Shimazu domain maintained a sugar trading office to handle exports to Japan, there was also a kelp trading office to manage transshipments to China where the seaweed was used in cooking. As their main city became a collection point for kelp, the Ryukyuans began eating it in large amounts. That kelp was harvested by Ainu under the economic and administrative control of the Matsumae domain, and thus the two minorities were linked via the political economy of the Tokugawa shogunate system.

CHAPTER 6

CHANGES IN THE MODERN AGE

6.1   Historical Setting

While Japan was confined to its own microcosm under the national seclusion policy of the Tokugawa shoguns, Europe and America were transformed by the industrial revolution and the rapid development of capitalism. Western nations acquired immense economic and military strength, and the great powers moved into Asia in search of markets and resources.

In 1853, a squadron of American warships suddenly appeared in Edo Bay. Commodore Perry presented the shogunate with a presidential letter demanding that Japan be opened for trade, and indicated that a failure to respond would be met by military action. By 1858 Japan had been forced to conclude commercial treaties with the United States, Britain, France, the Netherlands and Russia, designating several ports where ships from those nations could land for trade and foreign nationals would be allowed to reside. The treaties contained unequal provisions giving foreigners immunity from Japanese law and denying Japan the right to set tariffs autonomously.

In reaction to the treaties which had been forcibly imposed by foreign states, a movement arose that demanded the expulsion of foreigners from Japan. Meanwhile, trade developed under the treaty arrangements, with raw silk and tea as the main export products and woolens, cotton goods and arms as major imports. Domestic prices rose as a result of the foreign trade, making life difficult for the lower-ranking samurai and the peasants. All the open ports were located in the shogunal domains of the Tokugawa clan, and other feudal clans grew displeased with their monopolization of the profits. The petty samurai displayed increasing antipathy toward the merchants who profited from foreign trade. These veins of social discontent coalesced with the movement to expel foreigners, gaining a momentum that threatened to topple the shogunate. The petty samurai were the driving force of the movement, and their leaders decided they should overthrow the shogun and give power to the emperor, who for centuries had held sovereignty in name only. After minor military clashes between the shogunate and several feudal clans of western Japan which supported the rebellion, the shogun recognized that he had lost the capacity to govern and handed over to the emperor. That return of power to the imperial house in 1868, known as the Meiji Restoration, marked the start of the modernization of Japan.

The emperor soon moved from Kyoto to the abandoned shogun's castle in Edo, and Edo became the official capital, renamed Tokyo. The fiefs of the daimyo were abolished, and the centralized government that was formed under the emperor pressed strongly forward with the formation of a modern state along Western lines. Its chief aims were to stimulate an industrial revolution in Japan by transplanting modern industry from the West, and to build a modern army based on conscription. For those purposes it was deemed necessary to introduce a modern educational system and to ensure an ample supply of stout soldiers and labourers.

The learned men of the time who had acquired information from the West believed that one reason why the Japanese had poor physiques compared to Westerners was that they did not eat meat or dairy products. The populace was exhorted to consume meat and milk, especially after the news spread in 1872 that the emperor had eaten meat, and for the next few years such a diet was regarded as the mark of a civilized person. Meat was included in soldiers' meals, and was served at a number of Western-style restaurants which opened in the cities. The restaurants thrived as purveyors of exotic cuisine, with meat and beer proving to be the most appealing novelties. Western cooking was usually used to prepare meat, although there were some meat dishes based on traditional cooking, such as sukiyaki.

Meat dishes were part of the traditional cuisines of nearby Korea and China, and the Japanese might more easily have accustomed themselves to Oriental meat recipes since they were designed to be served with rice rather than bread and eaten with chopsticks rather than unfamiliar cutlery. Yet for some time after the opening of the country, Korean and Chinese restaurants were unable to win acceptance in Japan. Part of the explanation for this lies in the attitudes the Japanese held toward various foreign nations during the modernization process.

Due to their geopolitical situation, throughout history the Japanese had taken China as the model for civilization. But nineteenth-century Japanese intellectuals were aware that Europeans had successfully invaded China in the Opium War, and so had concluded even before the opening of the country that the civilization of Europe and America was what moved the world. When it came to modernization, China was discarded and Western civilization was adopted as the model. Western food was seen as civilized cuisine with much to learn from, while Chinese food was neglected as the cooking of stagnant Asia. Victory in the Sino-Japanese War of 1894–5 reinforced the tendency to scorn China. Chinese food was considered 'unsanitary' and in the Chinatown districts that had grown up in Kobe, Yokohama and Nagasaki the only customers at Chinese restaurants were local Chinese residents. It was not until the end of the First World War that the Japanese began to perceive Chinese food as tasty and economical, and Chinese restaurants appeared in significant numbers in the cities.

There was even stronger prejudice against Korean food. The heavy use of garlic and red pepper in Korean cooking was indeed ill-matched to the traditional taste of the Japanese who used very little spice, but the distaste was also associated with strong ethnic discrimination against Koreans. When Korea became a Japanese colony in 1910, the idea that the Koreans were a people 'who should learn from the Japanese' was so strong that pupils at Korean girls' schools were given classes in Japanese cooking. Only after 1945, when Japan was defeated in the Second World War and its colonial occupation of Korea ended, did Korean restaurants oriented toward Japanese customers appear in the cities of Japan.

Japan steadily expanded its territory and joined the ranks of the imperial powers, taking Taiwan (from 1895) and Korea as colonies, acquiring concessions and markets in southern Manchuria after winning the Russo-Japanese War of 1904–5, and receiving a League of Nations mandate over the Pacific Islands north of the equator (now Micronesia) at the end of the First World War. Capitalism and the attendant progress of the industrial revolution had provided the economic base for expansion. Factory production outstripped agricultural output in 1919, marking the transformation of Japan into an industrial state. Along with the changes in economic structure came rapid population growth, from 35 million in 1872 when the first modern census was made, to 55 million in 1919. Factors which enabled that growth included the expansion of domestic food production, colonial exploitation, and the development of industrial capacity for importing food.

The brief reign of Emperor Taishô, from 1912–26, was a time of peace and prosperity. Japan participated in the First World War and was able to obtain German holdings in China and the Pacific without major sacrifice. While Europe was exhausted by the war, Japan gained Asian markets which stimulated its economy. Liberal and democratic thought – critical of the military whose political role had strengthened after the Russo-Japanese War – gained considerable influence during the Taishô era, and the intellectual and political mood of the nation at the time has come to be known as Taishô Democracy. The urban middle class, mainly salaried white-collar employees, expanded rapidly and took the lead in developing new ways of life. They tended to wear informal kimono at home but Western clothing at work or when going out; to live in traditional homes which also had Western-style parlors; and to install modern kitchens equipped with gas and running water, and designed for standing rather than the traditional sitting or stooping postures. The middle class grew to like Chinese cuisine and began preparing Western-style food, previously served only in restaurants, at home. They also patronized coffee shops regularly. Their new diet brought increased consumption of sugar and milk.

The new dietary culture of the urban sophisticates and other new lifestyles associated with Taishô Democracy were nipped in the bud by dramatic social changes. The great depression triggered by the Wall Street crash of 1929 hit Japan the following year, bringing on the worst economic crisis since the formation of the modern state. Most heavily affected were the middle class who had been in the vanguard of dietary change. Soon after, as the wartime era began, significant regression of dietary customs became unavoidable among all segments of the population.

Acting contrary to government policy, Japanese army officers staged the Manchurian Incident of 1931 and the army proceeded to conquer all of northeast China and establish the puppet state of Manchukuo. The League of Nations condemned the aggression, prompting Japan to withdraw from the League and remain diplomatically isolated while the army gained steadily greater influence and pulled the country along the road to fascism. The Sino-Japanese War broke out in 1937, the Pacific War began in 1941, and, by the time Japan surrendered to Allied forces in 1945, the country had endured some fifteen years of continual war. Food supplies became unstable as the war dragged on. Rationing was begun in 1941, but the official rations were largely exhausted before the end of the war and much of the population was forced to go hungry. After the war the government gave food production the highest priority and worked especially to increase the rice harvest, but it was not until the mid-1950s that rice production was restored to its pre-war level.

The remarkably rapid economic growth of the 1960s brought qualitative change as well as quantitative increase in food. The traditional diet which was based on rice and vegetables came to include more fish, and meat began to appear commonly on the dining table. Along with the increased intake of animal protein and fats, spices came into use. Bread replaced freshly boiled rice at breakfast in many households. Cooking originating in Europe, China and Korea was adopted in the kitchen for daily meals. One result of the changes has been a steady decline in rice consumption since 1962. In place of the traditional staple-based meal pattern, in which the belly was filled with rice and the side dishes served to sharpen the appetite, a new pattern has emerged based on the enjoyment of several tasty side dishes.

The backdrop to those changes was the progressive industrialization of food and meals. Economic development entailed the growth of the food industry as a 'public kitchen' that furnished households with new and different foods, including items that had been introduced from abroad such as bread, ham and milk. Large-scale marketing and distribution networks promoted new foods that were partially or entirely pre-cooked and could be served at home with minimal effort. The outstanding example is instant *rāmen*, or Chinese-style egg noodles, first sold in 1958. Ready to eat just three minutes after hot water is added, packaged instant noodles have by now spread from Japan to many countries of the world. The economy also spawned a 'public dining room' in the form of the rapidly growing restaurant industry, serving many new foods that eventually found their way into the home.

In the Japanese economy of the early 1990s, food products constitute the fourth largest industry in terms of annual turnover, exceeded only by electrical equipment, automobiles and oil. Steel is next, followed by the restaurant industry. Such extensive industrialization of food has enabled the Japanese of today to enjoy a very rich and varied menu. Yet it has also spawned tangible fears that the family kitchen and dining room may be thoroughly devoured by societal trends.

6.2 The Resumption of Meat Eating

Meat was not widely eaten until the Meiji period (1868–1912), but meat eating was not unknown among the Japanese of earlier times, as explained in Chapter 3. Those engaged in the manufacture of leather goods, as well as the hunters and stock breeders who furnished hides, ate the flesh of four-legged animals as a matter of course, but these groups were considered social outcasts. Among the general population wild fowl were considered edible, as were whale and dolphin which were regarded as fish rather than mammals. Chicken was long held taboo as a foodstuff, but it appeared in seventeenth-century cookbooks. Eating the flesh of mammals for medicinal purposes was permissible, and sometimes healthy people ate it as a tonic. The usual 'medicine eating' fare was deer or wild boar (boar was known colloquially as 'mountain whale').

The Tokugawa shogunate (1600–1868) placed controls on religion, giving the secular administration higher status than religious authorities. Under that arrangement the religious energies of Buddhism and Shinto were gradually weakened, and by the late Edo period the religious bans on meat eating were growing lax. Some of the intelligentsia who had absorbed Western ideas (through the medium of Dutch books) claimed that it was merely superstitious to avoid meat, for it was a rich source of nutrition and rejection of it led to frailty. In Edo the sole shop dealing in meat for ostensibly medicinal purposes was joined at the beginning of the nineteenth century by several others selling the meat of wild boar, deer, fox, rabbit, otter, wolf, bear and serow. A contemporary writer of the nationalist school was outraged: 'I cannot bear to walk past those shops. These evil customs were all started by the Europeanized scholars. As a result the houses of Edo are filled with impurity which provokes the wrath of the fire deity, and many fires have broken out of late' [Oyamada 1909:174]. There was a vogue for 'medicine eating' among the townspeople, but presumably only a part of the population ate mammal meat and they did so on very rare occasions.

The meat of choice in the latter part of the nineteenth century was beef. Beef pickled in miso appears on a menu written at the beginning of the eighteenth century, and it was an open secret that a daimyo of Hikone (now part of Shiga) made gifts of that dish, which he called 'healthful meat', to the shogun and other daimyo [Itô 1990:176-83]. But people in general had strong psychological resistance to killing and eating cattle, which were important animals on the farms, and it was not until shortly before the collapse of the Tokugawa shogunate that restaurants serving beef appeared in the cities. A description of some of the earliest of those establishments is in the autobiography of the prominent educator Fukuzawa Yukichi, who enrolled in a school of Dutch studies in 1854:

> There were only two places in Osaka that served beef at that time, and they were low-class shops that were never visited by civilized-looking people. The regular customers were all either heavily tattooed street ruffians

147

or students from my own school of Dutch studies. We had no idea where the meat came from, whether it was slaughtered or had died of disease. It was very cheap, so we could fill up on beef and sake and rice, but the beef was very tough and smelly. [Fukuzawa 1899:63–4]

The Japanese-style beef stew which originated around that time (*gyûnabe*, the forerunner of sukiyaki) was made by boiling beef and welsh onion with miso or soy sauce, a recipe similar to those that had been used to cook deer or wild boar meat for 'medicine eating'.

During the 1860s the colonies of Westerners living in the treaty ports often attempted to purchase cattle from local farmers, who usually refused if they knew the animal would be used for food. Among the peasantry of the time a cow was regarded almost as a member of the family, and dead cows were given burials. The Westerners resorted to purchasing cattle from China, Korea or America which were butchered aboard ships and sold in the foreign settlements. But the shipments could not satisfy the demand as the foreign population multiplied. Finally, members of the Yokohama foreign community were able to make arrangements with stock breeders in the hills of the Kansai district, where most Japanese cattle ranches were located. Thirty to forty head of cattle at a time were shipped live from the port of Kobe to Yokohama, where a slaughterhouse was set up. Beef shipped from Kobe gained a reputation for being very tasty, and the regional product remains famous today as 'Kobe beef'.

In 1869 the Ministry of Finance established the Gyûba Kaisha (Cattle and Horse Company) for the purpose of producing and selling beef and dairy products. The cattle and horses that had been raised on the ranch lands of the Tokugawa clan were turned over to the company. It was given a monopoly on slaughtering in Tokyo and on the provision of meat to the beef restaurants and butcher shops that were proliferating in the capital at the time. As a government enterprise it had been designed in part to create jobs for out-of-work samurai, and all of the employees were drawn from their ranks. Unable to abandon the sense of privilege and authority that their class had until recently enjoyed, they conducted business in a haughty manner which gave the company a bad reputation. They were also slack in checking the quality of the animals purchased and heavy-handed in rigging the market, and were so unsuccessful that the company was closed down after one year. Nevertheless, the fact that the government had taken the lead in operating a slaughtering and milking business did much to promote the consumption of meat and milk [Itô 1990:228–9].

During the Boshin Civil War of 1868–9, fought between imperial forces and several daimyo of northeast Japan who hoped to maintain shogunal authority, many wounded soldiers were sent to hospitals in Tokyo. There they received Western-style treatment and were fed beef to restore their strength. Most refused it at first, but as the doctors advised them to eat beef if they wanted to survive, they complied. Many of them grew to like it so much that after their release they spread the word in their various home regions that beef was delicious and healthful. The imperial navy served beef to improve the nutrition of sailors' meals starting in 1869, when the Gyûba Kaisha was founded. The sailors butchered it themselves and excess meat was sold to the public. Later the army began serving meat as well. Military rations during the Sino-Japanese and Russo-Japanese Wars included tins of beef flavoured with soy sauce and ginger, called *yamatoni* which refers to its Japanese-style taste. The soldiers who ate it later helped spread the custom of meat eating through the country, and tinned *yamatoni* remained popular until about 1950 [Miyazaki 1987:45–6].

While soldiers grew to like the taste of meat because they were forced to eat it, the general population became familiar with it through city restaurants. During the early Meiji period meat was served in Western-style hotels and restaurants, and in restaurants that specialized in beef stew. The Western-style establishments had first appeared in the foreigners' districts of the treaty ports, and they spread to Tokyo and Osaka after restrictions on foreigners' activities were eased by the new Meiji government. The foreigners dining in those establishments were joined by high government officials, traders, intellectuals, and others who came out of curiosity to try eating Western food and using a knife and fork. The prices were so high that the common people could not often afford them. *Gyûnabeya*, or beef stew restaurants, were more accessible to the public because they were cheaper and also because the beef they served was seasoned with the familiar flavours of soy sauce and miso and eaten with chopsticks.

The first stew restaurant opened in Edo in 1865. At first the customers were mainly disagreeable ruffians of the type who liked to brag that they had eaten meat, and most people held their noses and walked quickly when they passed the shop. With the change of government a few years later, the adoption of Western civilization became national policy and stew restaurants gradually spread through the main cities.

A stew restaurant was the setting for a comic novel of 1871 entitled *Aguranabe* (The Well-Seated Stew Pot), in which one of the characters makes the following observations:

> Say, you there. Beef is really delicious, isn't it? When beef can be had, who would want to eat venison or wild boar? In the West nowadays they always eat beef, but in the old days beef and mutton could be eaten only by royalty and ministers of state, and never by the common folk. What a blessing it is that our country has become more and more civilized and regular folk like us are able to eat beef. Some people who reject modern civilization still think that eating beef is a barbarous custom. They say absurd, nonsensical things like, 'If you eat meat you will offend the Buddha and the Shinto deities, if you eat meat you are defiled' – but only because they are ignorant of Western science.
> [Kanagaki 1871 28–9]

Thus meat eating was held up as a symbol of modern civilization, and its rejection portrayed as reactionary ultranationalism. In the early Meiji period people absorbed civilization in part through their stomachs.

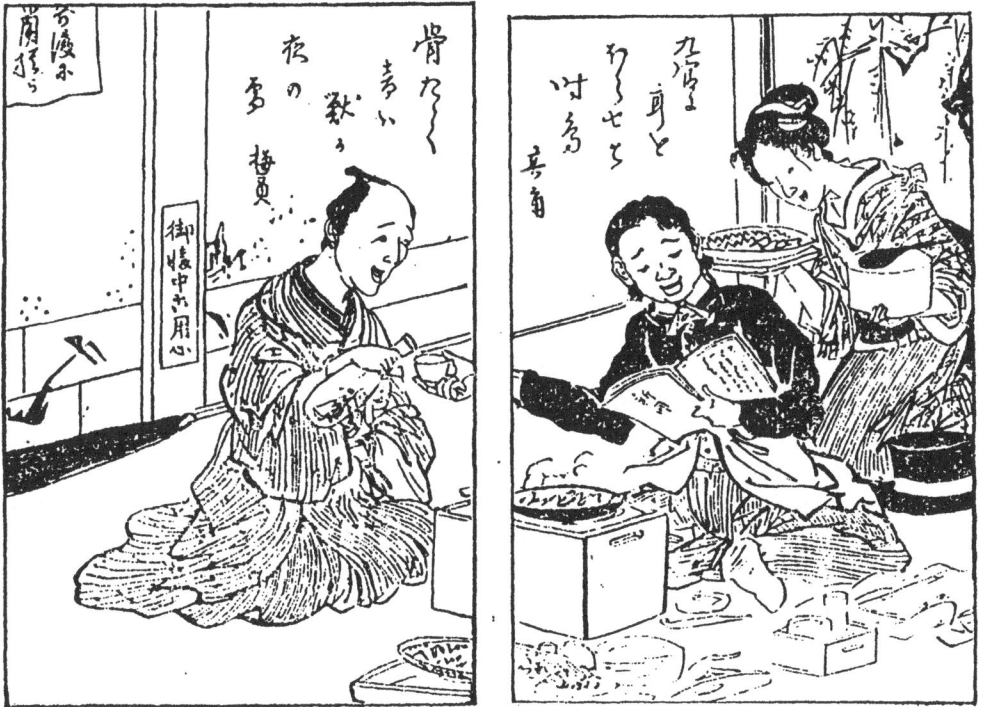

Figure 8
A fashionable diner of the early Meiji period. The Western clothes, newspaper, and *gyûnabe* stew – all unusual for the time – symbolize the powerful current of Western-style modernization that was beginning to sweep the country. (From *Aguranabe* 1871.)

A contemporary newspaper article noted that in 1877 the number of businesses serving stew or selling beef in Tokyo had grown to 558. Since stew is easy to prepare, it is likely that many residents of the large cities began to buy and cook beef at home around that time. Horse meat also came into household use as a cheaper alternative.

Beef stew spread quickly from the main cities to the provincial towns, for townspeople could treat beef simply as a new food. But this was not the case in farming districts, where cows were used as work animals and each was given a name and treated more or less as part of the family. Moreover, the farming population still maintained the traditional religious beliefs that classed meat eating as a defilement. It took longer for meat to be accepted by farm families, and when they did begin eating it, they often cooked the stew outside the house or spread paper over the household Shinto and Buddhist altars to avoid defiling the deities with the smell. Like Jews who keep separate pots for cooking meat and cooking milk, in some homes a certain pot was reserved exclusively for cooking meat so as to avoid contaminating other foods.

By the beginning of the twentieth century, resistance to meat eating was limited to the elderly. Beef stew had come to be eaten nationwide, regarded not so much as an ordinary meal but as a special treat. It was called sukiyaki in Osaka, Kyoto, Kobe and other parts of the Kansai region where, in contrast to Tokyo and eastern Japan, the stew was made with several types of vegetables and dipped in beaten raw egg before eating. By the 1920s the sukiyaki version had became prevalent throughout the country and attained the status of a national dish (see Section 9.4).

Large-scale breeding of pigs for food began when the government introduced a foreign species for that purpose in 1868. At first they were reared near the large cities and fed with leftovers from restaurants and inns. Pork was cheap and was considered a substitute for beef, and its consumption increased during the Sino-Japanese and Russo-Japanese Wars when beef was in short supply. It was used mainly as a beef substitute in stews until the second decade of the twentieth century, when it became common to eat pork cutlet as well as Chinese dishes that included pork. Mutton was considered odourous and generally avoided, goat was eaten only in Okinawa, and ducks were only rarely bred as poultry. Horses were commonly raised for food in Nagano and Kumamoto Prefectures and horse meat was eaten by lower-class urbanites who could not afford other meat. Otherwise, through the first half of the twentieth century, most of the meat eaten in Japan was beef, pork or chicken.

Daily meat consumption per capita from 1934–8 was 6.1 grams, including 2.2 grams of beef and 1.9 of pork. That would be enough to make a meal of sukiyaki, the favourite meat dish of the population at large, for each person about once a month. Thus some 70 years after the resumption of meat eating among the Japanese, it had spread through the population but was generally consumed only in small quantities [Miyazaki 1987:72–3].

6.3   Milk and Dairy Products

The dairy industry began in 1863 when a Japanese who had worked at a Dutch-operated milk shop serving the Western community in Yokohama opened his own shop there to sell milk to his compatriots. He opened another shop in Tokyo, and was called upon to teach Western milking techniques for the government's short-lived milk and meat monopoly, the Gyûba Kaisha. As the employees he trained there went on to open shops in various areas, milk became available in provincial towns during the 1870s [Adachi 1980:219–222]. Thus the government played a part in the early growth of the dairy industry. The Gyûba Kaisha also distributed propaganda such as the following, in which enlightenment about the medical efficacy of milk and dairy products was associated with nationalism:

> Our Company manufactures cheese, butter, powdered milk and condensed milk for the purpose of expanding the utilization of milk in the nation today. For the effects of milk are even more remarkable than those of beef. Milk is a wonderful and indispensable substance for patients with fever or pulmonary tuberculosis and for those whose bodies are weak, and it may be considered effective against every illness. To be used not only for illness, milk is drunk at daily meals in Western countries, and cheese and butter should also be used in the cuisine of our country in the same manner as *katsuo-bushi* (dried bonito shavings). By

utilizing milk to live a long life, maintain a healthy body and invigorate the mind, the Japanese shall save their name from dishonour.

In the early Meiji period, milk cows were kept in or near the cities, and milk was carried to customers' homes in iron buckets and sold by the dipper-full. Pasteurization was introduced just after 1900, scarcely a decade after it became widespread in the West, and thereafter milk was generally delivered in glass bottles. Mothers who had little breast milk provided much of the initial demand. Tinned condensed milk was shipped to areas without dairies, and was advertised with the catch phrase, 'No wet nurse needed.' Apart from young children, milk was widely drunk by the ill and those with weak constitutions. Daily milk drinking among the population at large dates from the 1950s.

The dairy industry of Japan before the Second World War was limited to drinkable products, beginning with whole milk and diversifying to condensed milk and, from the 1920s, powdered milk. Dairy products in the form of solid foods developed more slowly and, apart from ice cream, never caught on. Just as Westerners tend to dislike the smell of Japanese foods made from fermented soybeans, such as *nattô* and miso, so the Japanese generally find fermented or processed dairy products, which were not a part of their traditional diet, to be disagreeable. 'Stinking of butter' (*bataa-kusai*) was an epithet commonly used during the late Edo and early Meiji periods in reference to Japanese who ate Western food or affected Western manners. Until large-scale domestic production began in the 1930s, most of the butter used in Japan was imported and apt to have gone rancid during a long journey by ship. Butter and cheese production grew rapidly during the 1970s, when many households began eating bread with breakfast. Still, the Japanese generally prefer bland processed cheese, and only a small segment of the population have developed a taste for the distinctive odours of natural cheeses.

Although more than a century has passed since milk and dairy products came into use, Japan's consumption level is far lower than those of nations with historical traditions of dairy farming. Moreover, consumption is largely limited to beverages or desserts, in the form of whole milk and ice cream, although yoghurt and lactic acid beverages have gained popularity in recent years.

6.4   Entry of Foreign Foods

Sukiyaki, like the simpler beef stew that preceded it, was never haute cuisine but rather was a recipe used by the common people to adopt a new ingredient into their traditional set of everyday foods. In the face of the wave of foreign culture that revived meat eating and introduced other Western foods and cooking, there was no active response from the domain of traditional Japanese cooking. Refined restaurants turned to Western cooking techniques to devise meat dishes for their menus, showing no interest in any reorganization of the established system of Japanese cooking. Unwilling to alter their ingredients and techniques, the high-class restaurants preserved the culinary system that had evolved in the Edo period, thus fossilizing themselves as purveyors of a static traditional cuisine.

Consequently a new category of dining facilities appeared. Called Western restaurants, they served meals with non-traditional ingredients, especially meats, fats and oils. In the early Meiji years these restaurants, sometimes located in hotels, were extraordinarily expensive and catered only to a tiny upper-class minority. Then in the late 1880s Japanese cooks who had learned Western cooking in hotels and expensive restaurants began opening a new class of Western restaurant, called *yôshokuya*, which catered to the urban general public. By the turn of the century there were fifteen to sixteen hundred *yôshokuya* in Tokyo [Itô 1990:249–250].

Yôshokuya means 'Western-food restaurant' but in fact these establishments served Western cuisine that had been altered to suit Japanese tastes. Bread was rarely ordered, and the *yôshokuya* meal was usually served with Japanese-style boiled rice, on a plate rather than in the traditional bowl. Sauces were made from a base of soy sauce to match the taste of rice, and Worcestershire sauce was used on almost anything, for the Japanese took it as the Western equivalent of their own universal flavouring, soy sauce. For foods fried with oil, the *yôshokuya* changed original sauté recipes to deep frying, the method familiar for tempura. As there was little interest in a full-course meal, the diner would select one or two items à la carte from a general menu. The standard beverage selection was beer or sake; wine was hardly ever served or expected.

The typical dishes at a *yôshokuya* included rice and curry (*raisu karê*, today called *karê raisu*); hashed beef over rice (*hayashi raisu*); rice fried with bits of chicken (sometimes called 'pilaf'); omelette; steak; breaded deep-fried cutlets of pork, chicken or beef; croquettes; and breaded deep-fried fish or prawns. Having been popularized in the *yôshokuya* restaurants, these modified dishes of Western origin began to be prepared at home, especially in the cities. The most popular in either venue was *raisu karê*. Another offshoot was *tonkatsu* (pork cutlets; see Section 9.6).

British cooking was the main inspiration for the Western-style cuisine of Meiji Japan, in part because Western culture in general was transmitted to Japan mainly through the medium of English. Moreover, most of the Christian missionaries in Meiji Japan came from Britain or America, and cookbooks which were translated into Japanese at missionary schools played a large role in the dissemination of Western cuisine. Japanese curry recipes did not come directly from India, but were based on Anglo-Indian recipes using British ready-made curry powder. Hence the Japanese viewed curry as a Western food. Restaurant *karê* was made with a roux of browned flour and resembled Western curry sauce, but in the Japanese home the roux was omitted; instead salt and curry powder were added to boiled meat and vegetables (beef or pork with potatoes, carrots, etc.) and the mixture was thickened with unbrowned flour. *Karê* was always served over rice, and often was further seasoned with Worcestershire sauce and served with a garnish of vegetables pickled in soy sauce (*fukujin-zuke*). It was eaten with a spoon rather than a fork.

The complex aroma of the curry powder mixture was something quite exotic for the Japanese whose native cuisine used so little spice. Combined with meat, the new symbol of nutrition, and with the familiar staple rice, curry became the nation's favourite 'Western' dish. Since the Taishô period many noodle shops have served curry-flavoured versions of *soba* and *udon* soups including meat. Undergoing various Japanese-style modifications, curry has remained very popular, and Japan now consumes more turmeric than any other country of the world except India. With a flavour distinct from the curries of either India or the West, *karê* has become one of the national dishes of Japan.

China's proximity to Japan notwithstanding, Chinese food did not become popular until half a century after the reopening of Japan. Chinese restaurants began to open in the major cities after 1910, and once the cuisine became known it was rapidly and widely accepted. It was comfortable fare because it could be eaten with chopsticks and was well complemented by rice, since most of the Chinese residing and operating restaurants in Japan had come from the southern, rice-eating provinces of Guangzhou (Canton) and Fujian. Chinese restaurants were also inexpensive. By 1923 Tokyo had 1,000 Chinese restaurants, and about 5,000 Western restaurants, mainly *yôshokuya*. As in Western restaurants, most of the cooks who worked in Chinese restaurants were Japanese. Accordingly, except in the Chinatowns of Yokohama and Kobe where restaurants catered to Chinese customers, Japanese versions of Chinese cuisine were served.

The most popular Chinese restaurant dish was *shina* (China) *soba*—noodles in a pork or chicken broth topped with slices of pork and seasoned with black pepper. From about 1918 on, this dish was also widely sold by peddlers on the city streets at night, fitting in with the established evening custom of eating Japanese-style noodles at street stalls. The noodles used in *shina soba*, as well as the soup, the toppings, the flavouring and even the customary bowl (*donburi*) were all developed in Japan; neither the dish nor its constituents were to be found in China. After the Second World War it underwent further change, and under the name *râmen* this foreign-inspired food has become another of Japan's national dishes (see Section 9.7).

Western and Chinese cuisine were accepted largely because they provided foods that were lacking in the native cuisine – meat, oils and fats, and spices. As knowledge of modern nutritional science spread, meat dishes came to be seen as energy providers, and Western and Chinese foods were considered highly nutritious. The mass media also promoted new foods and nutritional awareness. Foreign-style recipes appeared regularly in women's magazines from the 1920s, and nutritious foods became a common topic of radio programmes and newspaper articles in the early 1930s.

Foreign foods which appealed to the Japanese were adopted first in the popular restaurants of the cities and gradually penetrated into private homes, becoming modified to Japanese styles during the process of diffusion. Dishes which in their native countries were parts of full-course meals were picked out singly, and their ingredients and recipes were altered to complement the tastes of rice and other Japanese dishes with which they were eaten. Japanese customs influenced even the utensils and methods for eating. In other words, a given dish was removed from the context of the dietary culture of its native country, and eventually took root as an everyday food in Japan by taking a place in the Japanized foreign lexicon that is the context of Japanese dietary culture.

Yet the popularity of foreign foods before the Second World War should not be overestimated. While Western and Chinese food did become widespread as restaurant fare in the cities, few of the dishes became established as items prepared in the home. Domestic capability for a limited repertoire of foreign dishes was limited to middle– and upper–class households in the large cities. During the 1930s some 50 per cent of the population were farmers who relied much more than city dwellers on self-sufficient economy. Their normal diet, in which fish and vegetables were the main side dishes and meat was a rarity, had such strong traditional colouration that it can be regarded as an extension of Edo-period customs.

6.5   Zenith and Nadir

The Great Kanto Earthquake of 1923, the most devastating in Japanese history, killed 100,000 persons in greater Tokyo and the fires that raged afterward destroyed some two thirds of the city's homes. Until then, Tokyo had retained many buildings and ways of life from the Edo period, but after the disaster it was reborn as a new city. The changes in the capital then spread to the countryside.

Some of the most visible changes in the city's dietary life after the earthquake were in restaurants. In popular restaurants such as *soba* shops, the customers had always removed their shoes and sat on tatami floor mats, but in the rebuilt restaurants they kept their shoes on and sat on chairs at high tables. The domestic kitchen also changed, for the fires caused by the earthquake had driven home the danger of cooking on charcoal or wood fires. The city converted rapidly to municipal gas, and at the same time most households began using municipally supplied running water. Previously, the typical kitchen was an earthen-floored room a step down from the other rooms of the house, where the cook bent over a wooden sink or sat at an oven-like wood-burning cooking stove (*kamado*) with holes on the top for pots and kettles. The modern kitchen was built as a regular room designed for standing, with a counter-top gas cooking stove and a sink with running water. It was often equipped with an ice-block refrigerator as well.

At about the same time the traditional small, tray-like individual dining table was replaced in most city homes by the *chabudai*, a low round table with collapsible legs at which four or five persons could sit. This reflected the changing disposition of the household. In the cities especially, where a higher proportion of the population were salaried breadwinners, the extended family of rural tradition had been replaced by the nuclear family, small enough to dine together at the same table (see Section 7.2).

Active, universal diffusion of knowledge about food and nutrition also began at this time. Modern cooking schools had opened as early as 1882, but were organized for upper-class young women and had little connection with the daily meals of the common people. From the 1920s cooking classes were frequently offered by women's clubs, girls' schools, newspaper companies and other institutions. Cooking programmes were aired on the radio and a daily 'economical and nutritional menu' prepared by the government's nutrition institute appeared in major newspapers. Women's magazines aimed at middle– and upper–class readers ran regular features describing easy methods for preparing Western-style foods. Thus the prototype of the present-day home, where foreign foods are routine elements of the daily meal, was already in existence.

By this time, modern industry had brought major changes in the food supply. Manufacturing for the national market had begun around the turn of the century, with the completion of rail and road networks that enabled food distribution on a large scale. Flour, sugar and beer factories led the way, followed by makers of tinned foods. Soy sauce and fine sake began to be produced with machinery, packaged in bottles rather than the traditional casks, and brews which previously had only local markets began to be distributed far and wide. Certain towns and their brand names became nationally famous for their excellence, notably sake from Nada (in Hyogo) and Fushimi (in Kyoto) and soy sauce from Noda and Chôshi (in Chiba). Western sweets and refreshments including chocolate, beer, spirits, lemonade and carbonated drinks came into production, not by hand on a small scale but in mechanized factories, and spread throughout the country. An entirely new product of food factories was monosodium glutamate (MSG), marketed under the brand name Ajinomoto ('source of taste'). It was crystallized from glutamic acid, which chemists had identified as a key flavour ingredient of kelp, traditionally one of Japan's favourite foods.

During the 1920s a set of new foods and beverages became established among the urban population: coffee, black tea, milk, lemonade, beer, whisky, ice cream, biscuits, and Western cakes and sweets. Their popularity was stimulated by new types of drinking and eating establishments that served as gathering places for city dwellers. The first coffee house opened in Tokyo in 1899, and during the Taishô Democracy years numerous coffee shops sprang up in the cities where people would pass part of the day over a cup of coffee or black tea. Milk bars, serving milk drinks and inexpensive cakes and furnishing newspapers and magazines for reading, were popular among students. In homes, coffee was rare but black tea was commonly drunk since it could be brewed much like traditional green tea, and there were plentiful supplies of black tea and sugar from the colony of Taiwan. The first beer hall opened in Tokyo in 1899, and during the twenties there were many popular pubs (called cafés) where waitresses served beer, whisky and cocktails.

But the new habits of the modern urbanites were stifled before they could spread through the rest of the country. The economic depression that began in 1930 was most strongly felt by office workers and other members of the urban middle class who had been the pioneers of dietary change. In the following year the

160

nation plunged into war, and as the invasion of China escalated through the 1930s, the government placed priority on military production. Living standards declined as the production of civilian goods decreased, and the food supply grew steadily worse. Under the wartime economic regime the slogan 'Luxury is the enemy' was propagated, creating a social atmosphere in which it was wrong to enjoy one's food. In 1939 it was decreed that on the first day of each month everyone would endure the same hardships as soldiers at the front; restaurants and pubs were forced to take the day off because the sale of alcoholic beverages was banned. Everyone was encouraged to eat simple meals. Office workers and students were urged to pack a 'rising-sun box lunch' (*hinomaru bentô*), named after the national flag because it consisted only of a red pickled apricot (*umeboshi*) on a rectangular ground of white rice. This was absurd in terms of nutritional balance, but the authorities were no longer concerned with the health of the nation. They demanded meals based on idealism.

After the Pacific War began in 1941, rice and other cereals were rationed and food coupons were required to dine in restaurants. As the war intensified, food imports were cut off by the Allied naval blockade and domestic agricultural production dropped as farm labourers were conscripted into military service or munitions factories. Serious food shortages resulted. Restaurants virtually disappeared because they could not get supplies, and the food distributed by the government fell short of minimal subsistence requirements. City dwellers were forced to become self-sufficient, and kitchen gardens sprang up on vacant lots in the towns and cities. The highly efficient sweet potato was the crop most commonly planted in these gardens, and by the end of the war rice distribution was so meagre that there was actually stronger traffic in sweet potatoes. As in the seventeenth century when its introduction led to population growth in western Japan, the sweet potato came to the rescue once more.

After the surrender of 1945, the American occupation forces alleviated the food crisis with massive imports of wheat flour and powdered skim milk. The government allocated that food for schoolchildren, and bread and milk came to be viewed as a child's lunch. That laid the groundwork for the later popularity of bread as a breakfast food in the home. Food shortages continued for several years after the end of the war, and the government gave utmost priority to raising food production. Finally, in 1955, rice production was restored to the level of the 1930s.

6.6   New Meal Patterns

The economy of Japan grew very rapidly from the late 1950s, and dietary standards rose along with personal income. Larger amounts were eaten, and the food selection changed. Once food consumption had climbed back to the quantitative level of the pre-war years, it became clear that the Japanese were not returning to the dietary pattern of the past, but rather were in the process of creating new eating habits. Major changes have occurred in the types of food that are eaten.

The post-war policy of augmenting food production reached fruition in 1962 when the annual consumption of rice per capita rose to 171 kilograms, the highest since rice cultivation began in Japan. Consumption of *mugimeshi*, a boiled mixture of rice and barley, had virtually disappeared, and those who still ate it chose it as a healthy food rather than because they could not afford enough rice. Yet since then rice consumption has steadily declined; in 1986 it was 71 kilograms per capita. This has been accompanied by a sharp drop in the farming population, with farm households comprising less than 10 per cent of the national population by the 1990s. Among the main agricultural products that are consumed, Japan now has self-sufficient production capacity only for rice, green vegetables and eggs. For all other foods the proportion of imports, ultimately financed by industrial exports, has been rising year by year.

The substitution of bread for rice is one of the reasons for the decline in rice consumption, yet the importance of bread in this regard should not be overestimated. By the early 1990s about 30 per cent of the adult population were in the habit of eating bread for breakfast. Well established though it is as a breakfast food, bread still is rarely eaten with the noon or evening meal. The urban lifestyle of rushing off in the morning to work or school, making it hard to find time to cook rice, has spread throughout the country and hence many people make do with store-bought bread. In large cities of other rice-staple countries, such as Singapore and Manila, it has also become common for white-collar employees to have bread for breakfast. Bread as a staple is thus chosen for convenience, when the time and effort required for a rice-centred meal are impractical.

Overall, rice consumption has declined not so much because bread has appeared on the scene, but because the proportion of the rice-based meal taken up by other dishes has increased. As a result of economic expansion, more different kinds of dishes are placed on the meal table, and so more room in the stomach is taken up by what used to be considered side dishes. The regular evening meal in a typical home used to consist of rice, soup, and pickles plus one or two additional dishes of vegetables or fish. Today there are three or more additional dishes.

Under the customs that formerly prevailed, one's rice bowl was refilled several times in order to fill the belly, and serving more than one or two of the tastier, more costly side dishes was considered extravagant or even greedy. Eating was looked upon in an ascetic way, not as something to be enjoyed but as the means of ingesting sufficient energy to maintain the body and perform work. To use a modern metaphor, the body was a car and rice was its staple petrol, while the other dishes were merely motor oil, used in small amounts to keep the petrol burning smoothly. In the days when that way of thinking predominated, except in the small number of wealthy households, a large array of side dishes appeared only on extraordinary, festive occasions.

By the late 1960s extreme differences in income had been substantially eliminated and Japan had become an affluent society. When asked in surveys to classify themselves as upper, middle or lower class, 90 per cent of the people marked the 'middle' column. With affluence, people came to expect enjoyment with their food, and the ordinary home meal expanded to include more dishes. Likewise, more time was spent at the table. Under the traditional moral code a meal was not supposed to take time, but was to be finished quickly before resuming one's work or study. In the early 1960s the average total time spent eating three meals on a weekday was 70 minutes, but in 1970 it had become 90 minutes [NHK

1986:21]. These changes reflected the shift from meals based on the staple grain to meals based on the other dishes, from ascetic meals to pleasurable meals.

The growing emphasis on non-staple dishes brought diversification of the common diet, largely through the adoption of foods and cooking of foreign origin. Western and Chinese cuisine, once only seldom eaten, became part of the daily menu at home as well as routine restaurant fare. In a 1981 national survey in which 5,000 people were asked for their favourite foods, the following came at the top of the list [NHK 1984:2–3].

1. Sushi (fingers of rice topped with raw fish)
2. *Sashimi* (raw fish)
3. Sukiyaki
4. *Tsukemono* (pickles)
5. *Udon* (wheat noodles)
6. *Chawan mushi* (custard with eggs, vegetables, and chicken or fish)
7. Tempura (batter-fried seafood and vegetables)
8. Salad (usually Western-style vegetable salad)
9. *Yakiniku* (Korean-style barbecued beef)
10. *Râmen* (Chinese-style egg-noodle soup with pork)
11. Prawns breaded and deep-fried
12. Grilled fish
13. *Oden* (hotchpotch of fish cakes, vegetables and tofu simmered in broth)
14. Vegetable stir fry (with a bit of meat; Chinese-style)
15. Chilled tofu (soybean curd) in block form
16. *Karê raisu* (meat and vegetable curry with rice)
17. Steak
18. *Soba* (buckwheat noodles)
19. *Sunomono* (vegetables or seafood marinated in vinegar)
20. *Yakisoba* (variant of chow mein)

Eight of the 20 items have foreign roots – four Western (salad, breaded prawns, curry, steak), three Chinese (*râmen*, stir fry, *yakisoba*), and Korean barbecue. Each of these dishes either contains meat or is prepared with oil. They have become favourites as the

Japanese adopted foreign foods to supply those elements which were lacking in the traditional diet, notably meat, fats and oils. Non-traditional foods that have become necessities in the family kitchen include butter, margarine, salad oil, jam, coffee, black tea, milk, ham, sausage, bacon, black pepper, bouillon cubes and powdered Chinese soup stock, Worcestershire-style sauce, and catsup.

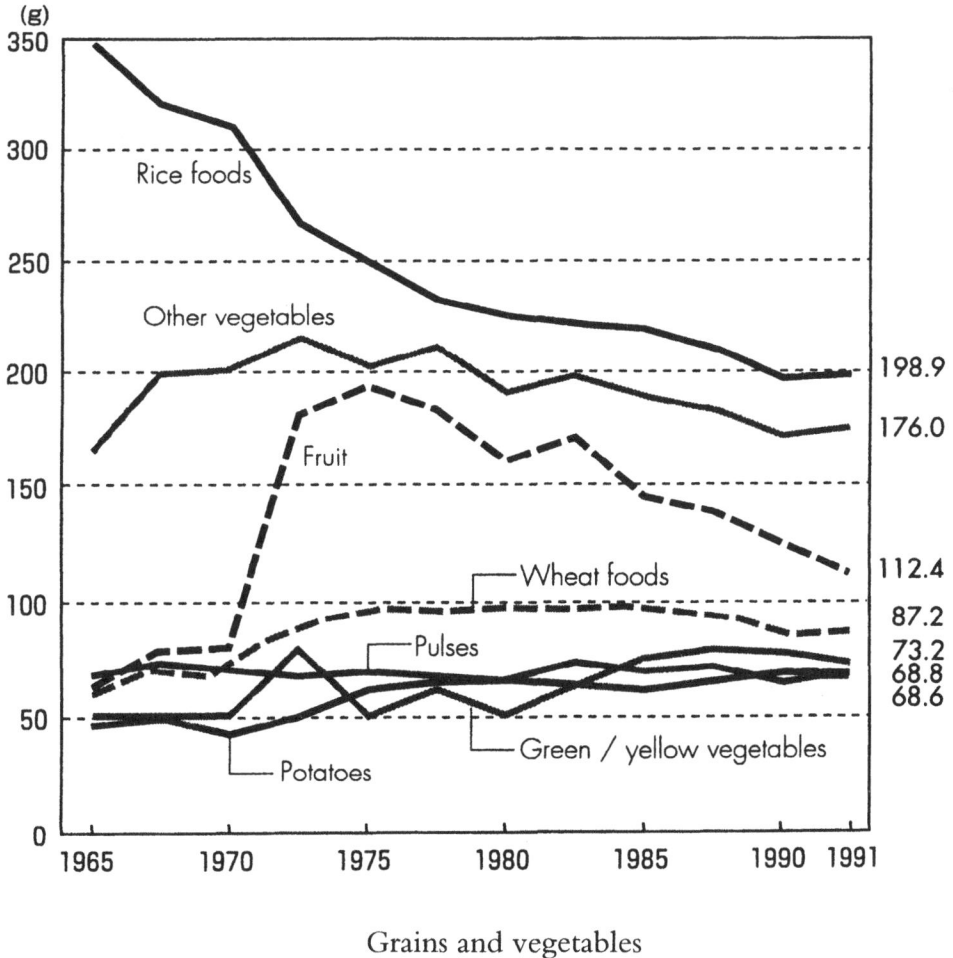

Grains and vegetables

Figure 9   Recent trends in food intake of the Japanese (per capita daily consumption)

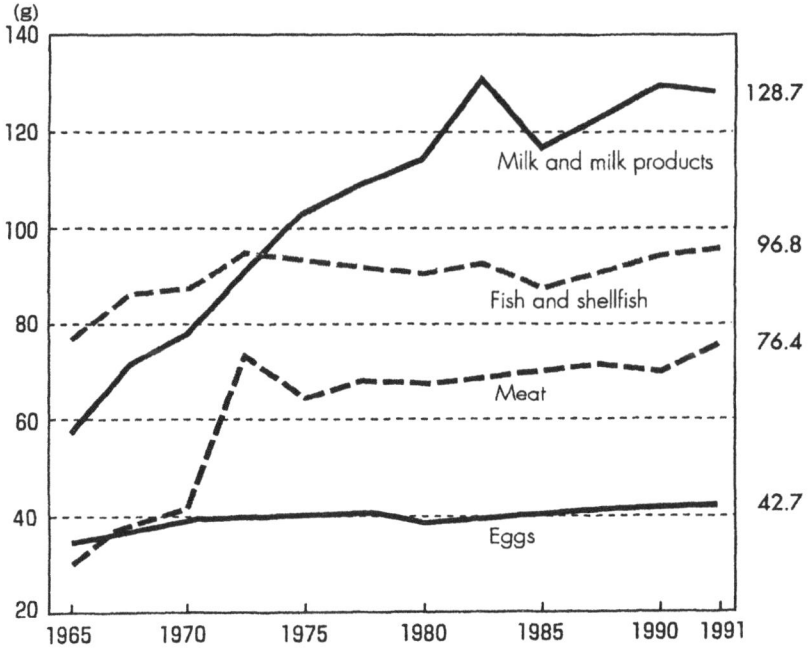

Animal-derived foods

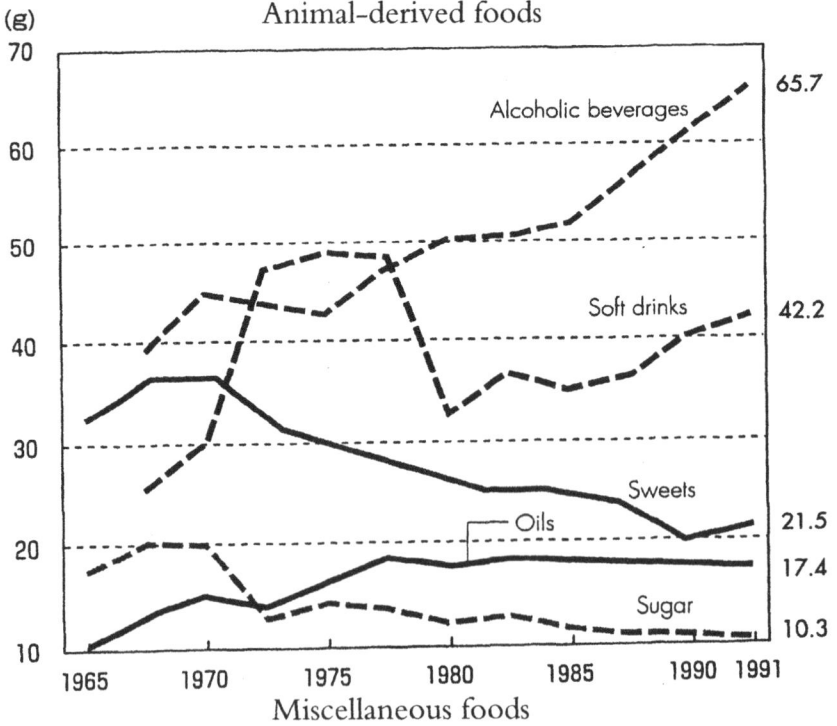

Miscellaneous foods

That foreign foods are now commonly eaten does not mean the traditional cuisine has been driven out. Traditional foods and cooking have survived while meal menus have been enriched by the addition of foods and cooking methods of foreign origin. Likewise, the fact that meat is now commonly eaten does not mean that fish is less so. Japan today consumes far more fish than it did in the years before the Second World War. The graphs in Figures 9A, 9B and 9C, drawn from Ministry of Health and Welfare statistics, show the transition of per capita daily consumption for three food groups. Besides rice, declining consumption is found for sugar and sweets, a reflection of the dietary trend toward affluence in food and eating. For the other foods, consumption levels have remained stable or risen since 1965. Dairy products, meat, and sake are foods that have come to be consumed in increasing quantities. [Kôseishô 1993:39–40].

6.7   Integration of Foreign Foods – A Model

Equipped with a gas stove, a stainless steel or enamelled sink, a microwave oven and a toaster, the Japanese kitchen today is not unlike a Western kitchen. A frying pan and wok are virtually indispensable, and most homes have silverware and Western-type plates on hand. Seven out of ten households use a Western-style table and chairs for meals. And as just discussed, home menus commonly juxtapose dishes of Western, Chinese or Korean origin with traditional Japanese foods. Hence contemporary Japanese home cooking is often called international or Western. But is it really so?

A survey conducted by the author in 1972 investigated this issue. Fifty families were asked to record the types and quantities of all food eaten during one week, and were interviewed about their ideas of the relation between foods of foreign origin and Japanese foods. Even though a quarter of a century has elapsed and the sample was rather small, the model that was drawn up from the survey results remains applicable today without need of revision. Shown in Figure 10, the model is a simplified version of the analytical results, omitting snacks, sweets and beverages. It describes the conjunctive relationships of staples (rice and bread) with other 'Japanese', 'Western' and 'Chinese' dishes [Ishige 1975:165–180].

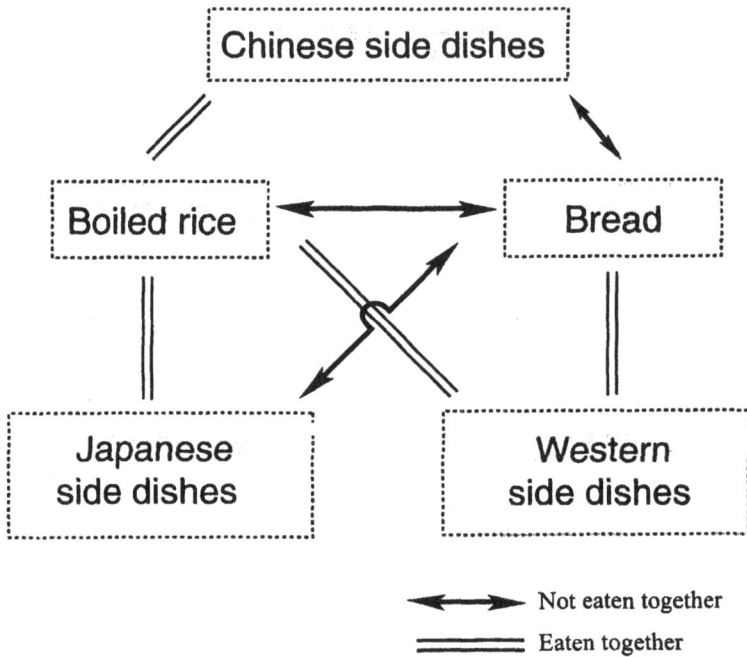

Figure 10   Correlation of main and side dishes.

The traditional idea that a meal contains two kinds of food – the staple and the other dishes – remains strong today. The survey confirmed that with the exception of meals in which a staple and another food are put together as a single dish (e.g. sushi, noodle soups, or sandwiches) meals always consist of the staple (rice or bread) and another dish or dishes. The respondents perceived bread as a food of Western origin. A meat-based meal in Europe may include buttered rice as well as bread, while in Hawaii, the US state with the highest rice consumption, restaurants serve meals with both rice and bread. But the Japanese believe only one staple grain should be served at any one meal. The survey responses included not a single report of rice and bread at the same meal; it was always one or the other. Since rice and bread are so clearly seen as mutually exclusive, all other dishes can be classified into the two broad categories of foods associated with rice and foods associated with bread.

All of the foods associated with bread are of Western origin, as opposed to Japanese or Chinese-style dishes. When bread is served in the home it is with the morning meal, and it is eaten with such foods as ham and eggs, salad, cheese, butter and jam, and such beverages as coffee, black tea, fruit juice or milk – all recognizably Western in origin. In the rare instances where a Japanese or Chinese-style dish was eaten at breakfast together with bread, it was left over from the previous evening. Traditional green tea was never drunk when bread was eaten. In the home it is quite unusual for bread to be served at a meal other than breakfast. It is in restaurants that the noontime or evening meal may include bread, and then only with Western-style food. In other words, the menu of bread-associated dishes is a closed system, consisting entirely of Western-style foods and excluding Japanese or Chinese-style foods. This shows that bread meals have never been modified to a truly Japanese form, but have retained a strongly foreign character.

The rice-associated food group has just one solid characteristic, which is that the beverage served after the meal is green tea. Otherwise the meal might include almost any combination of Japanese, Western or Chinese-type dishes. For example, a meal of rice and miso soup served with raw fish, omelette and stir-fried vegetables – representing those three different streams of cuisine – would not be especially unusual. It is noteworthy that a meal consisting wholly of Chinese-style food is never seen in the home, only in a restaurant. The survey found that even when a home meal included two Chinese-style dishes, there was always another non-staple dish of Japanese or Western-style food. Unlike the bread meal which always consists entirely of Western-style food, a purely Chinese meal is not found in the home as a closed system. This signifies that Chinese cuisine, for which the Japanese have a stronger affinity because it is served with rice and eaten with chopsticks, is more fully integrated into the diet than Western cuisine, which retains an emphasis that is characteristically foreign. Korean dishes which have recently become popular in homes, notably barbecued beef and *kimchee* pickles, would occupy the same niche as Chinese dishes in the model (Figure 10).

Thus, while the menu of today's Japanese home-cooked meals may seem at first glance to be westernized or sinicized or thoroughly international, it is in fact no haphazard combination of cuisines, for it contains regular combinations of associated components, i.e. a pattern. As a description of that pattern, Figure 10 represents the framework of the acculturation process that the domestic menu has undergone since the Meiji period. We may surmise that in the future, except for bread breakfasts, foreign foods will continue to be adopted into the everyday diet only after becoming associated as 'side dishes' with rice. The foreign foods that are selected will be those that have been modified to Japanese forms in which they can be eaten with chopsticks rather than knife and fork, and do not require special sauces but, if desired, can be flavoured with soy sauce or Japanese-style Worcestershire sauce. Hence rather than the westernization or sinicization of Japanese home cooking, we should think in terms of the Japanization of foods of Western and Chinese origin. For the course of change in the modern Japanese diet has not been one of striving to alter the local cuisine into Western or Chinese forms, but rather of reorganizing the traditional meal by selecting foreign elements and adapting them to Japanese forms.

A significant category of eating in Japan is that which is done while drinking alcoholic beverages. In the traditional cuisine the types of foods that are served with sake, which is of course a rice liquor, are the same as those served with rice. In the model of present-day eating patterns (Figure 10), sake can again be substituted for rice, since the snacks or other foods that are served with it commonly include Western and Chinese-style dishes as well as the more traditional Japanese fare. Beer, which became popular in Japan nearly a century ago, and whisky-and-water, a common drink since the late 1960s, are also in the rice column. Wine was for many years associated only with Western food and considered unsuitable for Japanese or Chinese-style dishes, and thus fell into the bread column. Since the 1980s, however, as wine began to grow in popularity among the population in general, it has begun to be matched with Japanese dishes, for example white wine with tempura. In the near future certain wines which are well-suited to Japanese food may move to the rice column.

PART TWO

THE DIETARY CULTURE
OF THE JAPANESE

CHAPTER 7

AT THE TABLE

7.1   Gohan -- **Framework of the Meal**

Like their neighbours in China, Korea and Southeast Asia, the Japanese use several different words to refer to rice in its various forms: The rice plant in the paddy is *ine*; the threshed grain with the hull intact is *momi*; hulled rice is *kome*; rice that is cooked and ready to eat is *gohan*, or *meshi*, a less polite word often used in men's speech.

The words *gohan* or *meshi* are also commonly used to refer to an entire meal. When a housewife has finished cooking a meal she calls out that *gohan* is ready. When a businessman wants to adjourn for food and drink he invites his associates to continue discussions over *meshi* at a restaurant.

For the Japanese, a meal consists of two categories of food, the staple (usually rice, i.e. *gohan*) and the other dishes (*okazu*) of fish, meat or vegetables. The same conception runs throughout the rice-growing regions of East and Southeast Asia. In all those regions, moreover, a word that means cooked rice is also used as a synonym for 'a meal'. In standard Chinese *fàn* means a meal, and also refers to the staple, cooked rice, as distinct from the other dishes (*cài*). In Thai *ah hán* means a meal, but in common parlance the word for cooked rice, *khào*, is used to refer to a meal, especially in the phrase *gin khào*, 'eat rice', which is used to mean 'eat a meal'. In the Thai conception a meal consists of two types of food, *khào* or cooked rice and *gap khào* or 'rice accompaniment'. The same principles are evident in Korean and in other Southeast Asian languages, regardless of linguistic family differences.

Rice in Japan, as in other nations where it is the daily staple, is normally boiled and eaten with no flavouring added. It is the non-rice dishes that are the domain of contrived flavour and fragrance. Neutral in flavour, rice is considered a complement to the taste of any other dish. In the traditional conception of the meal, one was supposed to fill up on rice while eating small amounts of the side dishes to enhance the appetite. A meal without rice would have been thought of as improper. Alternating mouthfuls of rice and some other dish was the correct way to eat, and uninterrupted ingestion of the non-rice dishes was considered vulgar.

In former times the basic meal of the common people consisted of rice, a soup (usually vegetables simmered with miso paste), a side dish of vegetables or fish, and pickles. (In inland areas, however, sea fish was a delicacy served only on rare occasions.) Additional helpings of rice and soup were expected, but only a single small plate or bowl of the side dish would be served to each person. Festivals and annual observances were occasions when the common people ate special treats, and every effort was made to include as many supplementary dishes as possible in such feasts. What was regarded as a special treat was not a great quantity of a single choice dish, but small amounts of a number of foods that were normally unavailable. The traditional Japanese meal has no counterpart to the entrée of the West. Hence the impression of some Westerners that an elegant restaurant meal consists only of drinks and endless hors-d'oeuvres. If we had to designate a main dish, it would be rice or sometimes sake.

The order in which the meal was eaten changed over the centuries, and also varied between such established formats as *honzen* and *kaiseki ryôri*. In the *honzen* banquet, sake was drunk with the food and rice was eaten last. The *kaiseki* meal of the tea ceremony began with rice, and an array of other dishes was then taken along with sake. Japanese meals today usually consist of the courses and sequences described in Figure 11.

Alcohol is rarely consumed with breakfast or lunch, but it is a part of the daily evening meal for a growing proportion of the adult population. While alcohol is being drunk, rice is generally not eaten. This is a carryover of the traditional idea that alcohol − being rice wine − and boiled rice are in essence the same, and thus it is strange to eat them together. To avoid having sake and rice in the mouth together, sake is drunk while eating a variety of non-rice dishes. It is only after drinking one's fill that the first rice is eaten, and from that point the drinking cup is left untouched.

Only soup and pickles are eaten with rice in a traditionally served meal. At a formal banquet, if a soup is included among the dishes served while drinking sake, then another soup will be served when the rice is brought out. Pickles are formally supposed to be eaten with rice, but on some occasions they may be served with sake, to add variety to the menu.

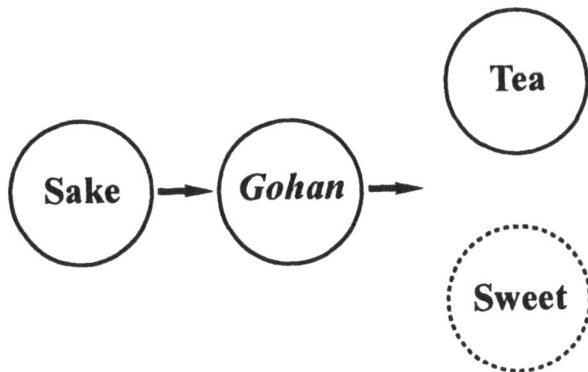

Figure 11   Courses of the typical Japanese meal today.

After rice, the meal is concluded by drinking green tea. When there is no soup, the rice is often served with green tea poured over it and a topping of pickles and other garnish. This mixture, called *chazuke*, is alternately eaten and drunk from a bowl. Fruit or sweets may occasionally be served with tea, but tea alone will suffice to round out the meal. Desserts were on the menus of traditional banquets, but were not part of the ordinary home meal. In traditional households today, fruit and sweets may be taken with tea between meal times, but are not served with the meal. Nowadays a growing proportion of home meals do include dessert, owing to the influence of Western eating patterns.

Sake as a rule is never drunk alone but is complemented with one or more types of food. The accompanying dishes, which are called *okazu* when eaten with rice, are called *sakana* when served with sake. *Sakana* is a homonym for the word that means fish, and though they are now written with different ideographs, both words derive from the term meaning 'side dishes served with sake'. Yet despite the different generic names, the foods served with rice and those served with sake comprise the same broad range of fish, vegetables etc. They are the side dishes, while the main dish is either rice or rice wine. Rice and sake thus play interchangeable roles in the traditional conception of the meal.

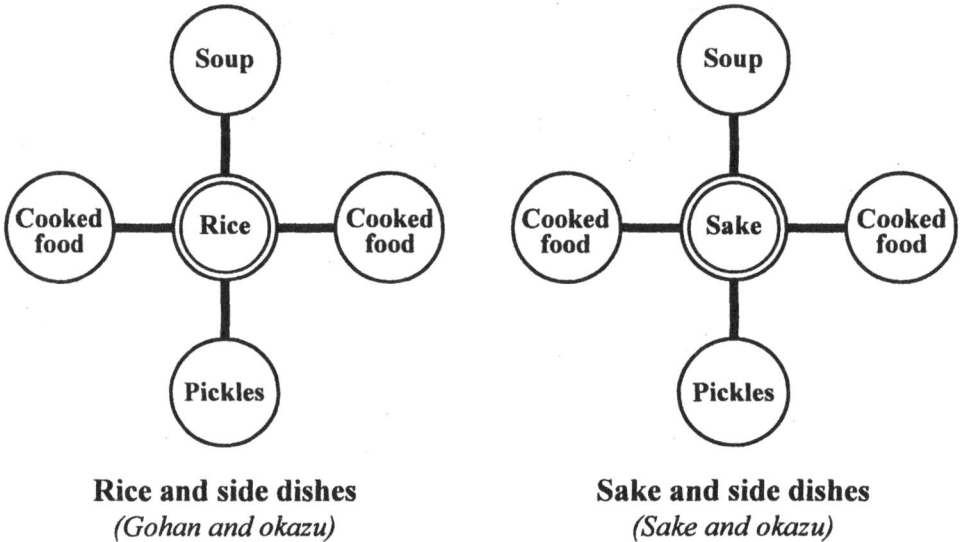

Rice and side dishes   **Sake and side dishes**
(Gohan and okazu)   *(Sake and okazu)*

Figure 12   Side dishes with rice and with sake.

7.2   The Rise of the Table

A Jesuit missionary who lived in Japan in the sixteenth century noted that, 'Whereas our [Western] dining table is in place before the food is set out, their dining table is set with food and then carried out from the kitchen' [Frois 1982:558]. The traditional Japanese residence had no room that was reserved only for dining. A meal could be eaten anywhere because each person's food was served on a small portable table known as a *zen*. For a special occasion such as a wedding or funeral when a large number of people took a meal together, the sliding paper-door partitions could be removed so that almost the entire house served as a single large dining area. In daily life a room adjacent to the kitchen, which may have had a small hearth set in the floor, would normally be used for meals, but once the meal was finished and the portable tables

178

removed, that room would typically revert to some other use, such as a workspace or bedroom.

Historically, the personal *zen* table took various forms, and special types were used for ceremonial purposes. The *zen* in everyday use among the common people from the eighteenth century onward was a square box with a simple lacquer finish. Eating utensils were stored in the box. For use, the lid was removed and placed upside down on the box to form a tray, on which the plates and bowls of food were set. Alternatively, the box had a tray attached to the top and a drawer to store the utensils. The items kept inside included chopsticks, a rice bowl, a soup bowl, one or two small plates for side dishes, and a cloth for wiping the utensils. The tray measured 25 to 30 cm per side and the box was 15 to 20 cm high. This small table would be completely filled by a bowl of rice and a bowl of soup, a small plate of vegetables or fish and another small plate of pickles – the everyday menu of the common people. Single servings of the side dishes were set out beforehand, but extra helpings of rice and soup could be had, served by the housewife from pots beside the table. The eating utensils stored in the personal table were thoroughly washed only about three times in a month. The usual procedure after eating was to pour hot water or tea over the utensils and drink it, and then wipe them with the cloth and place them in the box. When the meal was over, the packed *zen* were stored in a regular place in the kitchen.

The part of the room furthest from the kitchen was the place of honour, occupied by the head of the household or the retired grandfather, and the servants sat closest to the kitchen. Between the two ends sat the other family members in order of status, men before women and elders before juniors. The housewife sat either between the youngest family members and the servants, or next to her husband so as to serve him personally. Thus the order of the *zen* tables reflected the traditional family relationship structure based on male superiority and respect for elders.

[Mitani]

Figure 13   Zen: meal stands and meal trays of the Edo period. Each design has its own name. (Mitani 1975).

Before the morning meal one or two miniature bowls of rice would be placed as an offering on the household altar, which might be either Shinto or Buddhist. It was also customary to lay out an extra meal (called a *kagezen* or 'image table') for a family member who was away on a journey or military service, as a means of praying for a safe return. In traditional belief, after death people become Shinto or Buddhist deities and act as protectors of their descendants. The daily meal was conducted with the attitude that it was attended not only by those actually present, but also by ancestors and absent family members. Thus it had something of the character of a minor religious observance, and the meal was therefore expected to be conducted with propriety in a hushed atmosphere. Eating in silence was the ideal, and loud conversation was not tolerated.

A low dining table large enough for several people, called a *chabudai*, came into use from the beginning of the twentieth century. It was either rectangular or round, typically about one metre in diameter, and stood about 30 cm high on four folding legs. The *chabudai* evolved as a modification of the Western dining table, shortened to match the custom of sitting on the tatami-mat floor, and with folding legs for portability, in keeping with the multipurpose nature of the dining room. The new dining table was adopted first by the emerging urban middle class of salaried workers and their families, and appeared rather later in the homes of urban merchants and in farming areas. Merchant families usually ate together with live-in assistants and servants, and therefore preferred to keep serving their meals on individual tables. Farm households, with their labour-intensive lifestyle, were generally so large that the *chabudai* designed for five or six people could not accommodate everyone. The conservative nature of the rural population also tended to delay their adoption of the new table. Salaried workers in the cities, on the other hand, lived in nuclear families and were quick to discard the old-fashioned *zen* in favour of the *chabudai*.

In contrast to *zen* table service, with its ascetic tenor and undercurrent of tension among the diners, the togetherness of the *chabudai* meal offered what amounted to a new ideology. In a book published in 1903 the socialist leader Sakai Toshihiko proclaimed:

> Mealtimes are gatherings of the family. Mealtimes are when the family comes to fruition as a happy circle. Therefore the meal should definitely include all family members, all at once, all around the same table. Whether the table be round or rectangular, Oriental or Western, it must be a single table. The old-fashioned *zen* ought to be abolished.
>
> When everyone eats at the same time at the same table, naturally everyone should eat the same food. Some men reserve for themselves certain special foods that are kept from the rest of the family, an outrageously insensitive and unreasonable practice.
>
> To my way of thinking, even the maids should be fed together with the family. Furnishing the maid with the

181

same food that the family eats will not put much strain on the household budget. [Sakai 1979:104–5, 220].

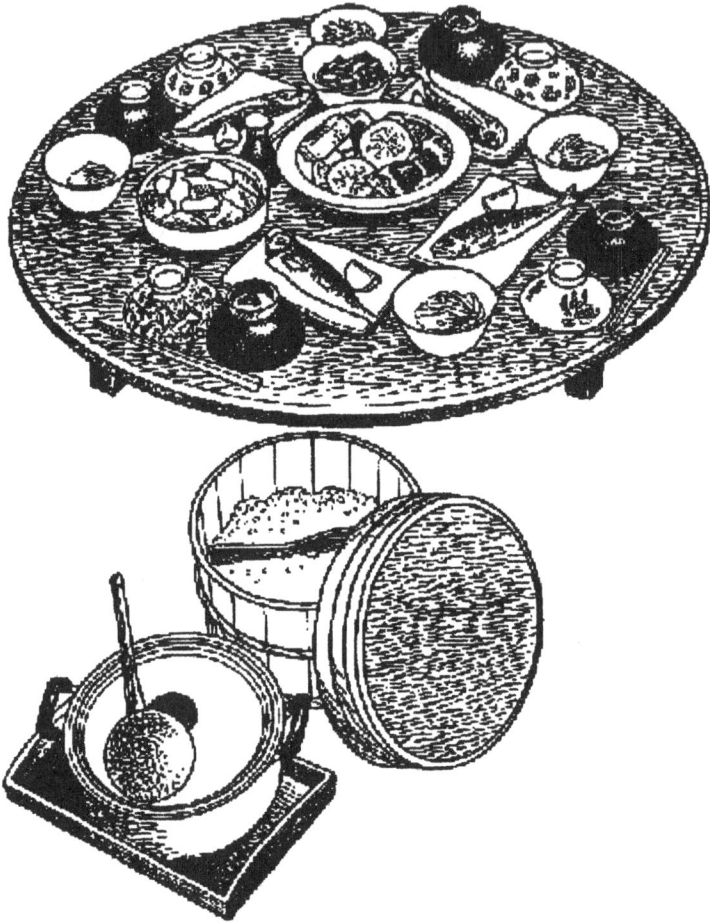

Figure 14   A typical meal of the 1950s, set on a *chabudai*. Each place has a ceramic rice bowl and lacquered soup bowl, chopsticks, a plate with a cooked fish and a section of lemon, and a bowl of other cooked food. At the centre is a bowl of simmered *daikon* radish, and to its left is a bowl of pickles. From these the diners will take bits to their individual rice bowls using the top ends of their chopsticks, rather than the tips which touch their mouths. On the floor in the foreground is a wooden container of boiled rice and a pot of soup.

182

Sakai saw these as indispensable steps for realizing a 'family of democratic beauty' in a 'common society worth respecting and hoping for'. Similar assertions were made in women's magazines during the Taishô Democracy years. Yet the use of a *chabudai* was not in itself enough to bring the happy family circle to fruition, according to a survey in which 300 persons born before 1915 were interviewed about changes in the family meal. [Ishige and Inoue 1991:30–7] In most homes silence was enforced even at the common table; children were scolded if they talked too much; when there was conversation among the family the topic was usually supplied by the father and frequently concerned his work; when children were addressed they were usually lectured about the need to study harder; and scenes of the family chatting merrily and laughing together at meals were rare.

Convenience was the reason most commonly cited by our respondents for the change from the personal to the family table. Separate plates and bowls with individual servings remained the rule, although the pickles might be served on a single plate for everyone's use. Even so, it was easier to set out the food on a single table than on many small ones, and to move just one table to create the dining space. Cleanliness was the next most frequent response. It was more sanitary to use a common table because the housewife directly handled the eating utensils, washing them and placing them in a cabinet after each meal, whereas the utensils kept in the personal table were merely rinsed and wiped by the user nine days out of ten. While this made more work for the housewife, the spread of modern ideas of sanitation supported the popularity of the *chabudai*. The added work is one reason why the new tables caught on first in the cities, where running water was fairly common and hence washing was easier. In the households of our respondents, by 1925 the low *chabudai* was more common than the personal *zen* table, and by the late 1930s the *zen* had become unusual. After 1945 Western-style dining tables with chairs became more and more common, outnumbering *chabudai* from about 1971 (see Figure 15).

The use of a table and chairs in the home was advocated as early as 1919 as a founding tenet of an organization, formed mainly by intellectuals, which promoted modern lifestyles. But tatami floors made it virtually impossible to use chairs without redesigning the Japanese home, and high dining tables remained rare. They first appeared in significant numbers from about 1950, for serving lunch

(Famiy)

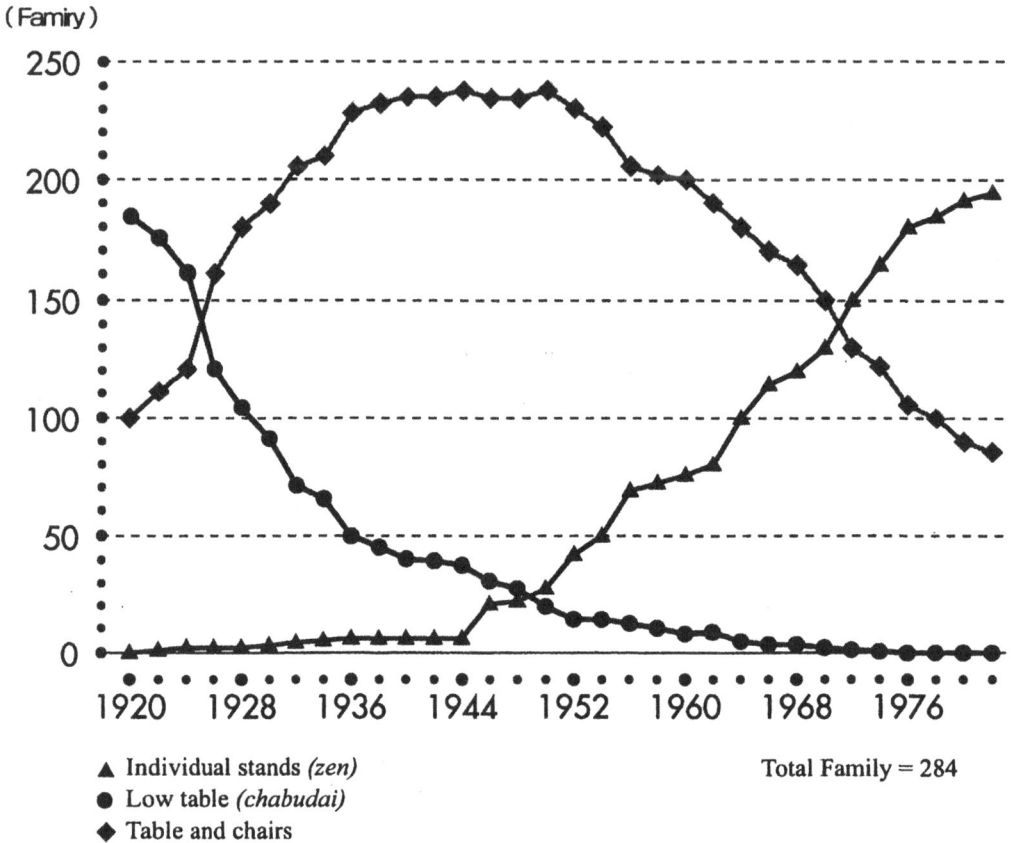

▲ Individual stands *(zen)*
● Low table *(chabudai)*
◆ Table and chairs

Total Family = 284

Figure 15   Diffusion of the high family meal table

in farmhouses. When farmers and farm workers came to the house for the midday meal, they had to wash their muddy feet before stepping up to the tatami floor to eat. But the traditional farmhouse also had a large dirt-floored kitchen where a table and chairs could be set up for eating without washing the feet, and this was promoted by the Ministry of Agriculture and Forestry as part of a programme to improve farm life in the post-war years. Eating on chairs began to spread among the non-farm population from 1956, when public agencies began erecting blocks of reinforced-concrete flats throughout the country. The council flat had just two small rooms plus a kitchen, and to save space the designers envisioned the kitchen as the dining area. As Western-style furniture was expensive at the time, and there was some doubt as to whether people would want to eat in the kitchen, at the beginning a kitchen table was furnished so the occupants had only to buy chairs. Concrete residences were virtually unknown in Japan until this time and the council flat became an object of admiration, which led to a vogue for high dining tables. Privately developed blocks of flats sprang up rapidly thereafter, and they were routinely designed for dining tables. As the immovable dining table became a fixture of modern life, more and more Japanese homes acquired a permanent dining area. By the early 1990s about 70 per cent of all households used a table and chairs for daily meals.

The diffusion of the high dining table coincided with the establishment of democratic politics and the decades of rapid economic growth. The extended family with its authoritarian head disintegrated as the nuclear family pattern spread even to rural homes, and gender differences were levelled as women made notable advances in society. As the farming population declined and the great majority of jobs came to be located in offices and factories, the home tended to lose its character as a production site and become purely a place of consumption. Fathers lost their status as vocational teachers, and with intensified economic activity large numbers of men began working late, so more and more often the evening meal included only the mother, who ran the household, and children. By the 1970s, economic development had brought televisions, refrigerators and cars to virtually every home. The differences between city and country disappeared as an urban lifestyle spread throughout Japan.

Consistent with these circumstances, our survey found that in today's households the topics of mealtime conversation tend to be furnished by the wife and children rather than the father. Encouragement of cheerful conversation during the family meal is now the rule, and eating in silence has become the exception. The topics run from ordinary small talk to daily events at home and at school, and tend also to include news and entertainment [Ishige and Inoue 1991:64–82]. The latter topics are stimulated by the television which many families now have in the dining room and switched on while eating. The happy family circle, which early in the century was ideologically expounded yet not delivered by the *chabudai*, has been realized, but with the addition of the television which turns the dining room into a miniature restaurant cum theatre.

Economic expansion enriched the selection of non-rice dishes in the meal, and the larger space required for plates and bowls was another reason why the dining table replaced the smaller *chabudai* and *zen* tables. The dining area in most homes is either part of the kitchen or opens on to it, and meal service has tended toward multiple courses of hot food, sometimes with the next dish being prepared while the previous one is eaten. Still, the traditional style of laying out all the food at the start of the meal, as was the rule on the *zen* and the *chabudai*, remains dominant. If the larger number of different foods making up today's meal were all set out separately for each individual, the family table would overflow. As a result many homes have adopted a style of service resembling the typical Chinese meal, with each of the dishes except rice and soup placed on a platter in the middle of the table, from which everyone helps themselves.

The spread of the high dining table also coincided with the new popularity in the home of foods originating in China and the West. For centuries, meals of exclusively Japanese cuisine had been taken while seated on a tatami floor, and such was the framework in which table manners developed and stabilized. At a meal where one sits in a chair, where Japanese, Western and Chinese foods may be eaten all at once, where chopsticks may be supplemented or replaced by knife, fork, spoon and hands, just what sort of dining etiquette is to prevail? The traditional formalism of the household meal has indeed collapsed, but the standard that might replace it has not yet fully developed. The most desirable procedures for adults as well as children are not yet clear. In short, household table manners today are in a state of anarchy.

Religion, meanwhile, is on the wane. Offerings are rarely placed on the household altar in homes that do not have an elderly resident, and the ritual of setting out a meal for an absent family member has disappeared. Thus the daily meal has lost its character as a simple, sacred observance amid domestic life. Yet while the deities and ancestors starve, those living in this world are routinely served a variety of foods such as formerly could be eaten only on special feast days. The Japanese of today celebrate a perpetual festival without deities.

7.3   The Tabletop as Landscape

'Japanese food is enjoyed with the eye, Western food is savoured with the nose, Chinese food delights the tongue.' This saying developed during the past century as most Japanese became familiar with foods of foreign origin. In their perception, the native cuisine is notable for its beautiful presentation, Western food for the aroma of spices and herbs, and Chinese cooking for its outstanding taste. (A proper list of world cuisines should no doubt include the rich aromas and tastes of the Indian subcontinent and the Middle East, but until the 1980s restaurants serving the foods of those regions were rare in Japan.)

Japanese cuisine is well known for its aesthetic presentation, but in fact the use of beautiful crockery and the special exertion required to fill it with 'food for show' are typically found in a high-class restaurant rather than in the ordinary home. Food for show is nourishment to which artistic value has been added. As such it provides enjoyment of a visually sensual nature, and yet the fundamental sensory functions of a meal are to provide a feeling of fullness and to satisfy through taste. In ordinary home cooking, every effort is made toward those fundamental purposes, while little energy goes toward visual appeal. Indeed, throughout the world the pouring of energy into preparing food for show is the province of professional cooks at work in fancy restaurants, palaces or the homes of the very rich.

In France, decorative banquet cooking reached its peak in the nineteenth century, and the serving style has since tended toward simplification. Illustrations of luxurious French banquets of the time show that architecturally styled decorations were common; even a miniature Parthenon or Egyptian pyramid could appear on the table. Platforms or stepped pedestals were constructed to hold the food, and the alignment of plates as well as the placement of food on the plate were quite geometrical, based on symmetry.

European table setting in general is shot through with the principle of symmetry.

The formal gardens of Europe are likewise geometrically and symmetrically arranged in an architectural manner with platforms and stairways. The intent is to create a harmonic beauty by emphasizing artificial composition. In contrast, Japanese gardens are non-geometric and asymmetrical in a style reminiscent of natural landscape. Traditional Japanese aesthetics has displayed a marked tendency to avoid symmetry and geometry, which are considered overly artificial. The garden is regarded as an abstract representation of nature, and since nature has a fundamentally unbalanced arrangement, geometric forms such as the line, circle or cube are not used. The miniature mountains and ponds that are typically constructed are shaped differently for each garden.

Japanese haute cuisine since the eighteenth century has sought to present the philosophy of the garden on the dining table. One popular trend has been to serve food in *sansui* (landscape) forms. The word *sansui* literally means 'mountain and water', using those two elements to symbolize the whole of nature. The term is used for landscape painting as well as formal garden design; no conventional Japanese garden lacks the mountain–and–water motif. When *sashimi* is served according to the *sansui* convention, at the far end of the plate (from the diner's viewpoint) threadlike strips of *daikon* radish are piled high in the shape of a mountain and tiny pieces of green vegetables are placed around it to represent trees and shrubbery. At the front of the plate the slices of raw fish are arranged as an image of waves. In this sort of three-dimensional presentation, the mountain is not an equilateral pyramid but an uneven triangle, conventionally higher on the right and lower on the left. A triangle with unequal sides is also preferred in a two-dimensional serving design. For example, when small amounts of three types of food are set on a single round plate, a typical arrangement is to place two at the front with a space between them, and the third at the back and to the right. In this case the food at the rear would be the finest of the three.

In Chinese banquet cooking, a typical aesthetic array of hors-d'oeuvres would use slices of meat and vegetables to create a figurative motif, such as a phoenix or dragon. In Japanese cooking, on the other hand, presenting food as a pictorial expression is quite unusual and generally considered unrefined. Even in the *sansui* serving style, the design is based on philosophically abstracted forms; the uninitiated diner might look carefully at the food without any idea of mountains or water coming to mind. As in Europe, in Chinese cooking the emphasis is on symmetrical placement of the food, something which is never seen in Japanese service. One reason why symmetry is prominent in China is that even numbers are auspicious in that culture, whereas in Japan odd numbers are preferred. A plate of Japanese food typically contains three, five or seven varieties, but rarely an even number.

In China and Europe the diners surround the table during the meal, and symmetrical serving styles are preferred because they appeal visually to all sides. In Japan, like the landscape garden that is designed to be seen to best advantage from a particular spot of the house that adjoins it, the traditional cuisine is set out on the premise that it will be viewed from one direction only. The eyes of a person seated at an old-fashioned single-serving *zen* table look down from above. Many pieces of Japanese tableware are asymmetrical yet designed to be oriented in a certain way when placed atop a *zen*. Containers are also made to be viewed from a certain side. The aesthetic of Japanese cuisine consists in the creation of a miniature Japanese garden atop a tiny personal dining table.

7.4   Chopsticks and Table Manners

A British friend of mine married a Japanese woman and moved to Japan. In order to accustom him to Japanese life, the first thing his wife taught him was how to use chopsticks. Saying 'You mustn't humiliate yourself when eating with Japanese men,' she took out two small ceramic bowls, placed a handful of shelled peanuts in one of them, handed him a pair of lacquered chopsticks, and ordered him to move the peanuts one at a time to the other bowl. It is no simple thing to pick up and hold a slippery peanut with the pointed ends of smoothly lacquered chopsticks. If he accidentally dropped a peanut on the table, she would not allow him to retrieve it with his fingers, but made him use the sticks. Finally, when all the peanuts were successfully lodged in the second bowl, she told him to return them to the first one. The transferring procedure was repeated a seemingly endless number of times. 'I felt like Sisyphus at the time,' my friend told me. 'But you know, the result is that I can use chopsticks as well as any Japanese.'

For a child to eat a meal by oneself without relying on mother's hand, the first thing that must be learned is the proper way to hold chopsticks. The key point is that rather than moving both of them, the chopstick that is in the lower position when held is kept in a fixed position while the upper one is moved to grasp the food. As shown in Figure 7.2, the ring finger holds the lower chopstick in place, the thumb lightly supports both, and the index finger controls and moves the upper chopstick. With proficiency in the proper way of holding chopsticks, one is able to use them with great dexterity; it is even possible to pick up a single sesame seed.

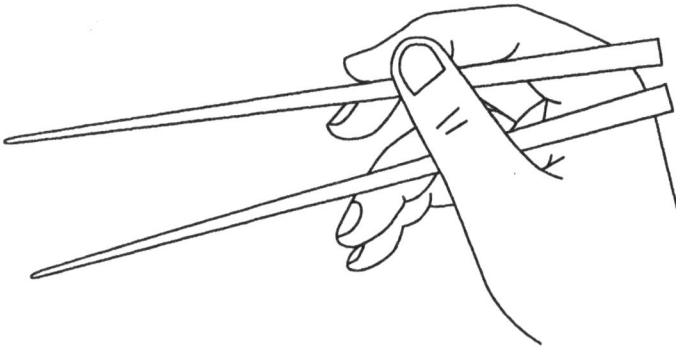

Figure 16   The correct way to use chopsticks.

The most convenient length depends on the size of the hand and fingers. Children's chopsticks are naturally shorter. Those considered suitable for adult use range from 17 to 23 cm, the shorter ones mainly for women. Married couples frequently receive gifts of paired sets of longer and shorter chopsticks. Japanese chopsticks narrow steadily to tips that are almost pointed, which allows them to be used for very small bits of food. The tips of Chinese chopsticks are not pointed and moreover they have an average length of 27 cm, hence they do not lend themselves to very delicate use. In a Chinese meal the diners take their own portions of food (except rice and soup) from platters in the middle of the table, for which long chopsticks are convenient. The Chinese use spoons for food that is difficult to pick up with their chopsticks. The Japanese have long eaten only with chopsticks, and it is often said that due to the constant training of making minute movements with the fingertips at every meal, they are quite skillful in using their hands for precision work; however this has not actually been proven.

In the table etiquette of Japan the greatest importance is attached to the use of chopsticks, and there are a number of incorrect ways of holding or using them which are considered marks of vulgarity. Breaches of etiquette include the following:

Clutched chopsticks *(nigiri-bashi)*: Grasping the chopsticks with the palm of the hand. This is not merely childish behaviour; grasping a pair of pointed chopsticks may be taken as a menacing move.

Piercing chopsticks *(sashi-bashi)*: Piercing the food with one or both chopsticks in order to pick it up.

Scooping chopsticks *(yoko-bashi)*: Placing the chopsticks against each other and using them like a spoon.

Cramming chopsticks *(komi-bashi)*: Using chopsticks to push back food that is already in the mouth.

Licked chopsticks *(neburi-bashi)*: Licking off food that is clinging to the chopsticks.

Crying chopsticks *(namida-bashi)*: Allowing soup to drip like tears from the tips of chopsticks.

Racking chopsticks *(kaki-bashi)*: Placing the mouth on the edge of a plate or bowl and using the chopsticks to rake in food.

Chewed chopsticks *(kami-bashi)*: Biting the tips of the chopsticks.

Dragging chopsticks *(yose-bashi)*: Using chopsticks to pull or pick up a plate or bowl.

Hesitating chopsticks *(mayoi-bashi)*: Moving the chopsticks back and forth indecisively over various dishes of food.

Roving chopsticks *(utsuri-bashi)*: Applies to two situations: eating a bite of one dish and then immediately eating a bite of another; or continually eating only non-rice dishes. The refined diner alternates a bite of a non-rice dish with a bite of rice or a sip of sake.

Probing chopsticks *(kara-bashi)*: Touching of food with the chopsticks and putting them down without eating it. Considered a distrust toward the provider of the food.

These are only some of the dos and don'ts for chopsticks. It is said that 'table manners begin with chopsticks and end with chopsticks'.

There are bone chopsticks in China, and most chopsticks in Korea are metal, but in Japan they are traditionally made of bamboo or some other wood (and nowadays sometimes plastic). Those in normal use in homes today are lacquered wood, or plastic with a similar external appearance. Ordinary lacquered chopsticks will endure several years of use. A given pair, identifiable by size, colour and decoration, is reserved for a particular user, for chopsticks are never shared, even with one's family members. Accordingly, restaurants usually provide a pair of disposable chopsticks for each customer. In most restaurants these are *waribashi*, a small piece of plain wood that is split almost in half lengthwise, which the customer extracts from its paper and splits in two. *Waribashi* have been in use since the restaurant business first flourished in the eighteenth century. Higher-class restaurants provide pairs of disposable chopsticks made either of unlacquered high-grade wood, or bamboo with the natural green skin on one side.

Disposable chopsticks are used because of the taboo against sharing chopsticks with another person. This is related to the Shintoist concept of defilement, which remains deep-seated in the Japanese mind (see Section 3.2). It is commonly believed that something which has touched someone's mouth picks up that person's character and might, if used by another, transmit a contamination which is not physical but spiritual and cannot be washed away. I once surveyed some seminar students on Japanese

192

ideas of cleanliness, and included the following question: 'Suppose you lend an article that you use to someone else, who uses it and then thoroughly cleans it before returning it to you. Which article would you have the strongest sense of psychological resistance against reusing afterward?' An undergarment for the lower part of the body and a personal pair of chopsticks were the leading responses.

When chopsticks are not in the hand, they are set on the table with the tips on a small chopstick rest (*hashi-oki*), typically made of ceramic, lacquer or bamboo. This avoids contact with the table surface so that the part that enters the mouth is kept clean. The chopstick rest became common only in the 1960s. Previously each pair of chopsticks was set on the table in a narrow box with one of the long sides fashioned as a sliding lid. The diner would remove the chopsticks from the box at the start of the meal and replace them at the end, using the edge of a plate or bowl as a rest when it was necessary to put them down in order to drink soup or tea.

In traditional table service the foods were almost always set out on small plates as individual servings. Thus in principle one's chopsticks came into contact only with one's personal serving of food. Yet there were times when everyone at the meal would take pickles from the same large bowl, or take pieces of a large fish or other special dish served on a single large platter for all. Even among members of the same family, touching common food with the personal chopsticks was considered a breach of etiquette (known as *jika-bashi*, 'direct chopsticks'). Instead special serving chopsticks, which belonged to no individual and thus were neutral, were used to take food from the common platter on to one's own plate, from which it would be eaten with one's own chopsticks. If serving chopsticks were not provided, the personal chopsticks were reversed and the top ends, which never touched the mouth, were used to take individual portions. Household observance of this custom gradually faded from the late 1950s, when foods of Chinese and Western origin became popular in home cooking. Often those foods are placed in the middle of the table and all family members serve themselves with their own chopsticks in the Chinese style, with only rice and soup served in individual bowls. Yet this style of eating is limited to groups that are intimately related; in restaurants, serving chopsticks are still used.

193

7.5   Etiquette – As You Like It

Until the 1950s, the more affluent Japanese homes had two dining spaces. One was the *zashiki* or drawing room for entertaining guests. Not used for regular family meals, it would be kept closed except on *hare* or special occasions when guests were present. The *zashiki* is a tatami-mat room with a *tokonoma* alcove at the far end, and custom dictates that the guest of honour sit in front of the *tokonoma* facing away from it while the host sits at the opposite end of the room closest to the door. Today's high-class Japanese-style restaurants maintain the style of the classic residential *zashiki*.

The other eating area functioned as the *ke* or everyday space for family meals. Traditionally this room was adjacent to the earthen-floored *doma* that contained the cooking range and sink. The name of the dining room varied by region but in the countryside it was most commonly called *daidokoro* (kitchen) and in the city *chanoma* (living room; literally 'tea room'). Despite the name 'kitchen', the farmhouse *daidokoro* did not house the key cooking functions of boiling rice and washing. The floor was usually of wood rather than tatami, with an open wood-burning hearth (*irori*) about one metre square set in the centre, over which a kettle or pot could be suspended to boil tea or miso soup. The urban *chanoma* had a tatami floor and was typically furnished with a charcoal-burning brazier for heat. In either case, this was the room where food was served for the whole family, but it was not reserved exclusively for eating. At other times it might be used as a place to chat or have tea or even to spread out bedding for the night, for the rooms of the traditional Japanese house were multipurpose spaces where equipment for various activities would be set up and removed.

A single space reserved for eating is emerging in today's home. As most families now use a Western-style table for meals, there is often a separate dining room next to the kitchen. Alternatively, in many cases the dining table is placed in the kitchen.

In a banquet meal or in a home meal where drink plays an important part, the rice is served last, as noted above. The table setting and dining etiquette described here are for the typical family meal in which rice and soup and side dishes are taken together. Normally the table is not adorned with flowers, nor are napkins or a tablecloth used. Chopsticks are placed crosswise on the table immediately in front of the diner with the tips on a chopstick rest.

Behind the chopsticks, a ceramic bowl of boiled rice is placed at the diner's left, and a lacquered wooden bowl (or a plastic bowl with similar appearance) containing soup is placed at the right. This pattern, which was probably fixed by the eighth century, assumes that the chopsticks are held in the right hand, placing the rice bowl which is most often picked up and put down nearest the left hand, and the next most frequently held bowl, for soup, at the right. The diner's serving of the side dishes (*okazu*) sits on ceramic plates or shallow bowls behind the rice and soup.

Rice and soup bowls with lids have become rather rare in the home but are still sometimes used. When removed, the lid of the rice bowl is placed at the diner's left and the lid of the soup bowl at the right. In the light *chakaiseki* meal that may be served with a tea ceremony, the lid of the soup bowl is upturned and placed on top of the rice bowl lid.

At the start of the meal each diner says *itadakimasu*, a polite expression meaning 'I receive what is provided'. With its open syntax (typical in Japanese) the phrase leaves open to interpretation the question of who has provided the food; during the Second World War it was generally understood that the emperor was the provider. At the end of the meal each diner says *gochisô sama* or 'thank you for the wonderful meal'. These set phrases for starting and ending the meal date only from the 1940s, and have been universalized by being taught in the schools. Previously, in some families one would start and finish the meal by bringing the hands together as if praying silently at a Buddhist altar, but in most homes there were no prescribed salutations [Ishige and Inoue 1991:111–12].

Chakaiseki etiquette specifies that one begins the meal with a mouthful of rice, followed by a drink of soup, and then extends the chopsticks to take a morsel from a side dish. For the ordinary meal at home the order is different, starting with a drink of soup, then a mouthful of rice and then a bite of a side dish. Rotating consistently from soup to rice to side dish was formerly considered the refined way to eat, but with the increased number and amounts of side dishes on the modern table, enforcing that procedure today would overstuff the stomach with rice and soup. Nowadays as long as the order is sustained for one initial round, it is not impolite to eat mouthful after mouthful of the side dishes without touching the rice or soup. In other words, show good form at the start, then eat what you please.

Unless food is served on a large plate, it is permissible to lift up the bowl or dish in the hand to eat. The rice and soup bowls in particular should be picked up, for it is impolite to eat from either when it is on the table. It is acceptable to take as many refills of rice and soup as desired. Placing the bowl on the table with one mouthful left in the bottom is the signal that one wants another helping. In traditional etiquette it was bad form to leave any food uneaten, but now the side dishes tend to be so generously served that it is becoming necessary to excuse not finishing them. It is still impolite to leave any of the rice or soup, as those portions can be adjusted by not taking further helpings.

When dining abroad, the Japanese are often criticized for making slurping sounds when eating, which happens because they are not used to eating soup with a spoon. In traditional Japanese table manners it is impolite to slurp one's soup or make noise when chewing. The exception is noodles. Noodle lovers attach great importance to the feeling of the noodles slipping smoothly down the throat, and consequently suck them down in a single breath without chewing well, an operation that inevitably produces some noise.

When drink is taken with the meal no distinction is made between an aperitif, a beverage accompanying the food or an after-dinner drink. Traditionally, sake was the only drink. Today it has become common to drink beer with Japanese-style food. Some people drink wine with meals, others drink whisky mixed in the Japanese manner with ice and water, and many take the edge off their thirst with beer and then switch to sake. At banquets it has become customary to serve beer for the opening toast. From the Edo period, sake was normally drunk hot even in the heat of summer, but since the 1980s when there was a boom for refined sakes (*ginjôshu*) that are preserved by chilling, many people have come to prefer chilled sake. A traditional drinking method that is sometimes used at banquets as a means of expressing respect is to borrow the cup of a higher-ranking guest, drink from it, and return it after it is drained. In order to wash the cup for this practice, water would be placed on the table in a special vessel called a *haisen*, which has become rare as the custom has gone out of fashion in recent times.

Traditional Japanese table manners developed on the premise of eating from tiny individual tables while seated on the floor and using Japanese tableware for Japanese cuisine consisting mainly of rice. Today the daily meal is often eaten in chairs around a large table, Western or Chinese-style utensils may be used, foods of foreign origin are commonly served, and the increased variety of foods on the table has made rice a less important part of the meal. The traditional etiquette has not successfully made the transitions required to cope with these physical changes in the meal. Hence, rather than being bound by the old rules, the way to eat today is to use some common sense and proceed as you like. Certainly the stricter forms of dining etiquette, such as the rules for the *chakaiseki* tea meal, are now best ignored in daily life.

CHAPTER 8

IN THE KITCHEN

8.1   The Secularization of Fire and Water

The Japanese house is a raised-floor structure. The rooms are built on a platform a step higher than the ground, and shoes are removed before entering the raised space. The traditional house also includes a space that is separate from the raised interior rooms, called the *doma*, where in former times almost all the work of preparing food was done. The *doma* ('earthen space') had a plaster-covered floor at ground level and was connected to the outside via the side door. It housed the *kamado*, a cooking stove with a hollow centre for burning fuel and two or more openings in the top surface for holding pots. There was also a sink and a water jar, and a storage area for cooking and eating utensils. The food preparation carried out in the *doma* included hulling rice in a special mortar. Some houses in the towns had wells dug beneath the *doma*, but water was usually drawn from a well outside the house and stored in an earthenware jar. This layout was the rule for Japanese homes up to the beginning of the twentieth century.

Some simple cooking might be done in the room used for meals by suspending a pot over the small *irori* hearth, but there was a strong tendency to relegate water and fire to the *doma*, away from the main rooms of the house. Wood was burned for fuel, but neither the *irori* nor the *kamado* was fitted with its own chimney. Smoke could escape only through a chimney in the roof, which meant the room would fill with smoke and soot when a fire was burning. Furthermore, most homes were built of wood and some had paper-covered *shōji* and *fusuma* doors as room dividers, leaving them highly vulnerable to fire. Chairs were not used, and if water were spilled on the tatami mats or wooden planks of the floor it would become difficult to sit. For these reasons, cooking with its use of fire and water was mostly kept out of the living area, in the *doma*. There, a paper charm invoking the god of water was typically placed near the water jar, and virtually every kitchen had a charm affixed to a post near the cooking stove to revere *kōjin*, the god of the kitchen hearth who was believed to prevent fires.

The housewife was the keeper of the fire. It was her duty to make sure the coals never died out so that a substantial fire could always be coaxed from the ashes of the stove. It would be highly embarrassing if the fire went out and she had to get fresh coals from a neighbour. The fire of the family hearth was actually regarded as a sacred being and treated with deep respect. In order to protect the sanctity of the fire from the defilement associated with bloodshed in Shinto beliefs, in some districts it was customary for a woman to prepare her meals in a different building from her family during menstruation and before and after giving birth. In areas of Honshu west of the Kinki region, the fire would be changed at festival times. In the mountain farming villages of what is now Okayama Prefecture, for example, various types of wood were used for cooking on ordinary days but during a festival period only pine was suitable as fuel for the fire that would yield the ritual feast [Kanzaki 1989]. During the most important festival period, the New Year, it is still common today throughout Japan to visit a shrine on New Year's Eve and obtain embers from a sacred flame to light a new fire for the first meal the next morning. (The largest and best known such rite is the Okera-mairi at the Yasaka Shrine in Kyoto.) In another widespread observance, on New Year's morning the first water (*wakamizu*) is drawn from a well with ritual incantations and used for special purposes including the year's first meal. These acts to mark the arrival of the new year are also thought to renew the divinity of each home's fire and water.

The customs by which the fire and water of each household were held sacred began to disappear with the march of modernization in the twentieth century. After the spread of matches and the popularization of the gas range, a freshly ignited fire would be used every time food was cooked, and with the arrival of indoor plumbing, water could be had simply by turning the tap. The elements had been domesticated, and so they lost their sacred significance.

Kitchens with gas and plumbing became common in Tokyo when the city was rebuilt after the earthquake of 1923, and then spread to the rest of the country. As it became possible to use fire and water in domesticated forms it was no longer necessary to relegate them to the *doma*. They were installed within the regular interior, in the kitchen with a raised wooden floor which appeared adjacent to the room used for eating. Equipped with a water tap, work surfaces for cutting and dishing up food, a gas range, and cupboards to store dishes, spices and foodstuffs, this new room was the template for the kitchen of today. Kitchen work in the *doma* was done mostly while bent over, to feed and tend the wood fire in the stove or to wash foods and eating utensils in buckets that sat on the floor, but the internalized kitchen was designed to allow work to be done in a standing position. This was something of a revolution, for up to that time every indoor activity in Japan had been done while seated on or near the floor. Yet while cooking in the modern kitchen was done standing up, the eating of the meal in the adjoining room was still done while seated on tatami, which meant the housewife had to stand up and sit down repeatedly in the course of handling the food at mealtime. It was not until the 1970s, when the Western-style dining table with chairs came into general use, that the preparing and consuming of the meal were brought to a fairly uniform height.

The typical Japanese kitchen of today seems to overflow with pots and pans and tableware. There is too much to fit in the cupboards. Pots sit out on shelves while ladles and other utensils hang from wall racks. It is rare to see a kitchen resembling the European model in which all of the cooking and dining implements are systematically stored away, because there are so many kinds of utensils and tableware involved in today's kitchen work. Meals at home formerly consisted only of Japanese cuisine, but now they frequently include foods of foreign origin. Western cooking requires frying pans and large Western-style plates and cutlery. Chinese cuisine involves a wok and tableware with Chinese designs, especially bowls for the popular *râmen* noodles, while Korean barbecue is made on an electric grill. A few small ceramic sake cups and flagons were all that was needed for drinking at home in the old days, but now a home is not complete without an array of different glasses for beer, wine and whisky. The traditional teapot and teacups for Japanese tea are supplemented with Western-style cups for black tea and coffee, and Western teapots and electric coffee makers have now become common in the home. In short, the twentieth-century acceptance of foreign foods and beverages has brought an avalanche of specialized equipment that has left the Japanese kitchen in a state of confusion.

8.2   From Wood Fire to Electric Rice Cooker

Even among nations that eat rice as their staple food, the Japanese are unusually finicky about the taste of rice. Most tourists returning from China, for example, report that they sampled numerous tasty delicacies in fine restaurants, but the rice tasted awful. Of course that opinion carries the baggage of cultural preference for a particular type of rice and taste, and the question of whether or not it transcends ethnocentrism deserves to be asked. At any rate, when eating abroad, what the Japanese tend to worry about first is the taste of the rice. The reputation of a traditional Japanese restaurant would be destroyed if something were lacking in the taste of its rice, no matter how fine an array of other specialities is presented. A meal has two categories of food, the rice and the side dishes, and naturally it is best for both to be delicious, but if it comes to deciding which has priority, tradition dictates that it will be the rice. According to the taste of the Japanese over the centuries, as long as there was good rice and a few pickles to stimulate the appetite, the meal was a success. With that mentality, the housewife of former times would take great pains to cook tasty rice every day.

Rice was cooked on the *kamado* in a deep, heavy iron pot used exclusively for this purpose, called a *hagama*, *tsubagama*, or simply *kama*. The bottom part of the *kama* was hemispherical and the upper part cylindrical. Where those sections joined there was a projection shaped like a lowered hat brim, which functioned to seal the pot over the *kamado* opening that was often slightly larger. This design directed all of the heat from the stove into the pot and heightened the thermal effect on the bottom part. It also prevented boiling rice water from falling onto the flame even when the lid was lifted or some water boiled over. The *kama* was covered with a thick and very heavy wooden lid.

Figure 17   The rice pot (*kama*) and stove (*kamado*) of a pre-modern kitchen. When removed from the stove, the pot with its rounded bottom is set on a doughnut-shaped straw mat to prevent it from tipping. The paper sign pasted to the post is a reminder to take care with fire.

After uncooked rice has been washed to remove impurities, it is soaked for 30 to 60 minutes in water so that the grains absorb some moisture, then drained in a colander and placed in the pot with the correct amount of water for cooking. Once the lid is in place and the pot is on the flame, it should not to be opened until the rice is done. Steam pressure is used to cook the rice, hence a firm or heavy lid is required, and any reduction in pressure caused by lifting the lid during the cooking process will yield undesirable results. Inasmuch as the lid cannot be lifted midway to add water, the correct amount must be supplied at the start. The rule of thumb is 1.2 parts of water to rice, and this can vary between 1.1 for freshly harvested rice which has a high water content, or 1.3 for rice that has been stored for nearly a year and dried out. With too little water the rice at the bottom of the pot will be burnt, and with too much the rice will turn watery and soft. Housewives cooking rice in *kama* concentrated very carefully on precisely adjusting the water amount.

Adjusting the fire was also a delicate operation. The flame was kept low at the start, then quickly brought up high, and as soon as the steam began to force its way out between the lid and the pot, the firewood was removed from the stove. From there the rice cooked on the heat which remained in the stove. The same pattern of heating is still used, even with modern appliances. If strong heat is applied from the start, only the rice that is touching the surface of the pot will be thoroughly heated while the rice nearest the top will remain uncooked; uneven conditions at the start affect the cooking all the way to the end. Therefore, a low flame is used at the beginning to warm the entire area inside the pot slowly. At the next stage, when the flame is turned up, the rice begins to stew in the boiling water, and if this process is allowed to continue the starch will melt and the sticky water will push the lid up and boil over. Just before it boils over, the firewood is removed from the stove, and the low heat of the remaining coals is utilized. This causes the fluid to be absorbed and the starch to coat the surface of the grains, while the small amount of liquid left over is heated by the remaining coals and turns to steam. These two phases of boiling and steaming constitute the Japanese technique of rice cooking. The crucial point is the timing for withdrawing the firewood. Too early and the rice will be half done, too late and it will burn. The marks of a well-cooked pot of rice are starch gone uniformly sticky, no water left in the bottom, and nothing burnt except the single layer of grains touching the bottom, which have been scorched just slightly to form a dark skin of melanoidine which exudes an appetite-enhancing smell.

The entire process must be accomplished without lifting the lid to observe the condition of the cooking rice. Hence, strict procedures for adjusting the fire and the water, as well as long experience, were required. Even a skilled housewife might occasionally fail. To control the fire successfully, she listened to the sound of the water boiling in the pot, watched the way the steam escaped and smelled the small amount of vapour that escaped. While rice was cooking a housewife never left her position in front of the stove.

The cooked rice was transferred from the pot to a lidded wooden bucket called an *o-hitsu* (or *meshi-bitsu*) which was carried to the eating space. Rice cooked in the morning would be kept until evening in the *o-hitsu*. Because it was made of wood, usually of fragrant cypress, it retained warmth well and absorbed moisture to prevent the rice from spoiling. The companion to the *o-hitsu* was the *shamoji*, a small wooden rice scoop shaped like a paddle. It was the housewife's job to use these utensils to fill each person's rice bowl. In doing so she would regulate the allotment, giving larger portions to the growing children or, when the rice was mixed with barley, selecting parts that were richest with the tastier rice for the head of the household.

Primogeniture was the rule in traditional Japan, and it was customary for the family of the first son to live together with his parents. Rather than the head of the household, it was his wife who managed the daily budget. In the era of household self-sufficiency, the budget centred around the food supply, and thus it was left to the wife to plan and manage the yearly allotment of rice and other foods. Even after her son was married, the wife (now identified more as the mother-in-law) would continue managing the household, but as she grew older the time would come when she entrusted the management to her daughter-in law. That transfer of responsibility was called 'passing the *shamoji*'. The tool for serving rice was thus taken as the symbol for household food management, a sphere that encompassed not only the *o-hitsu* which preserved the day's supply of cooked rice, but also the storehouse which held the grain harvest and other supplies. This symbol retains its potency in contemporary Japan, as the members of the country's largest women's league, the Federation of Housewives, carry *shamoji* when they march in political demonstrations.

During the twentieth century there were numerous attempts to make the world's most difficult rice cooking technique, a test of skill and delicate judgment, simpler and easier. The spread of municipal gas networks made precise heat control easier, and a new type of *kamado* fueled by gas was devised. Many new rice-cooking devices incorporating gas or electric heat sources appeared during the 1920s and 1930s but none received household acceptance on a broad scale. Then, in 1955, an 'electric pot', which cooked a mixture of grain and water into boiled rice at the push of a switch, came on the market and the automation of rice cooking advanced very quickly. Today most households have an electric rice cooker with electronic control circuitry. A timer is set to cook the rice whenever it is needed, and a thermostat keeps it ready to eat at any time. Since it is also the hot storage device, the rice cooker tends to be kept near the dining table and the *shamoji* is dipped directly into it. In other words, rice cooking is no longer kitchen work, and the housewife's painstaking effort for delicious rice is a tale of bygone times. Needless to say, the iron *kama* and wooden *o-hitsu* have disappeared from the kitchen.

8.3   The Knife – A Sword for the Kitchen

For the samurai, Japan's warrior of the past, his sword was more than just a weapon. A sword embodied the samurai's soul: it represented the character of its owner. The samurai therefore sought possession of swords made by master craftsmen. He lavished great care on his sword, keeping it polished to a fine sheen. It was a greater honour for a samurai to receive a fine sword rather than gold as a reward for service rendered to his lord.

For Japanese cooks, the *hôchô*, or Japanese kitchen knife, is the equivalent of the samurai's sword. The *hôchô* is so much a symbol of a cook that in Japan a cook is known as a 'knife wielder'. Whereas all the pots, pans and other utensils in the kitchen of a Japanese restaurant belong to the establishment, the *hôchô* is the private possession of the one who uses it. When a cook moves from one restaurant to another he takes his own *hôchô* with him. A chef gauges the skill of a new cook by examining his *hôchô* to see where it was made and how it has been maintained. Just as the Japanese sword was engraved with the name of its maker, the handmade *hôchô* (still a common sight) bears the name of the smith. And for an apprentice cook, the gift of a knife that has been used by the instructor amounts to a veritable treasure.

Cooks of traditional Japanese cuisine are known today as *itamae*, which literally translates as 'before the board'. Originally the term *itamae* was reserved for the chief cook, whose station was in front of the cutting board. The cooks who work in the kitchen of a large restaurant have specialized responsibilities, with one in charge of preparatory work such as washing vegetables and scaling fish, another devoted to the grilling of fish and other foods, and another in charge of boiling and stewing. The duty of the *itamae* or top chef of the kitchen is to slice the food, and from his station at the chopping board he also supervises the entire kitchen. The knife wielder was accorded this high rank because to him was entrusted the job of artistically slicing *sashimi*, the preparation of which requires no cooking as such but demands the highest skill.

Skillful use of the *hôchô* has been highlighted since the Heian period (794–1192), when banquet hosts would sometimes demonstrate their proficiency for the entertainment of their guests. Standing before a cutting board with a *hôchô* in his right hand and long chopsticks called *manabashi* in his left, the host would cut up a fish and prepare *namasu*, the type of *sashimi* that was eaten at the time. *Manabashi* were special tools used only when slicing fish or poultry, to allow the cook to work without touching the flesh, and were never used for eating. They were in use as late as the Edo period in the kitchens of fine restaurants, but by the nineteenth century the custom had begun to die out. The classic *Essays in Idleness* (*Tsurezuregusa*), written about 1330, tells of a nobleman who so loved cooking that he spent 100 days practicing the technique of slicing carp, thereby acquiring unequaled mastery of the *hôchô*.

During the Muromachi period (1336–1568) the cutlery skill that had evolved for show at banquets was passed on to the cooks working in the kitchens of senior nobles and samurai, and codified into formal kitchen knife procedures (*hôchôshiki*) for slicing fish and poultry. Since that time, the word *hôchô* has also been used to signify cooking in general, or the cook. This was the era when the Shijô and Ôkusa schools of cooking were established, each with its own sets of fastidious rules for such things as the sizes of knives and cutting boards, the order of the slicing work and shapes of the sliced pieces, and even the positions for placing sliced fish and poultry on the cutting board. The Heian-period master chef and nobleman who is said to have started the Shijô school was later deified as the protector of cooks, and is venerated at a shrine in a suburb of Osaka. Chefs gather there on the annual festival day to perform *hôchôshiki* as a votive offering, and it is a great honour to be chosen to participate in this ceremony. Apart from a few famous restaurants where traditional techniques are performed for show, that annual shrine ceremony is the only public opportunity to see *manabashi* used for slicing.

Figure 18   A cook slicing a fish with the aid of long chopsticks (*manabashi*) on a four-legged cutting board. From an early sixteenth-century book illustrating various professions.

The cutting edge of the Japanese sword has long been renowned as the sharpest in the world. Before Japan's borders were closed in the seventeenth century, swords were one of the main items exported to China and Southeast Asia. Japanese swords are forged, by a unique method, of steel obtained from iron sand and melted in a specially designed forge before being patiently hammered. High-grade kitchen knives are handmade by the same process. In the days when swords were commonly produced, the same smith often made both swords and *hôchô*.

The blade of a Western kitchen knife is made entirely of steel. While a steel knife-edge is sharp, it is too hard for slicing through soft flesh, such as that of fish, or for doing fine work. To cut and slice food for Japanese cooking, a cook requires a *hôchô* that provides the right amount of friction between blade and food and offers the right feel when the blade hits the cutting board. To meet these requirements, the cutting edge of the *hôchô* is wrapped in soft iron, as is that of a Japanese sword. The addition of soft iron not only gives a sharper cutting edge but also allows more delicate operations because the entire knife becomes more flexible.

Whereas Western and Chinese kitchen knives have blades tapered at equal angles on either side, the blades of many traditional Japanese *hôchô* are tapered on one side only in order to suit specific purposes. In using an asymmetrical *hôchô* the side without the taper seems to cling to the material being cut, resulting in a smooth, evenly cut surface, while the tapered side works to push aside the piece being cut. It is the asymmetrical blade that allows soft sashimi to be sliced so neatly and radish to be cut thinner than paper. The superior smoothness of cutting with a single-taper blade has been scientifically proven by electron microscope analysis of the cells on the cut surfaces of food.

The Shôsôin repository in Nara, built to preserve articles used by the household of Emperor Shomu (r. 724–749), holds some 9,000 items including the two oldest *hôchô* extant. Measuring about 40 cm in length including the wooden handle, these knives with single-taper edges are shaped like short sabres. *Hôchô* remained sabre-shaped for several centuries after the time of Emperor Shômu, with single or double-sided edges, although from the fourteenth century some had blades wider than the handle. Documents from that time indicate that two types of knives were in use, the wider-bladed *nagatana* for chopping vegetables, and the more purely sabre-shaped *hôchô* for slicing fish. During the Edo period, when techniques of traditional Japanese cooking grew more sophisticated, the shape of the *hôchô* was further diversified to suit various uses [Miura 1993:21–33].

There is surely no country in the world with a greater range of kitchen knives fashioned for different purposes. Japanese cooks use *hôchô* with different shapes and names for preparing fish, slicing sashimi, and for cutting vegetables, eel, noodles, sushi, watermelon and other items. This variety dates from the late eighteenth century when the development of restaurants led to the establishment of numerous specialized areas of cuisine, for which particular knives were devised. These special knives, of course, are used by professional cooks. For home use, a set of three knives — *nakiri-bôchô*, *deba-bôchô* and *sashimi-bôchô* — is considered quite sufficient.

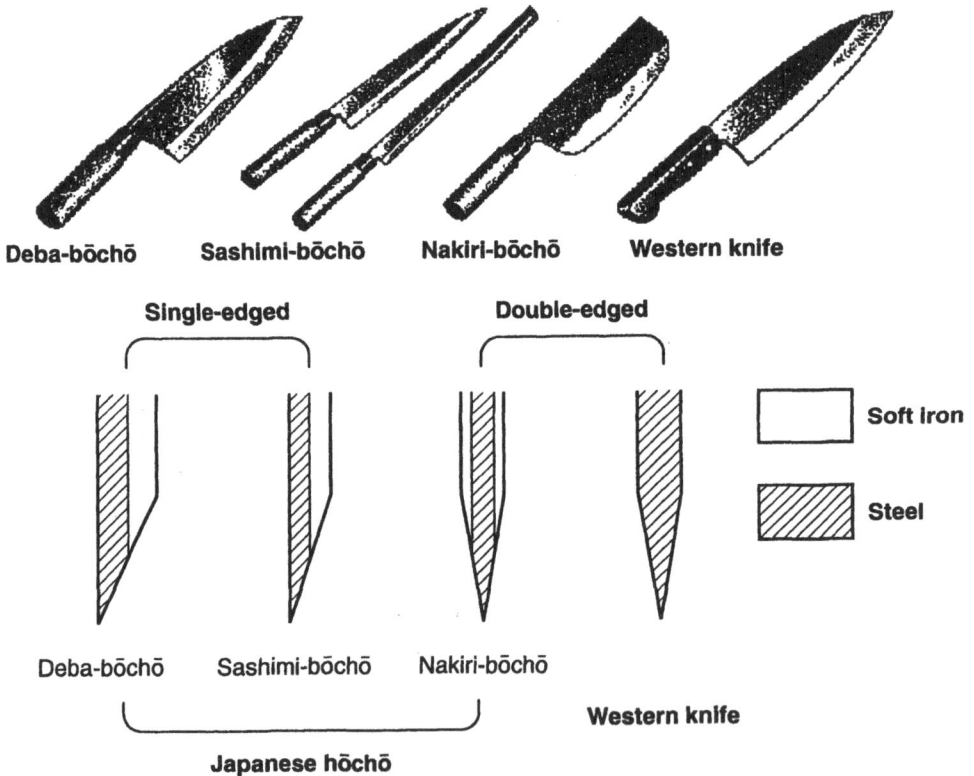

Figure 19   Common types of *hôchô* and their cutting edges. A triangular *deba-bôchô*, a *nakiri-bôchô*, and a long *sashimi-bôchô*, all with edges tapered on one side.

The *nakiri-bôchô*, which is used primarily for cutting vegetables, has an edge that is tapered on either one or both sides. Although similar to Chinese knives in shape, it differs in that the blade is extremely thin, while Chinese knives are thick and heavy enough to be used for chopping up meat and bone. The thin blade of the *nakiri-bôchô*, brought down perpendicular to the cutting board, allows hard vegetables to be cut up. The double-taper cutting edge is generally used in homes, while professional cooks prefer a single-taper design which allows finer work.

The *deba-bôchô*, is a thick, triangular knife with a single-taper edge that can be used to chop up fish and poultry with bone. It is also handy for filleting fish, as its sharp point pierces the flesh and its blade drawn along the backbone cuts the flesh cleanly away.

The *sashimi-bôchô*, a long, narrow knife with a single-taper edge, is used for preparing sashimi and for other fine cutting. Sashimi usually consists of pieces of a fillet from which the skin has been removed, sliced into pieces of uniform thickness. Because of its soft texture, raw fish would crumble if a knife were brought down upon it from the top. In preparing sashimi, therefore, one pulls the *sashimi-bôchô*, straight toward oneself so that the long blade draws through the piece of fish. Kansai chefs prefer to use a *sashimi-bôchô*, with a pointed tip, as opposed to the square tip that is popular in the Kanto region.

All three of these knives were considered necessities for the well-equipped kitchen. They were wielded mainly by women, for cooking was traditionally considered to be women's work. Yet men were expected to provide the strength necessary for cutting up a large fish or chicken, and also to relieve women of the cruel duty of slaughtering a live chicken or a large fish. This meant that men often had occasion to use the *deba-bôchô*, especially in rural areas not served by butchers where poultry was raised and slaughtered at home, and in fishing villages. These days, however, there is little use for the *deba-* or *sashimi bôchô* at home, since even in rural areas the supermarket sells filleted fish, prepared sashimi, and various cuts of meat and poultry. Cooking or slicing a whole large fish at home is now rare, and done only as a sort of hobby. A *hôchô* that is handmade in the traditional manner using iron sand is now quite expensive, and it is also troublesome to maintain, requiring regular grinding with a whetstone to keep the fine edge that is so essential to the functioning of the tool. For these reasons, more and more

211

homes now rely on just one triangular, stainless steel multipurpose knife that might be called a thin version of a Western meat cleaver. Yet while the multipurpose kitchen knife may look like a Western knife, in most cases it has a single-sided edge, because the Western style symmetrical knife edge has not gained acceptance in Japan.

In cultures where chopsticks are used for eating, all of the food must be cut in the kitchen to a size suitable for easy handling with chopsticks. Hence the cutting board is a kitchen necessity. The kitchens of China, where heavy knives are frequently used for chopping, are equipped with chopping blocks that are actually thick rounds cut whole from a tree, capable of withstanding heavy swings of the blade. In Korea and Japan where thin, lightweight knives are used, the cutting boards are not so thick and are rectangular in shape.

The Japanese name for a cutting board is *manaita*. Etymologically, *ma* is a prefix meaning 'genuine', *na* was an ancient word for fish, and *ita* is a board. Thus a *manaita* is 'a board for fish cooking', and likewise the above-mentioned *manabashi* are 'chopsticks for fish cooking'. These names signify that the main thrust of traditional cuisine was focused on fish cooking. As previously explained, traditional kitchen work was not done standing up, but rather while bending over or seated on the floor. Accordingly, the traditional cutting board was a low table-like board with short legs, designed for doing work while seated on the floor. The oldest Japanese cutting board unearthed in archaeological excavations, dating from the latter half of the fourth century, has a pair of legs shaped like the crosswise supports of wooden *geta* clogs. In later times cutting boards were usually small tables with four legs. In one design that became common in the eighteenth century, slots are cut in the lower side of the cutting board and a pair of boards are inserted as supports. From the 1920s, as kitchens designed for standing work proliferated, the cutting board became a simple thick, rectangular slab that could be placed on the work surface or over the sink.

Today, as in the past, one side of the cutting board is reserved for cutting fish and meat, while the other is used for vegetables. When cutting boards were fitted with legs, most households had separate boards for those two purposes. Traditionally, the Japanese divided food into the two categories of *shōjin* and *namagusa*. In the *shōjin* ('ascetic') category were vegetables including seaweed, legumes and cereals. Fish and meat were *namagusa*, from an adjective that means 'smelling of raw flesh or blood'. In Buddhism, which was widely practised by the nobility and the samurai and had also spread to many commoners in medieval and pre-modern times, vegetarianism originally was the mark of a true believer who obeyed the religion's basic injunction against taking life. In actual practice, however, flesh was regarded as a tasty treat. Fish was frequently eaten, being avoided only by the clergy of certain sects that enforced a strict vegetarian diet, and there were no ordinary homes that served pure *shôjin* food. At the same time, virtually all Japanese observed the Shinto religion with its notions of purity and defilement. It was felt that the taking of life was unclean in a ritual sense (*kegare*), and that once a cutting board had been used for *namagusa* food it would contaminate the fundamental purity of vegetable food. Hence the need for two cutting boards. In some areas of Japan this distinction led further to the use of separate pots for *shôjin* and *namagusa* foods.

The old custom of using long *manabashi* chopsticks to avoid touching the flesh when cutting fish or poultry had less to do with hygienic considerations than with a psychological sense of cleanliness. Yet this was not done to avoid defiling the cook who touched the flesh while preparing the food. Instead it was meant to prevent the impurity of the cook's person from contaminating the food and being transmitted to the diner. For Shinto did not classify animal foods as impure. On the contrary, fish and poultry were used as offerings to deities in Shinto ceremonies where purity was of primary importance. A few Shinto shrines still maintain the practice of using *manabashi* to prepare food for festivals. The fundamental notion behind this tradition is the maintenance of spiritual purity by avoiding contact with human hands. As in festivals, which are moments of communion between deities and humans, it seems likely that the custom of using *manabashi* at banquets, which were elaborately ceremonial occasions of sharing food, was evolved so as to prevent any ritual impurity that the cook may hold from contaminating the food.

8.4   Restaurants – The Public Kitchen

Japan has an extraordinarily high density of commercial dining establishments. There are about half a million licensed restaurants according to 1991 national statistics. This includes many coffee shops which specialize in hot and cold beverages, but also offer light repast such as sandwiches. Not included in the restaurant category are bars and cabarets where the main business is serving alcholic drinks. On a per capita basis there are about four restaurants for every thousand people, which is surely one of the highest densities in the world. That distribution is not overly concentrated in the great urban areas, as it was in eighteenth-century Edo (see Section 5.4). It has been noted, for example, that the provincial cities of Japan have far more restaurants than those of England [Dore 1986:87].

The national government classifies dining establishments into five categories: restaurants, noodle shops, sushi shops, coffee shops, and miscellaneous. The fact that noodle shops and sushi shops are separate categories is indicative of the large proportions of those specialist establishments. Within the first category of 'restaurants' are the four subcategories of Japanese restaurants, Western restaurants, Chinese and other Asian restaurants, and unclassified restaurants. The great majority of 'other Asian' restaurants serve Korean cuisine, with most of the exceptions serving cuisines from Southeast Asia. Those in the 'unclassified' cateogry chiefly serve Japanese cuisine, frequently including Japanized Western and Chinese dishes. When those 'unclassified' restaurants are tallied together with the Japanese restaurants, noodle shops and sushi shops, the 1991 statistics include a total of about 230,000 Japanese-style dining establishments. By comparison there were about 23,000 Western restaurants and about 63,000 Chinese and other Asian restaurants.

Statistics aside, present-day Japanese restaurants can be pragmatically classified as *ryôtei* (high-class restaurants), *itamae kappô* (small restaurants), *taishû shokudô* (popular eateries), specialist restaurants, *nomiya* (public houses) and *yatai mise* (street stalls).

Ryôtei serve Japanese haute cuisine. Some do business in such non-traditional settings as downtown skyscrapers, but the typical *ryôtei* occupies a detached wooden building in the style of the traditional Japanese house. The guests are seated on tatami-mat floors and each party has a private room. In most cases the dining room faces onto a garden designed for viewing, and has a *tokonoma* alcove which is adorned with a fresh flower arrangements and a hanging scroll by a famous painter or calligrapher. The food is served on expensive and sometimes antique ceramic and lacquerware, hence the pantry of one of these exclusive restaurants is like a storeroom for *objets d'art*. Trays full of dishes, with the food arranged for visual appeal, are carried out and served by women wearing traditional kimono. In short, this type of restaurant is expected not only to provide fine food, but also to be a place for aesthetic appreciation as well. This is because the high-class *ryôtei* have inherited the traditions of the *kaiseki* cuisine served in the tea ceremony, including the spirit of tea as a synthesis of the spheres of architecture, interior design, flower arrangement, painting, ceramics and cuisine (see Section 4.2).

Normally the *ryôtei* does not have an à la carte menu. Unless a specific menu was ordered with the reservation, the restaurant serves a meal chosen by the staff, consisting of about ten courses. Prices are generally high, sometimes exceptionally high. Only the very wealthy dine at traditional *ryôtei* with their pocket money. Most of the guests come for a business-related meal without spending their personal resources. However, the *ryôtei* business has declined sharply during the recession of the 1990s, leading even some of the most renowned establishments to make special offerings to maintain their clientele and attract the general public, such as relatively inexpensive menus, or luncheons served on tables with chairs.

Ranking next below *ryôtei* are the small *itamae kappô* establishments. *Itamae*, literally 'in front of the board', refers to the cook standing at the cutting board. The original meaning of *kappô* was 'cutting and boiling', and the word now means 'cooking' or 'restaurant'. Put together, the two words refer to a sort of 'dining kitchen' with the cook and the diners in the same room. The customers order directly from the cook and converse with him as they watch him prepare the food (the cook is almost always male). Usually the diners are separated from the kitchen by a counter made of a single long board and they sit on high stools directly facing the cook, like customers at the bar of a public house. For the most part, *itamae kappô* offer cuisine of high quality. The cook usually serves the food himself so there is no need to hire additional staff; nor do such establishments spend much money on decor or tableware. This allows meals not very different than *ryôtei* quality to be enjoyed inexpensively. *Itamae kappô* first became popular in the major cities during the 1920s.

The *taishû shokudô* (literally 'popular dining hall'), also known as *meshiya* (rice shop), is a casual and plebeian place where people go to eat cheaply. It offers set meals and à la carte dishes similar to those on family meal tables. Some *taishû shokudô* have cafeteria-like displays of small ready-to-eat dishes set out in glass cases. These restaurants reflect contemporary household cuisine, offering a mixture of Japanized Western and Chinese-style dishes (see Chapter 6) as well as traditional Japanese mainstays. Typical fare includes noodle dishes, curry with rice, pork cutlet, and rice with toppings.

The existence of numerous restaurants specialized in specific types of dishes has been a feature of the Japanese food service industry since the Edo period. There is a large variety, although the majority fall into several well-known categories. Most common are noodle shops, usually serving both *soba* and *udon*, and sushi shops, and in many towns these two types of restaurants occur with about the same frequency. Eel restaurants offer *kabayaki* – boned eel that is skewered and grilled with the skin, basted with sweetened soy sauce, and served on a bed of rice. There are specialized tempura restaurants. At *fugu* (puffer) restaurants, the chefs must be licensed in the art of preparing the deadly puffer fish so that it is harmless to the diner. *Tonkatsu* (pork cutlet) restaurants offer breaded and deep-fried slices of pork served with shredded cabbage and rice. The pork recipes gave rise to *kushikatsu* ('skewer-cutlet') restaurants where a large variety of fish, shellfish, vegetables and other ingredients are available, breaded and deep-fried on skewers. Cantonese-style dim sum shops may be found. Chinese-style noodle soups are offered by specialist *râmen* or, less commonly, *jiao zu* shops. Curry restaurants usually offer only curry-rice dishes. As in other countries around the world, there are now growing numbers of fast-food restaurants offering such Western fare as hamburgers, fried chicken or pizza.

A *nomiya* or *izakaya* is the Japanese equivalent of a pub, serving sake and other alcoholic beverages. The *nomiya* dates from the Edo period, when members of the artisan class were the backbone of the clientele. Today that has changed to the white-collar 'salarymen' who make up a large part of the population, and many Japanese pubs fill up in the evenings with men in suits on their way home from the office. It used to be considered immoral for women to go out drinking, but since the 1980s small groups of young women are often seen. As a rule the Japanese like to eat lightly while drinking, and the pubs accommodate them with a variety of hors-d'oeuvres that go well with alcohol. A typical *nomiya* may offer as many as 30 items, including simple fare that can be quickly prepared such as raw or grilled fish, and ready-made foods such as *nattô* (fermented soybeans) or *shiokara* (salt-cured preserves of seafood and their entrails). Common winter fare for pubgoers is *oden*, a hotchpotch of fish paste products, tofu, octopus, *daikon* radish, taro, eggs and the like, simmered in stock for several hours and served with hot mustard. Rice and miso soup are also commonly available. Thus before heading home one can eat dinner at a local pub by having a few drinks accompanied by two or three small dishes, and finishing up with a bowl of rice.

Yatai are stalls set up temporarily on the street, usually opening after dark and staying open until the wee hours to provide late-night meals. In the nineteenth century, stalls were carried around by peddlers on their backs. Later they were placed on rubber tires, and since the 1970s automobile *yatai* have proliferated. The most common type of fare used to be traditional Japanese noodles (*soba* or *udon*), but nowadays Chinese-style *râmen* noodles predominate. *Oden* specialist stalls function more or less as sidewalk pubs. *Yatai* developed originally in the large cities, where people were active at all hours of the night in the workplace or the pleasure quarters. Now much of Japan has adopted urban lifestyles, with many rural residents commuting long distances to work and returning at night, and there is also more leisure time in the evenings. Along with these trends the late-night *yatai* have spread even to small rural towns.

CHAPTER 9

ON THE MENU

9.1   **Soup and** Umami **Flavouring**

Few people in the world are as fond of soup as the Japanese. A Japanese-style meal ordinarily includes a soup, with the exception of a meal where a very watery rice dish such as *kayu* gruel or *chazuke* (green tea poured over rice and flavourings) is served. For centuries, 'one soup and one side dish' in addition to the staple rice (*ichijū-issai*) has been regarded as the minimum complete meal.

A survey of farming families in the Kakunodate district of Akita Prefecture in northern Honshu found that in the past they ate miso soup up to a hundred times a month, which indicates that some people took soup even between meals [Miyamoto 1977:253]. Furthermore, the amount of soup taken with a traditional meal was rather large. Today, with the increased variety of side dishes accompanying the meal, there are now many people who eat just one bowl of soup, but extra servings of rice and soup are allowed at the typical home meal and it is normal to take a refill of the standard 180 cc soup bowl. Two bowls, however, is usually considered the limit. More than that is regarded as greedy, as is suggested by the proverb *Baka no sanbai shiru* (Three bowls of soup for the fool).

There are two categories of soup and they are known by different words, *shirumono* and *suimono*. During the Edo period the soup served when a meal was eaten was called *shirumono* and a soup served while sake was being drunk before rice was eaten was called *suimono*. In a *honzen ryōri* banquet, which often included two soups, the soup served at the same time the rice bowl was brought out was the *shirumono*, and that served at another point in the meal was the *suimono*. Thus, precisely the same soup might be called by two different names, depending on whether it was served with food or with drink. Today, however, this custom has died out and the two names tend to be used interchangeably.

Just as European soup can be classified as being either consommé or potage, so Japanese soup can be classified as being either *sumashi-jiru*, clear soup, or *miso-shiru*, miso soup. *Sumashi-jiru* broth consists of stock and salt with a tiny bit of soy sauce added for colour. *Miso-shiru*, made by dissolving miso (fermented soybean paste) in stock, is a thick colloidal solution coloured either light brown or reddish brown by the miso, which gives off a characteristic aroma.

In addition to broth, both types of soup contain bite-size pieces of fish, vegetable or tofu which are cooked in the stock before the flavourings are added. When the soup is served, the solid bits of food are eaten with chopsticks. A soup may also be seasoned with small amounts of a class of traditional aromatic soup flavourings called *suikuchi*. The most common of these is chopped leek, but there are also herbs and spices native to Japan, principally the chopped leaves of aromatic *mitsuba* (*Cryptotaenia japonica*), and the chopped young leaves or ground seeds of *sanshô* (Japanese pepper, *Zanthoxylum piperitum*). Other seasonings which may be used according to the time of year and the main ingredients of the soup are the grated peel of the *yuzu* citron (*Citrus junos*), and ginger.

Japanese soup is always served in lacquer bowls, never in ceramic ware. Not only does lacquer ware keep the contents warmer, but the Japanese feel that it also looks warmer to the eye. Today real lacquer ware is being replaced in most homes by plastic bowls which require less care but are nevertheless difficult to distinguish in look and feel from the traditional lacquered wood bowls. Coloured either red or black, the soup bowls may have designs on the outside but are left undecorated inside for aesthetic reasons: the plain red or black background plays up the colour of miso soup and sets off the solid ingredients in the transparent *sumashi-jiru*. A diner picks up the soup bowl in the left hand and drinks the soup from the rim of the bowl, eating the solid ingredients with chopsticks. Japanese soup is 'drunk', unlike Western soup which is 'eaten'.

While miso soup is considered to be common, everyday fare, *sumashi-jiru* is regarded as a more refined soup. The taste of miso soup is determined by the strong taste and flavour of miso itself. No shortcuts can be taken, however, in producing the flavour of *sumashi-jiru*. Its delicate taste is the product of the harmonious blending of fine-quality soup stock with such flavourings as soy sauce, salt or sake, such solid ingredients as fish or vegetables, and small amounts of seasonings. This is why it is said that *sumashi-jiru* is, along with the handling of the *hôchô*, a supreme test of a cook's skill. And the foundation of a tasty *sumashi-jiru* is the soup stock.

Japan developed a way of preparing stock that is different from the Chinese and Korean methods. On the mainland, flesh and bones are boiled to make soup stock (pork or chicken in China, chicken or beef in Korea). The bones used to make a simple stock will probably be discarded afterward, but as a rule, the ingredients used to make stock in China and Korea stay in the soup or are used in another dish.

In Japan where meat was not widely eaten, with very few exceptions, meat and poultry products were traditionally not used in soup stock. Japan instead developed several kinds of foods that are used almost exclusively for making *dashi*, Japanese soup stock. These include *katsuo-bushi* (dried bonito), *niboshi* (dried sardines), *konbu* (kelp) and dried shiitake mushrooms. These ingredients do not appear in their original form in the finished product but merely work behind the scenes, having served their purpose when their essence is drawn out within a short time in hot water. In the cases when stock ingredients are reused, they are boiled down in soy sauce as a class of foods called *tsukudani* which are enjoyed not for their own taste but for their chewy texture.

Katsuo-bushi has long been used as an ingredient of *dashi*. In olden times it was made by boning the bonito, boiling it, and then drying it first over a fire of rice straw and then in the sun. Around 1670 the process was improved by adding the steps of wood-smoking to impart fragrance, and finally the cultivation of mould on the surface of the dried fish. The mould served to reduce the water and fat content of the fish and break up the protein into various amino acids. Moreover, the mould and the smoking had the effects of heightening the unique flavour and fragrance and allowing it to be preserved for long periods of time with no change in quality.

Katsuo-bushi thus made does not look at all like a fish product, being as hard and heavy as a piece of mahogany, so solid that it does not easily break even if struck with a hammer. In the kitchen, a special type of plane is used to shave *katsuo-bushi* into flakes thinner than paper. These are placed in hot water just before it boils, and allowed to stand for a few minutes after the water boils and the flame is turned off. The water, when strained, yields high-quality stock which is called *ichiban-dashi* (first stock) and is used for *sumashi-jiru*. Most of the essence of the *katsuo-bushi* is extracted in the first stock. Still the remaining flakes can be boiled again, this time in about half as much water and for a long time, to extract the last bit of essence. The *niban-dashi* (second stock) that is thus produced is too weak in taste and fragrance to be used in dishes where delicate flavour is required, and serves instead as stock for richly flavoured dishes that include large amounts of miso or soy sauce. The flakes strained from a second stock are completely flavourless and can only be discarded.

As an alternative to the somewhat costly *katsuo-bushi*, a means was developed in the mid–nineteenth century for obtaining *dashi* from *niboshi*, anchovies or small sardines that have been boiled in salted water and dried in the sun. Boiling several of these *niboshi* in a litre of water produces a *dashi* that, although not as delicate in taste as that obtained from *katsuo-bushi*, is adequate for everyday *miso-shiru*. Once extracted of its essence, *niboshi* loses all its flavour and can be used only as cat food. Until the production of *niboshi* began, the Japanese fishing industry used most of its anchovy catch to make fertilizer, as very little of it was in demand to be eaten fresh. Hence it might be said that in our daily bowl of *miso-shiru*, we are consuming the essence of fertilizer.

Konbu is the Japanese word for *Laminaria japonica* and several other types of kelp which grow on reefs along the coasts of Hokkaido and northern Honshu. Dried to a form resembling thick black paper, *konbu* is used to make stock by placing a piece in water, heating it slowly and removing it just before the water comes to a boil. Timing is crucial in making *konbu* stock because boiling it produces a smell and a bitter taste. While *konbu* used for stock is sometimes reused as *tsukudani*, there is no flavour left after the essence has been extracted and it is usually thrown away.

The finest soup stock is made from both *konbu* and *katsuo-bushi*. The *konbu* is lifted out of the water just before it comes to a boil, *katsuo-bushi* is added and the water is brought to a boil, and the strained stock is used to make high–grade *sumashi-jiru*. Recent scientific research has provided evidence that when glutamic acid which is the main flavour constituent of *konbu dashi* and inosinic acid which is the main flavour constituent of *konbu* are used together, there is a multiplier effect which produces a remarkably strong level of the taste that is known in Japan as *umami* (deliciousness).

The *shiitake* mushroom (*Lentinus edodes*), which is native to Japan, was originally gathered in the wild and began also to be cultivated from the end of the seventeenth century. When dried *shiitake* are soaked in water, their distinctive fragrance and flavour are released to create soup stock, and the rehydrated mushroom is ready to be cooked and eaten. The techniques for obtaining *dashi* from *konbu* seaweed and *shiitake* mushrooms were developed by Buddhist monks who, forbidden to eat animal products, sought ways of varying their vegetarian diet.

In the traditional Japanese diet, the meals of the common people also consisted mainly of rice and vegetables. Fish was a special treat that was usually unavailable, except in fishing villages. When making a soup of fresh fish (called *ushio-jiru*, 'sea water soup'), the fish itself flavours the water and stock is not needed. But the vegetables and tofu that were ordinarily eaten lack the rich flavour of meat or fish. Hence in making soup or other boiled food it was necessary to supplement the flavour of the broth. This was one reason for the development of foodstuffs that are used especially for *dashi*.

Indeed the context for the development in Japanese cooking of extraction techniques for making soup stock was the absence of meat, fats, oils and strong spices from the traditional diet. Foods rich in animal protein and fats need only to be cooked in salty water to be tasty because the meat's amino acids and fats are released in cooking. This is why beef stew tastes good even without the addition of stock. Cooking vegetables alone in salty water, however, is not at all satisfactory (with the exception of root crops and nuts). In Japan, boiled vegetables are often eaten with soy sauce, which contains salt, because soy sauce also contains amino acids which enhance the flavour of the food. In European cooking, butter sauce or oil dressing is poured over vegetables to ameliorate the effects of salt. Oils and fats serve to mellow the taste of salt, while the fragrance of oil cancels unpleasant smells and whets the appetite. In Middle Eastern and Indian cooking, spices are used in great quantity and their strong aromas cancel the other flavours, a method that works well for a cuisine in which a balance of subtle tastes is not the primary concern.

Western scientists submit that the human tongue can distinguish just four basic tastes – sweet, salty, bitter, and sour. Japanese scientists are altogether opposed to that theory, on the grounds that it cannot explain the deliciousness of *dashi* which is so important to the Japanese. There is no way in which those four categories can be mixed to provide the taste of *katsuo-bushi* or *konbu* stock.

Successive discoveries concerning the composition of *dashi* have been made in Japan during the twentieth century. The first important work was done by Professor Ikeda Kikunae of Tokyo Imperial University (now the University of Tokyo), who discovered in 1908 that the *umami* of *konbu* derived from glutamic acid. The following year, glutamic acid was isolated from wheat, artificially formulated, and produced in crystallized form as the chemical flavouring monosodium glutamate, which was soon marketed under the brand name Ajinomoto. Subsequent work showed that the *umami* of *katsuo-bushi*, *niboshi* and meat comes from inosinic acid, while that of *shiitake* mushrooms is composed of guanylic acid, and those taste ingredients also went into industrial production. Eventually it was demonstrated that gustation of the substances that make up *dashi* involves a taste that has properties differing from the four established categories, and is transmitted to the brain by a different mechanism. Accordingly, these constituents have come to be known in the scientific community as 'umami substances' [Kawamura and Kare 1987].

Nowadays shaving flakes of dried bonito with a plane has become quite rare in the home. Yet the use of chemical flavourings in pure crystal form is also declining, as most homes now use liquid or powdered *dashi* concentrates that are made mainly from natural ingredients.

9.2   Sashimi – Cuisine That Isn't Cooked

The traditional approach to cuisine in Japan differs markedly from the thinking of other countries and civilizations. Underlying the European and Chinese concepts of cuisine there seems to be the idea that cookery is the art of transforming materials that are not yet edible into palatable items, and the corollary that an important goal of cookery is the creation of taste sensations that do not occur naturally. The Cantonese offer an extreme version of that approach with their boast that, 'We can eat anything with legs except desks, and anything with wings except airplanes.'

In contrast, the philosophy of traditional Japanese cookery emphasizes that food should be enjoyed as close as possible to its natural state, with the minimum of artificial technique. Japanese chefs have always said that the ability to select fresh ingredients and enhance natural flavour is more important than cooking technique, and what a cook must avoid is too much cooking. Japanese haute cuisine is based on the paradoxical cooking philosophy that the ideal way of cooking is not to cook.

The perfect example of cuisine that isn't cooked is *sashimi*. Raw fish is sliced to a size that can be grasped with chopsticks, dipped in soy sauce with grated wasabi (*Wasabia japonica*, similar to horseradish), and placed in the mouth. A cuisine that utilizes no heat whatsoever, it consists of little more than slicing fish and arranging the pieces on a plate. Nonetheless, the Japanese consider sashimi the most refined form of cuisine. Sashimi and its prototype, *namasu*, occupy the throne of Japanese cuisine, and raw fish is an indispensable part of a first-class meal.

Those who are unfamiliar with sashimi may assume that raw fish has an unpleasant 'fishy' smell, but anyone who has tried it knows there is no disagreeable odour. This is because sashimi is made from only the very freshest fish. In evaluating the taste of a fish dish, the point that comes first and foremost is not the quality of the sauce or the technique of the cook, but the freshness. The maxim for fish cuisine is, 'Eat it raw if you can, otherwise grill it, and if that won't work, simmer it.' In other words: minimize the cooking. The freshest fish is prepared with minimal technique (slicing) and minimal seasoning (soy sauce and fresh wasabi). This is sashimi. Fish that is no longer fresh enough for sashimi but has not yet started to smell fishy is prepared with the next simplest technique of grilling, usually over an open flame after sprinkling with salt. Finally, fish that is not really fresh requires the relatively complicated technique of simmering and active seasoning with soy sauce, miso, sake or other ingredients.

The anthropologist Claude Lévi-Strauss proposed a scale of culture with regard to modes of cookery:

Roasted food, being directly exposed to fire is in a relationship of *non-mediatized conjunction*, whereas boiled food is the product of a two-stage process of mediation: it is immersed in water and both food and water are contained within a receptacle.

So, on two counts, the roast can be placed on the side of nature, and the boiled on the side of culture. Literally, since boiled food necessitates the use of a receptacle, which is a cultural object; and symbolically, in the sense that culture mediates between man and the world, a boiling is also a mediation, by means of water, between the food which man ingests and that other element of the physical world: fire' [Lévi-Strauss 1977:222-223].

If we accept his theory, then the Japanese notion of fish cuisine, with its higher regard for grilling than boiling and its ideal of eating fish in the most natural, uncooked state, should be considered an anti-cultural value system. Could this be so?

Eating raw fish is not something that is limited to Japan. In the Pacific islands there is the custom of eating fish seasoned with citrus fruit juice, coconut milk and salt, and in Peru there is *cebiché*, a popular raw fish dish. In China a dish that existed from ancient times consisted of thin slices of raw meat and fish dressed with a vinegar sauce. As culinary systems for heating food ingredients grew more advanced, the Chinese gradually stopped eating raw meat, fish and vegetables. The eating of raw fish survived in Guangdong and Fujian provinces, but since freshwater fish were often eaten in this fashion, the cuisine was banned after the Communist revolution to prevent exposure to parasitic worms. Today, Chinese raw fish dishes are available in Taiwan and Singapore. In Korea there is a dish of raw beef and fish dressed with a sauce made mainly of red pepper paste and vinegar.

In Japan the word sashimi first appears in literature of the mid-fifteenth century. Before that time raw fish dishes were always called *namasu*, a term which appears in literature from as early as the eighth century. Namasu is thinly sliced raw fish that is eaten with a vinegar-based dressing poured over it. The dressing may contain spices, such as a salted paste of grated ginger and the sharp-tasting *tade* (water pepper, *Polygonum hydropiper*), or miso. Namasu may be served as part of the *kaiseki* meal before a tea ceremony. Though there was a time when the words namasu and sashimi were synonymous, sashimi took on a different meaning when the current style was established in the Edo period. Namasu is cut into long cord-like pieces and dressed, whereas sashimi is sliced into bite-size pieces and dipped in soy sauce and wasabi. Since the use of soy sauce for seasoning spread from urban areas in the Edo period, the modern way of eating sashimi appears to have originated with city dwellers. Wasabi was a wild plant until sashimi became popular in the Edo period and the supply could no longer meet the demand, after which it became domesticated.

Sashimi is usually sea fish. Carp and other freshwater fish are also used, but the odour of freshwater fish is generally not well liked. Since the fish must be very fresh, sashimi tends to be expensive. Before modern refrigeration and transport technologies were developed, people in inland areas had very few chances to eat sea-fish sashimi, which made it the symbol of a great feast. From the 1960s sashimi has been a regular item on the Japanese dinner table; nowadays even people in remote mountain villages can buy it ready-made (that is, pre-sliced) at the local food store.

9.3   Sushi – From Preserved Food to Fast Food

Sushi shops in Japan have a special atmosphere, quite different than other eating and drinking establishments. This is because the workers, in particular those who actually prepare the sushi, have inherited the temperament of the Edokko, or 'child of Edo'. The term Edokko actually refers to people from the city's *shitamachi*, the large merchant and artisan district that was the centre not only of trade but also entertainment, fashion and urban lifestyles including snack shops. The modern form of sushi originated in Edo (present-day Tokyo) around the beginning of the nineteenth century and quickly became very popular there as a snack food. It then spread rapidly throughout Japan, and along with the techniques for making it, the provincial sushi chefs who apprenticed in Edo picked up the *shitamachi* style of receiving customers.

High-spirited, generous and hot-tempered, quick to quarrel and quick to reconcile were the *shitamachi* workmen of Edo. In keeping with their brand of vigorous enthusiasm, the customer entering a sushi shop today is showered with loud calls of welcome.

Tradition requires sushi chefs to speak up in a succinct but spirited fashion when interacting with customers, saying things such as 'What would you like?' or 'Yes, sir!' This is a sharp contrast to local manners, especially in the traditionally soft-spoken Kansai region, where customers are apt to find the calls rough and almost scolding. Sushi chefs should be swift in manner, with a lively but graceful carriage. They normally wear a *happi* coat, which is the traditional garment for tradesmen such as carpenters and gardeners, and often cover their heads with a twisted hand towel. Long hair is forbidden. This is hygienic but has more to do with the workman's tradition of short hair which dates from the 1870s, when men started cutting off their topknots.

There are virtually no women working as sushi chefs. Sushi workers today may explain that they handle the rice and raw fish with bare hands, and this is men's work because it would be intolerable for the fragrance of cosmetics on a woman's hands to be transmitted to the food. What they really mean is this: it is men's work because it is one of the last occupations that still maintains the proud manliness of the Edo workman.

The main category on the menu at almost all of the sushi shops in Japan and around the world is *nigiri-zushi* (hand-formed sushi), a small fistful of vinegared rice with a dab of *wasabi* and a slice of raw fish laid on top. This is also called *edomae-zushi*.

A sushi shop usually has two types of seating, at tables in the back of the room and on stools before the long counter or sushi bar. Customers at the tables mainly order the set menus that include a variety of different fish toppings. The chef then prepares trays of eight or ten pieces which are carried out by a waiter. Depending on the types of fish and the thickness of the slices, the sets eaten at tables fall into two or three price ranks which are usually clearly indicated beforehand on the menu.

When the wallet is not very full, it takes some courage to sit at the counter. There one is expected to order small amounts of various kinds of sushi according to preference, and the prices are usually not listed. The prices vary widely according to the availability of fresh fish as well as the type of fish. For example, *toro* (the fatty portion of the bluefin tuna), when it comes from fish caught in waters near Japan rather than those caught in the Atlantic or Indian Ocean and then frozen for transport, is far more costly in the form of a *nigiri-zushi* topping than the same weight of foie gras.

Along the back of the counter is a refrigerated glass case containing the day's supply of fish and shellfish. After inspecting the offerings and perhaps consulting with the chef, the customer places an order. The chef then slices the fish, makes the lumps of rice and serves up the order, often within a minute. An order usually consists of two pieces. As customers order different kinds of fish one after another they may also taste the thrill of wondering, 'What is all this going to cost me?'

To prepare *nigiri-zushi* the chef takes a lump of vinegared and salted rice in the palm of one hand and uses the first two fingers of the other hand to form it into an oblong shape. He then applies a dab of *wasabi* to one side of the fish slice and presses that side onto the slightly sticky rice, and the sushi is ready to eat. Although it is a very simple food, it takes expertise based on long training to form the sushi properly and to prepare the slightly tart rice. The fact that this well-liked food cannot be made at home helps to explain the large number of sushi shops in Japan.

Sushi is dipped in soy sauce before placing it in the mouth. In some shops the sauce is diluted with small amounts of water or *dashi* stock. The taste of fresh fish is better appreciated by dipping not the rice side but the fish side of the sushi and placing the same fish side on the tongue, but doing this with chopsticks is rather difficult. One must pick up the *nigiri-zushi* with the chopsticks, twist the wrist to dip the fish topping in the sauce, and then get it onto the tongue keeping the fish side down. Without skill and care, the fish may fall off. However, there is no need to do it the hard way. Eating *nigiri-zushi* with the fingers is not bad manners, but rather a mark of people who know sushi well. The original *edomae* sushi was sold at outdoor stalls where the customers were served standing, and it was always eaten with the fingers. Thin slices of pickled ginger are also served with sushi. As the diner switches from one variety of fish to another, eating a bit of this ginger extinguishes the flavour of the previous fish and refreshes the mouth to make it ready for the next one.

Present-day sushi shops also offer sushi rolls (*norimaki-zushi*), which are prepared by spreading sushi rice over a dark thin sheet of processed *nori* seaweed (laver), adding the main ingredient, and rolling it into a wrapped cylinder which may be cut into several bite-size pieces. Some of the common types of sushi rolls are *kanpyô-maki* containing strips of gourd that have been dried and cooked in sugar and soy sauce, *kappa-maki* with sticks of cucumber, *shinko-maki* with strips of *takuan* (pickled *daikon* radish), and *tekka-maki* with strips of raw tuna. Another item on the menu at some shops is 'scattered' or *chirashi-zushi*, also known as 'five-item' or *gomoku-zushi*. Served in a largish bowl called a *donburi*, it consists of a bed of sushi rice topped with artfully arranged slices of raw fish, boiled and peeled prawn, shreds of paper-thin omelette and other colourful ingredients.

All of the above kinds of sushi are relatively new, having appeared from the late eighteenth to early nineteenth centuries. Yet sushi has existed in Japan for more than a thousand years in the form of the preserved food *narezushi*, which is also found throughout Southeast Asia and in rice-growing regions of China (see Section 2.5). It is still made along the shores of Lake Biwa. Various kinds of fish have been used to make *narezushi*, but nowadays *nigoro-buna* (crucian carp, *Carassius auratus grandoculis*) is used almost exclusively because it turns out so deliciously. This product is also known as *bunazushi*.

To prepare *narezushi*, fish are caught during the spawning period from April to June, the scales and organs are removed (with the exception of the eggs), and they are first pickled with a large quantity of salt. In late July the fish is rinsed to remove the excess salt. Boiled rice is spread on the bottom of a wooden cask and covered with a layer of fish, followed by several more alternating layers, an inner lid, a stone weight, and water up to the top. The water prevents oxygen from reacting with the rice and fish, and the salt acts as a preservative. Over time lactic fermentation of the rice takes place, a tart taste permeates the fish, and the fish protein breaks down into tasty amino acids. Fish weighing about 300 grams each will be softened and ready to eat by the New Year. Fish of one-kilogram size take about two years. After removing the mixture from the cask, the pasty remains of the rice are scraped off and the fish is sliced as a side dish for sake or rice.

From the fifteenth century, Japanese sushi developed in a direction different than other Asian areas, beginning with the appearance of *namanare-zushi*. 'Namanare' means 'raw-mature' and describes an intermediate phase between those states. *Namanare-zushi* is ready to eat between several days and a month after the mixture of fish and rice is enclosed under a weighted lid. At that point the rice has a slightly acidic or vinegary taste, but retains its granular form, and the fish is still basically fresh. The rice is eaten with the fish rather than discarded. Whereas *narezushi* is fish eaten as a side dish, the emergence of *namanare-zushi* was the point where sushi took on the character of a complete snack, combining staple and side dish.

Narezushi developed originally as a method for preserving a large amount of fish caught at one time so it would be edible later in the year. In contrast, *namanare-zushi* was made in small quantities for use at festivals or feasts, and so was a luxury food rather than a preserved food. That meant that the types of fish were no longer limited to those caught seasonally in large quantities, and sushi diversified to include various sea fish, and even vegetables which were processed into vegetarian sushi. In place of the big cask used for large amounts of sushi, a small amount was made in a shallow wooden box, by topping a bed of rice with a layer of sliced fish, and applying an inner lid weighted with a stone. The finished product was sliced into long pieces. This is the forerunner of today's *hakozushi* ('box sushi'), an Osaka speciality made by pressing rice and cooked fish in a rectangular box.

The next new direction in sushi making, devised in the late seventeenth century, was to produce a rice-and-fish combination with a tasty acidic flavour, not through fermentation but by simply adding vinegar to the rice. Thus lactic acid was replaced by acetic acid. This new 'quick sushi' was given a name that means exactly that, *hayazushi*. Later, in the early nineteenth century, it became popular on the streets of Edo as *nigiri-zushi*, a convenient form that involves neither the vinegar dressing used for *namasu* nor the storage technology of preserved sushi. This was the final stage in the transformation of sushi from a preserved food into a fast food. The fact that vinegar is still always added to sushi rice to give it a slightly tart taste means that a culinary tradition survives unbroken, if only barely, in the form of contemporary sushi [Ishige and Ruddle 1990:21-8].

9.4   Sukiyaki and Nabemono

Many people outside Japan have heard that Japanese cattle are fed beer and massaged in order to produce the finest beef. What they may not know is that the practice is rare, limited to the few 'royal' animals who will end up on the tables of the country's most exclusive restaurants. The result is beef that is quite tender and very nicely marbled with fine white fat. It is used in thin slices for first-class sukiyaki and *shabu-shabu* cuisine.

The word sukiyaki seems to have originated as a compound of the words for plough (*suki*) and grilled (*yaki*). Several cookbooks from the Edo period describe a *sukiyaki* which consisted of fish or fowl grilled on an iron ploughshare over a charcoal fire. (The blade of the traditional Japanese plough is flatter than the Western counterpart and hence more suitable for grilling.) In the decades following the Edo period at the end of the nineteenth century, beef entered the national diet in the form of *gyûnabe* or beef stew, as described in Section 6.2. In some rural areas where the religious concept of meat as an impurity remained strong, the household altar was protected by cooking beef stew outdoors or in a barn, using a ploughshare instead of a pot. The use of the ploughshare for cooking disappeared by 1900, as it was replaced by a shallow cast-iron pan called a *sukiyaki-nabe*.

In the early twentieth century, *gyûnabe* was a dish eaten in the Kanto region which consists of beef boiled with welsh onion and tofu, while in the Kansai region beef stew was *sukiyaki*, which incorporated a variety of vegetables and was served with raw egg for dipping. After Tokyo was destroyed by the earthquake of 1923, Kansai-based sukiyaki restaurants expanded to Tokyo, and as the Kansai dish became more common, the term *gyûnabe* became obsolete.

Sukiyaki ingredients and recipes still differ from region to region, and from home to home as well. Like English people arguing about how to make a good cup of tea, once a debate on how to make sukiyaki begins there will be no end. Although many variations are possible, standard sukiyaki can be defined by listing the ingredients that cannot be left out. The thinly sliced beef is preferably high-grade sirloin, soft and moderately marbled with fat. As for the welsh onion (*negi*), Kanto chefs prefer them thick and white, while thinner and greener varieties are used in the Kansai region. The tofu is *yakidofu*, firm soybean curd with the surface slightly grilled. *Shirataki* are thin noodles of *konnyaku*, a gelatinous paste made from the root of devil's tongue, *Amorphophallus konjac*. (*Konnyaku* is a flavourless food and while it has no nutritional value because the starch is not digestible by the human body, it is an excellent source of fibre and is appreciated for its chewy texture.) Optional sukiyaki ingredients include wheat gluten (*fu*), onion, various kinds of spinach, and mushrooms.

Sukiyaki is cooked at the dining table. Formerly a portable charcoal stove was used, and today the sukiyaki pan is placed over a gas fire. In the Kansai style, first the beef is placed on the hot pan, sprinkled with sugar and broiled. When the scorched sugar has given the beef a caramel colour but the meat is still rare, the tofu, onion and *shirataki* noodles are added, followed by soy sauce for flavour. Tokyoites prefer the Kanto recipe which begins by wiping a hot pan with a lump of beef fat and sautéing the beef and onion. To this is added a broth called *warishita*, consisting of *katsuo-bushi* stock flavoured with soy sauce, sugar and *mirin* (a sweet liquid flavouring made from rice, mould and distilled spirits). After simmering, the noodles and tofu are added. In general the Kansai dish resembles a beef sauté, while the Kanto recipe preserves the *gyūnabe* tradition of boiling the beef in broth. Yet these are only standard outlines, and virtually every cook has a different way of making sukiyaki. The diners take the cooked food directly from the pan with their chopsticks, and dip each morsel in a small bowl containing beaten raw egg before placing it in the mouth.

Another popular beef dish that is cooked at the table is *shabu-shabu*. This is a Japanized version of the Mongolian hot pot, which is known in Chinese as *shuànyángròu* or 'briefly rinsed mutton' because the diner uses chopsticks to swirl a very thin slice of raw mutton in a pot holding boiling broth before dipping it in a sauce and eating. Introduced by Japanese who had lived in Beijing, *shabu-shabu* became popular in the Kansai region after the Second World War before spreading to the rest of the country. As sheep are not bred in Japan and most Japanese dislike the smell of mutton, thinly sliced beef, preferably marbled, is used. The sauce has also been adjusted to Japanese taste, and is quite different than the complexly flavoured Chinese original. The name *shabu-shabu* is onomatopoeia for the sound of the meat swirling in the broth.

Sukiyaki and *shabu-shabu* are *nabemono* (one-pot dishes), a category that also includes fish, chicken and tofu stews. The *nabemono* ingredients are boiled over a heat source set on or in the table, and the diner plucks them from the pot with chopsticks. Eaten directly from the boiling pot, *nabe* cuisine is very warming, and is hence a winter food. Preparing the ingredients is quick and easy, and everyone sitting around the pot shares the pleasure of playing chef. In many homes a *nabe* meal is eaten once a week during the winter. Earthenware pots are typically used for stews without beef.

Nabe made with the poisonous *fugu* or puffer fish is considered particularly effective in warming the body, and so holds pride of place among the dishes of this style. Thirty-eight species of puffer are fished in Japanese waters and the internal organs of most of them contain tetrodotoxin, a trace amount of which is deadly to human beings. Since tetrodotoxin is water-soluble, the edible portions are still contaminated after the liver, ovaries and other poisonous organs have been removed, and so must be rinsed with quantities of water. Japanese law prohibits amateurs from preparing puffer. The fish must be cut, cleaned and cooked by a licensed chef who has passed a rigorous examination. Hence *fugu* is normally eaten at specialized restaurants, although in the Osaka area, which accounts for 60 percent of the national consumption, puffer prepared by licensed professionals is available in some fish shops for those who wish to make *fugunabe* at home.

Fugunabe is made by boiling the fish in *konbu* stock with tofu and vegetables, and the diner dips it in a mixture of soy sauce, grated *daikon* radish and seasonings such as red pepper or citron juice. Many people have the idea that puffer is delicious because of its toxicity, but the taste itself has nothing to do with the poison. However, the bodily warmth resulting from eating *fugunabe* is due in part to the very small amount of tetrodotoxin that remains even after thorough rinsing, and perhaps also to the frisson of eating a dish which, when incorrectly prepared, actually kills people from time to time.

Puffer was a delicacy in ancient China and Korea. The eleventh-century Chinese poet Su Tung-p'o reportedly claimed 'The taste is worth dying for', but modern-day Chinese as well as Koreans rarely take the risk. In Japan, puffer bones are commonly found in kitchen middens dating back several thousand years. There are mentions in historical chronicles of death from puffer poisoning, and there once was a law prohibiting the custom of eating it. Since that did not work to curb people's fondness for it, the licensing system for chefs was established. Today, the Japanese catch cannot meet the demand and *fugu* is imported from China and Korea, and also bred domestically.

The current style of cooking and eating one-pot stews, exemplified by sukiyaki, dates from the Meiji period, but *nabe* cuisine has a much older history. The main difference is that instead of sitting around a single large pot, people in former times used personal cooking pots. As noted in the previous sections on table setting and chopsticks, Japanese table manners are based on separate servings and separate utensils. Traditionally it was taboo to take food from the communal pot with chopsticks that had touched one's mouth, and special serving chopsticks have been used to prevent the transmission of impurities or defilements from one person to another. For *nabe ryôri*, we know from Edo-period illustrations that each diner used a portable charcoal cooker with a scallop shell for a pot. This was also the tradition for *shottsuru-nabe*, a speciality of Akita Prefecture made with a local fish sauce, which nowadays is eaten from a common earthenware pot. In the past, intimate couples or parents and small children may have dipped their chopsticks into the same pot, but as a rule as soon as children were able to cook for themselves they were given their own shell pots and cookers.

Against the background of traditional customs, the practice of several people using their chopsticks to eat directly from the same pot signifies a mixing of personalities. A comparable image for sexual behaviour would be an orgy. It involves the breakdown of everyday reserve and a sense of fusion or solidarity among the diners. Hence this type of cuisine is often selected for groups of students or others who have come together from different places, as a way of building a communal bond.

Tabletop cooking of one-pot meals is found in China, Korea and Japan. In each of these countries, charcoal has been used since ancient times and portable cookers were also common, hence smoke-free cooking was possible wherever people ate. The use of wooden chopsticks was also a factor in the development of this cuisine, as eating from a boiling pot is impossible with the fingers and impractical with heat-conducting metal utensils. The custom of sharing the same cooking pot is much older in China and Korea, which did not have the taboos concerning purity and defilement which influenced the chopstick etiquette of Japan.

9.5   Tofu and Nattô – Meat for Vegetarians

A special feature of East Asian dietary culture is the development of a variety of foods made from the protein-rich soybean. In Japan, tofu (soybean curd) and *nattô* (fermented soybeans) are served regularly, and since the staple seasonings of miso and soy sauce are also made from soybeans, virtually everyone eats soy in some form or other every day.

Many Chinese believe the legend that a Han dynasty prince invented tofu some two thousand years ago. However, the written characters for tofu did not appear in Chinese literature until about CE 900, which has led to the theory that the Chinese began making it in the eighth or ninth century (the middle of the Tang dynasty) by adapting the cheese-making techniques of the northern nomads. Adding an acid or enzyme to milk coagulates the protein as cheese, and a similar process will change soy milk to tofu [Shinoda 1968]. If that was the original process then later advances were made, as tofu makers today utilize the solidifying effects of metal ions, and calcium sulphate or bittern is the typical coagulant.

The traditional, non-mechanized way of making tofu in Japan is as follows. Dry soybeans are soaked in water overnight, causing them to swell to about twice the original size. They are ground to a pulp in a stone mortar, mixed with water and boiled in a large pot for about ten minutes. The mixture is squeezed through a cloth bag to separate the soy milk from the lees, known as okara or *unohana*. A coagulant is added to the soy milk to separate the curd from the whey, and when it starts to congeal the milk is poured into a perforated wooden mould and pressed with a weight to drain the whey. When the tofu has solidified it is cut into blocks. Compared to Chinese and Korean tofu, the Japanese product is soft and delicate, and so it is placed in water to keep it intact for the customers.

Although okara is a very nutritious source of protein and fat, it is usually regarded as food for the poor. Many Japanese know the story of Arai Hakuseki, one of the greatest scholars of the Edo period and an adviser to the shogun: too poor as a youth to buy rice, he survived on the okara he received each day from a tofu maker, and when he became successful he repaid the kindness with a large gift of money. Okara is sometimes cooked with fish, shellfish, seaweed or vegetables and served as a side dish, but nowadays it is mostly used for livestock feed.

Soy milk is a beverage much loved in China, where it is commonly drunk hot in the morning. In the same way that cow's milk is curdled by adding rennet, soy milk is coagulated by adding bittern (*nigari*), a solution obtained by extracting sodium chloride crystals from concentrated sea water. Alternatively, bittern is secreted by sea salt that is exposed to the air and absorbs moisture. Tofu makers used to keep a quantity of salt in a large bag made of rice straw and collect the bittern that dripped from the bag. The main components of bittern are magnesium and calcium chlorides.

In the days before chemical preservatives and refrigeration, tofu makers produced only as much as they could sell each day. Many customers came early in the morning to get tofu for the miso soup they would eat at breakfast, and so the tofu maker, like the European baker, was hard at work well before dawn. Any tofu left unsold was processed into various forms to be sold the next day, including thin slices fried in vegetable oil, called *abura-age*; deep-fried balls of crushed tofu, yam, seaweed and vegetables, called *ganmodoki* in eastern Japan or *hiryôzu* in western Japan; and *yakidofu* or tofu grilled over a charcoal fire.

A technique to preserve tofu for a year or more was discovered in the early seventeenth century. This is freeze-dried tofu (*kôyadofu* or *kôridofu*). Eighty to ninety percent of the weight of tofu is water, and on a cold winter's night a cake left outdoors readily develops numerous fine ice crystals. The heat of the morning sun melts the ice, and the spaces formed by the crystals leave the tofu quite porous. When completely dry it becomes spongy and will keep for a long time. The name *kôyadofu* comes from Mt Koya, the Buddhist monastery complex where it was often made during the severe winters and, according to legend, was first discovered when a priest noticed how an offering placed before a Buddha statue had frozen and thawed. Today it is produced in factories with freezing and drying machinery. To cook freeze-dried tofu, it is first soaked in lukewarm water to make it soft, then the water is wrung out by hand and it is boiled in seasoned broth. The spongy structure makes it absorbent, so chewing it releases the soup into the mouth.

The oldest record of tofu in Japan is in a chronicle of the Kasuga Shrine in Nara from 1183. Over the next few centuries tofu production and cookery developed in Buddhist temples, especially those of the Zen sects which strictly prohibited the eating of animal products, for tofu is an excellent source of protein. Even today there are many restaurants specializing in tofu cuisine in the vicinity of famous Zen temples. During the Edo period (1600–1868) tofu became a daily food among townspeople and tofu shops proliferated in the cities. Rural areas, however, still had no tofu makers, and as it took much time and labour to make at home, the farm population regarded it as a luxury reserved for special events.

Among the hundreds of established dishes made with tofu, the Japanese are fondest of the simple *hiyayakko* (cold tofu) and *yudofu* (hot tofu). *Hiyayakko*, eaten in summer, is a block of tofu served cold and topped with sliced welsh onion, grated ginger, *katsuo-bushi* shavings and soy sauce. Alternatively, the tofu is cut into bite-size cubes and served in a bowl of cold water (nowadays often including ice) and dipped before eating in soy sauce mixed with grated ginger or Japanese mustard. *Hiyayakko* might be called tofu sashimi, whereas *yudofu* is the *nabemono* version eaten in winter. A pot of *konbu* stock is boiled on the dining table, and tofu is warmed in it and then served with a dip of soy sauce seasoned with welsh onion, powdered red pepper and other flavourings. The essence of this dish is to avoid overcooking the tofu. When it is put into the broth, the temperature of the broth decreases and the tofu sinks to the bottom. Soon it boils again and the tofu surfaces, and this is the best moment to take it out with one's chopsticks or a screen ladle. Overcooking makes the tofu turn hard and lose its unique subtle taste. This provides another window onto the philosophy of not cooking as the ideal way of cooking: the point is the natural taste of the tofu itself. Also, since tofu consists mostly of water, the taste is considered to depend on the quality of the water source.

Yuba is a close relative of tofu. When soy milk is heated in a pan without bittern, a protein-rich film coagulates on the surface, similar to the skin on heated cow's milk. It is lifted off with a thin stick and hung to dry like a piece of cloth, and when the water has drained the *yuba* is ready. It may be cut and rolled and served with wasabi horseradish and soy sauce, like sashimi, or boiled in stock seasoned with soy sauce, or used as a soup ingredient. Like tofu, fresh *yuba* is difficult to preserve, and so most *yuba* is sold in the dry form (*hoshi-yuba*) which looks like yellowed paper and is typically used as an ingredient of soup or stew. This is another food that was brought from China; the oldest Japanese documentation is from the mid-fourteenth century. It developed as an ingredient of temple cooking and today is commonly eaten in Kyoto, where the local culture is influenced by the high concentration of Buddhist temples.

The most infamous of the Japanese foods made from soybeans is *nattô*. This is fermented soybeans, or for those not partial to it, rotted stinking slimy soybeans. (Rot and fermentation are identical in scientific terms; the managed rot aimed at cultivating beneficial products is called fermentation.) *Nattô* might be compared to a ripe cheese. Many foreigners – and not a few Japanese – are disgusted by the strong aroma and flavour and gooey, sticky texture. It is traditionally made by wrapping small quantities of boiled or steamed soybeans in rice straw, inoculating them with a bacterium, and leaving them to ferment for about a day under hot, humid conditions. The product was standardized in the early twentieth century when scientists isolated *Bacillus natto* and distributed it to *nattô* makers. This enabled the production of *nattô* without straw in a clean and efficient way, with no interference from undesirable bacteria. Fermented soybean products similar to *nattô* are eaten in Korea, Southeast Asia and the southern Himalayas.

Nattô is served in a small lump and should first be stirred vigorously with chopsticks to make it looser and stickier. Then other ingredients such as a raw egg, chopped welsh onion, mustard or soy sauce are stirred into it, and the viscous mixture is placed on hot rice for eating. In Tokyo, until bread became popular in the 1950s, a typical breakfast consisted of rice, miso soup, *nattô* and pickles, and *nattô* sellers' calls were heard in the streets each morning.

Records of *nattô* date from the mid-fifteenth century, yet it is thought to be much older. In early times it was regarded as a low-class food for country folk, unsuitable for sophisticated cuisine, and this may explain its omission from writings generated in the metropolitan centres. It was the urban culture of Edo which brought *nattô* into wider popularity. The earlier custom of eating *nattô* minced in miso soup (*nattô-jiru*) gave way to seasoning it with soy sauce, which had come into widespread use in Edo during the seventeenth century, and serving it as a topping for rice at breakfast, or as a side dish. Nowadays *nattô* is commonly eaten in eastern Japan where strong traces of Edo culture survive, and more infrequently in other regions.

There is a lesser-known form of fermented soybeans called temple *nattô* (*tera-nattô*). To make it, boiled soybeans are inoculated with the same mould used to ferment soy sauce (*Aspergillus sojea*), immersed in brine for two or three months, and then dried. Unlike ordinary *nattô*, temple *nattô* is not sticky. The beans come out shaped like rabbit pellets, with a dark brown colour and a taste similar to *hatchô-miso*, a type of miso made with unmashed soy beans in a district outside Nagoya. It is served as a side dish for rice or sake, and sometimes ground up as a seasoning. Temple *nattô* resembles the Chinese food *dòu ch* and is known to have existed in Japan as early as the ninth century. It was originally called *kuki* and later *shiokara-nattô* (salty *nattô*) or simply *nattô*. Then as the version fermented with *Bacillus natto* became popular in Edo, '*nattô*' came to mean the sticky type, while the salty type continued to be produced at certain temples. Temple *nattô* is usually named for the place where it is made, such as the Kyoto specialties Tenryûji *nattô* and Daitokuji *nattô* or the Hamana *nattô* made at temples near Lake Hamana in Shizuoka Prefecture.

9.6   Vegetarian Temple Food

The Tokugawa shogunate collapsed in 1868 and as Japan began to transform itself into a modern nation, the central government took charge of religion and adopted a policy of eliminating the popular influence of Buddhism. Through the Edo period, Buddhist temples had been in charge of family records, including the government-mandated registration of births, deaths and emigration across district boundaries. Those administrative duties were transferred to the Shinto shrines, which were now agencies of the government. Buddhism and Shinto had coexisted and influenced each other for many centuries, but were now rigidly separated as the latter became State Shinto and the emperor, whose influence was being utilized for the sake of modernization, was decreed to be the highest Shinto priest. During the turbulence of the early Meiji years, a popular movement against Buddhism developed and many temples were attacked or destroyed. In this climate, in 1872, the government authorized the Buddhist clergy to live in the same manner as laypeople.

The Shinto religion had never discouraged its priests from consuming fish or alcohol (which may also be used in the ceremonial offerings at Shinto shrines), nor from marrying. In contrast, the doctrines of most of the Buddhist sects in Japan prohibited the clergy from having sexual relations or consuming animal flesh or alcohol. Also forbidden were five vegetables of the genus *Allium* which were considered to provide too much physical vigour and arouse sexual fantasy: garlic (*A. sativum*), red garlic (*A. grayi*), nira (Chinese chives, *A. tuberosum*), welsh onion (*A. fistulosum*), and *rakkyô* scallions (*A. chinense*). Officially, a priest, monk or nun violating these precepts was supposed to be expelled, but in truth not a few of them regularly flouted the rules. This made the Buddhist clergy a common butt of jokes. Here is one of the many stories mocking temple life that circulated in the Edo period.

A man set out for his local temple to pay homage at the family grave, and on the way he met one of the young novices heading toward the temple with a lunch box under his arm. 'I'm just on my way to the temple,' he said. 'By the way, what's in the box?'

'It's something important, so I'm not allowed to show it to you,' the novice replied.

'Well, I'm a good patron of the temple and a good friend of the head priest, too. I think there's nothing wrong with you showing me what's in the box.'

'All right, but you mustn't tell the head priest you have seen it,' the novice said, opening the lunch box to reveal an array of seafood delicacies.

'Don't worry, I won't say anything about this. You go on ahead and enter the temple first.'

After visiting the grave the man went to the quarters of the head priest, who welcomed him with the usual vegetarian foods and sake. He was not fond of vegetarian cuisine, and remembering the delicious-looking seafood, he said: 'Come now, I know you're hiding something wonderful. But we're good friends, aren't we? You don't have to keep anything from me.'

Not knowing what the man had seen, the head priest replied, 'So it's come out. Then there's nothing to be done.' He turned and called out, 'Come and meet my good friend,' and his mistress emerged from the back room.

ON THE MENU

The traditional religions of Japan are not intolerant, and many Japanese observe both Buddhist and Shinto rites. Other than the New Year, which is observed in Shinto fashion, the most important annual event for the Japanese is the Bon Festival, a Buddhist observance honouring the spirits of deceased ancestors. It is held for several days in mid-August (approximating the original timing in the middle of the seventh lunar month). In accordance with the Buddhist precept against killing animals, during the Bon period fisherfolk suspended their work and practicing Buddhists refrained from eating animal products. Even today, fishing is not normally done during the Bon period, but the custom of eating only vegetarian food is dying out, as more and more people have been buying frozen fish or eating beef since the late 1950s.

In another common Buddhist practice, vegetarian cuisine, or *shôjin ryôri*, was eaten in observance of the annual or monthly death day of a relative, especially a parent. Hence many Japanese families in former times ate Buddhist-style vegetarian meals on one or more days each month. But most people thought of a meal without fish as that much less appealing. Another joke from the Edo period illustrates the popular attitude: Two gentlemen spent the afternoon together and when they parted, one said, 'Tomorrow is my father's death day. Will you join me for *shôjin ryôri*?' His friend replied indignantly, 'I'm tired of eating the stuff on my own father's death day! Why should I eat it on yours?!'

Shôjin ryôri originated in the monastery as the cuisine of Buddhist practitioners who eat only vegetarian food. The discipline of approaching truth by abstaining from sexual relations, leading a pure life, and conforming to right conduct is called *shôjin* in Buddhist terminology. Part of that conduct is to obey strictly the injunction against taking the life of sentient creatures. Among the various styles of Buddhism in Japan, Zen contributed most substantially to the development of *shôjin ryôri*. Zen sects had just begun to flourish in Japan in the thirteenth century, an age of religious reformation when Buddhism was moving away from its Chinese roots and various new sects appeared with doctrines unique to Japan. One of the most successful of these, Jôdo Shinshû or the True Pure Land Sect, initiated a radical new doctrine that permitted monks to marry and eat fish. Only the Zen sects remained non-Japanized and continued for several centuries to carry on active exchanges with their Chinese counterparts. Consequently, Zen temples played a leading role in the introduction of Chinese culture to Japan during medieval times, not least dietary culture. As a result of bringing Chinese vegetarian cooking to Japan to improve the monastic diet, Zen temples introduced many tofu, *yuba* and temple-*nattô* dishes, which then spread to other sects and the public at large.

In the early seventeenth century a new style of vegetarian cuisine called *fucha ryôri* arrived when Ingen, a Chinese abbot, immigrated to Japan and established the Ôbaku Zen sect. *Fucha* cuisine is characterized by heavy use of vegetable oil and the frying of most ingredients, as well as the addition of a starchy broth at the final stage of cooking to produce a gravy-like consistency. It has some techniques in common with the modern Chinese vegetarian style of *sù cài*. The names of *fucha* dishes are approximations of Chinese words. Unlike Edo-period Japanese meals with each diner seated on the floor and eating from a separate portable table, a *fucha* meal was served to people sitting on stools around a common table who filled their individual plates and bowls from serving dishes set on the table. The *shippoku ryôri* of Nagasaki, which also developed during the Edo period from roots in Chinese cooking, is served in a similar way. Nagasaki was the only place where Chinese were permitted to live in Japan during the centuries of seclusion, and the Chinese there were traders rather than monks. *Shippoku* cuisine uses fish, fowl and game and is typically accompanied with sake, whereas *fucha* is vegetarian cuisine served with tea. Chinese cuisine enjoyed a surge of popularity among intellectuals during the eighteenth century, and restaurants specializing in *fucha* and *shippoku* cuisine were established.

In the absence of protein-rich animal foods, *shôjin ryôri* makes the most of protein found in the plant world, with many dishes that include the soybean products tofu or *yuba* (see the previous section). It also utilizes wheat gluten in the form of the bread-like food *fu*. The gluten is extracted from wheat flour by kneading it with water to a paste and immersing it in water to dissolve the starch. It is then steamed or boiled into cakes of *fu*, which is used as an ingredient of stews, soups and sweets. Since the Meiji period, *fu* has also been mixed with leavening and baked into *yakifu*, a dry spongy food that keeps for a long time.

The nutritional element that tends to be lacking in vegetarian cuisine is fat. *Shôjin ryôri* calls for vegetable oil and frying or deep frying more often than most other kinds of Japanese cooking. In addition, the high fat content of sesame seeds and walnuts is exploited by grinding them into pastes which are used as dressings for steamed vegetables.

For soup stock, *shôjin ryôri* relies on kelp and dried shiitake mushrooms (see Section 8.3). Up to the early Edo period, before Osaka became the cargo collection point for most food products, Kyoto's large demand for kelp to supply its hundreds of temples was filled with direct shipments from the north of Japan. Dried shiitake are soaked in cold water and the resulting brown liquid is used as soup stock, while the softened mushrooms are then used as ingredients of another dish. From medieval times Japan exported shiitake to China, but since the 1980s the trade in both fresh and dried shiitake has flowed the other way.

Key ingredients of *shôjin ryôri* including tofu, *yuba* and *fu* provide nutrition and unique textures, but not much taste. One way of providing flavour is to mix them with other ingredients. Alternatively a battery of cooking techniques may be used in succession, for example immersion in broth followed by sautéing or deep frying and then boiling, so that a plain-tasting food is ultimately savoured as a delicacy. Consequently, temple-style cooking usually requires much time and effort. In contrast to most other types of Japanese cooking, where the ideal dish is not cooked at all, *shôjin ryôri* relies heavily on artificial techniques, and idealizes skill. Often a special effort is made to create the appearance and flavour of seafood or meat with the vegetarian ingredients. For example 'grilled eel' which closely resembles the real thing in appearance, texture and taste, is made mainly from grated yam and sheets of pressed *nori* seaweed. While these imitations were no doubt devised by cooks who prided themselves on their technique, they also seem to show that the temple communities were never free from craving for animal foods.

9.7   Tempura and Oil

Tempura, the quintessential deep-fried food of Japan, is rather simple to cook but there are several secrets to making it delicious. The oil used for frying was originally sesame or rapeseed oil, but today almost any vegetable oil may be used including soybean, rice bran, corn, cottonseed or safflower oil. Using sesame oil improves the taste and aroma, but the oil must be kept very hot or the tempura will be soggy, and so tempura restaurants often mix another oil with sesame oil. The ingredients of tempura are seafood, usually prawns or small white fish, and vegetables which may include seaweed; meat is never used. If necessary they are first cut to a size that can be grasped with chopsticks.

The wheat-flour batter is called *koromo*, which means 'clothing'. It is made by adding a well-beaten egg to water, and mixing in flour. Care must be taken not to mix too thoroughly, or the batter may become doughy. Tempura that turns out like fritters, coated so thickly that the core food is unrecognizable, is a failure. The 'clothing' should not be like a blanket covering someone who cannot be identified as male or female, but light and translucent, revealing the skin of the wearer. For this effect only part of the flour is dissolved into the liquid, mixing loosely so that a layer of undissolved flour remains on the surface. Another secret is to use cold water; some cooks even add ice in summer.

The ingredients are picked up one by one with chopsticks, dipped quickly in the batter, and plunged into hot oil. A generous amount of oil is used for deep frying, so the food has room to swim. The most important thing of all is to keep the oil at the right temperature, about 175 degrees Celsius. The test is to dribble a bit of batter into the oil with a chopstick – if it sinks slightly and immediately resurfaces, the oil is just right. The flame must be carefully regulated, and fresh oil added if the pot becomes too hot. Skillfully fried tempura is golden in colour, crisp but not overdone, and releases juice into the mouth when bitten.

After frying, the pieces are drained on a rack or absorbent paper, and served while still hot. Usually the diner dips each piece in a small bowl of *tentsuyu*, which is prepared by simmering *dashi* stock with soy sauce and *mirin*. Grated radish or ginger may be added to the dip before eating, according to taste. There are some who maintain that a better way to enjoy the original taste of the ingredients is to eat tempura with only a pinch of salt. Tempura consisting entirely of vegetables is called *shōjin-age*, meaning deep-fried temple food.

The earliest record of tempura is from the end of the sixteenth century, and it probably came from a cooking method introduced by Portuguese missionaries (see Section 4.3). In the late Edo period the term meant different things in Kansai and Edo, according to an encyclopedia of customs from the mid-nineteenth century (*Morisada mankô*). The tempura of Kyoto and Osaka was what is now known as *satsuma-age* – fish paste mixed with starch, salt, soy sauce and mirin and deep-fried without batter – and even today elderly Kansai natives sometimes call this tempura. What we know today as tempura went by that name in Edo, but in Kansai was generally called *tsuke-age*.

Frying with oil or fat was rare in the Japanese diet that developed through medieval times. The main exception was the vegetarian food eaten in and around Zen temples, with its deep-fried bean curd and wheat gluten. It was during the Edo period that the general population acquired a taste for food cooked in oil, due to the spread of oil-based cooking styles introduced from abroad: Portuguese-inspired tempura in the sixteenth century, and the Chinese-style *fucha* and *shippoku* cooking that crystallized in Nagasaki during the seventeenth century (see the previous section). Only sesame oil, which was expensive, had been used for cooking until the Edo period. Then, as cheaper rapeseed oil came into production, mainly for lighting, and new oil-pressing techniques were introduced, the stage was set for the popularization of deep-fried foods.

Tempura is one of the national dishes of Japan that developed to its current form in the city of Edo, along with *soba* noodles, grilled eel (*kabayaki*) and standard sushi (*nigiri-zushi*). Tempura became popular in the 1770s as a snack food sold at street stalls, where the customers ate standing and did not use chopsticks. The morsels of fish, prawns and vegetables were stuck on bamboo skewers, coated with batter, deep-fried and eaten on the spot, as an inexpensive food for the common people. Tempura restaurants first appeared at the beginning of the nineteenth century, and by the middle of the century were listed in Edo restaurant guides, indicating that tempura had come to be appreciated by people of higher social standing.

A new type of deep-fried food called *tonkatsu* became popular in the twentieth century. *Tonkatsu* is a pork cutlet. It developed from the inspiration of Western cutlets, but along the way was localized into something quite different. A book of English recipes published in 1872, during the early-Meiji rush to emulate Western lifestyles, introduced cutlets as slices of veal or lamb seasoned with salt and pepper, coated successively with wheat flour, egg yolk and bread crumbs, and fried with a small amount of butter. By about 1900 breaded cutlets had become standard fare at the so-called Western-food restaurants in Tokyo. The Western foods served in those restaurants were generally Japanized versions, and the cutlets were no exception. The meat was changed to pork, which was especially well-liked in Tokyo, or beef. The butter was changed to lard for frying pork, or beef fat for beef. And the pan-frying technique was altered to a sort of deep-frying, filling the pan with enough fat to immerse the meat. Some restaurants then took the tempura approach of deep-frying the breaded meat in a pot of sesame oil. (Western-style cooking in the home, which was still uncommon at that time, was done with vegetable oil.) Finally, the seasoning for the cutlet was transformed as a liberal amount of *usutâ* sauce (the thick and relatively mild Japanese version of Worcestershire sauce) was added after cooking. This was because there was a popular impression that Worcestershire sauce was the Western equivalent of soy sauce, and hence a flavour enhancer for any Western-style dish. The cutlets also came to be garnished with mustard (*karashi*, which is sharper than Western mustard and is dissolved in water rather than vinegar).

Restaurants specializing in pork cutlets appeared from the 1920s in the *shitamachi* district of Tokyo. In these establishments the dish had changed further to its current form, starting with the name *tonkatsu* (*ton* means pork and *katsu* is a shortened form of 'cutlet'). In the Western-food restaurants the pieces of meat were thinly sliced and eaten with a knife and fork, but *tonkatsu* restaurants cut them as thick as steaks, and take pride in their ability to cook them evenly all the way through. After it is fried, the breaded meat is placed on a board and cut into strips which can be picked up with chopsticks. It is served with a pile of shredded raw cabbage, which works to refresh the mouth between bites of the greasy fried meat. Having been transformed into a food that is eaten with chopsticks, *tonkatsu* acquired Japanese nationality. Today it may appear together with more traditional Japanese cuisine, even at banquets. By the 1960s *tonkatsu* had spread throughout the country and was also prepared in the home. Several brands of sauce designed specifically for this food are marketed nationally, and a plastic bottle of *tonkatsu* sauce is a now a common item in the family kitchen.

Tonkatsu restaurants were followed by *kushikatsu* restaurants, which appeared first in the Kansai region. *Kushikatsu* means 'skewered cutlet' and actually consists of bite-size pieces of pork and welsh onion (*negi*) placed alternately on a short bamboo skewer. Several skewers are served as one order, coated with egg and bread crumbs and deep-fried like *tonkatsu*. The menu at a *kushikatsu* restaurant is by no means limited to pork, but may include as many as 50 different foods and combinations deep-fried on skewers, from beef, chicken and seafood to the full range of vegetables including such items as *konnyaku* starch. The different offerings are eaten with various sauces, including a thick sauce of the *tonkatsu* type, a seasoned and vinegared soy sauce for white fish, and mayonnaise for vegetables such as asparagus.

9.8   Noodles and Regional Tastes

The standard Japanese spoken today developed from the dialect of Tokyo, where the national government was relocated and centralized in the late nineteenth century. To forge a modern nation state from the many feudal domains, the government enforced the use of standard speech nationwide in education, government and the military. Until the early 1970s, when movements for the revival of local culture emerged, speaking a dialect in public was generally considered embarrassing and people with local accents had a sense of inferiority. That is, unless they were from Osaka or Kyoto, for those dialects were the proud exceptions. The two cities are close enough together that their dialects are not easily distinguishable and they are lumped together by outsiders as *kansaiben*. *Kansaiben* was and is spoken shamelessly, even on national radio and television. This is a result of deep-seated pride in Kansai society and culture, including a regard for Tokyo as an upstart rival. Kyoto was after all the capital for more than a thousand years, and Osaka was the country's commercial hub throughout the Edo period. Only Kansai with its historic traditions has been able to confront the mainstream of Tokyo-based standardization and centralization.

Kansai self-assertion has been even more conspicuous in food than in speech. After the capital was moved to Tokyo, dishes that had developed there when it was called Edo spread throughout the country, including such modern staples as sushi (*nigiri-zushi*) and tempura. Also, Edo-style versions of some other dishes such as grilled eel (*kabayaki*) began to edge out the local recipes in Kansai.

But the flow was largely in the other direction. In the modern category, the sukiyaki eaten in Tokyo originated in Kansai. In traditional cooking, virtually all the haute cuisine to be found in the Japanese restaurants of Tokyo is strongly influenced by the *kaiseki ryôri* of old Kansai, and it is difficult to find any dishes that developed in Edo. In recent times, Osaka-born *takoyaki* – diced octopus cooked in balls of batter at street-side stands – swept Tokyo and then the rest of the country during the 1980s.

A very common food that clearly demonstrates the marked difference in Tokyo and Kansai taste is noodles. There are a number of different kinds in Japan, but the most frequently eaten are *udon* and *soba*. *Udon* is made by rolling wheat flour dough and cutting it into long strings. *Soba* noodles are made from buckwheat (*soba*) flour with a small amount of wheat flour added, in the same way but cut more thinly. Both of these noodles are boiled and are served mainly in soup. Cooked *udon* is white and smooth, while cooked *soba* is ash brown with a slightly grainy texture.

The general public embraces the stereotyped notion that *soba* is the favourite in Tokyo and the rest of eastern Japan, while western Japan including Kansai is *udon* territory. Actually there are parts of the east where *udon* has been eaten more than *soba*, and many places in the west where the local speciality is *soba*. Buckwheat can be cultivated on cold and nonproductive soil that is unsuitable for rice or wheat production, and was therefore a historical staple in mountainous areas. Adjacent to the Kanto plain where Tokyo lies are the mountainous, buckwheat-producing prefectures of Yamanashi and Nagano, where *soba* noodles predominate. In western Japan, the Osaka and Sanuki Plains have mild climates and fertile soil, which allow a crop of winter wheat to be grown after the rice paddies are drained and harvested. Hence *udon* is the main noodle of those populous areas, and the Sanuki Plain in Kagawa consumes more *udon* per capita than any other part of the country.

Specialized snack shops serving *soba* or *udon* noodles appeared in the large cities during the Edo period. At first *udon* was considered the relatively higher-class food, for wheat was traded at strong prices while buckwheat was considered a poor man's crop that was grown to stave off hunger. By the end of the eighteenth century, Edoites had come to regard *soba* as the more refined of the two, and this was in fact due to refinements in the *soba* products sold on the city's streets. The flour for *soba* noodles was changed from pure buckwheat, which provides a somewhat rough texture, to a mixture of 80 per cent buckwheat and 20 per cent wheat, which is still the standard today. The result was noodles that were finer than *udon* and had the special aroma of buckwheat, and also slid easily through the throat, a characteristic that was prized because Edoites liked to slurp down their noodles very quickly. In addition, the broth was made tastier by adding larger amounts of *katsuo-bushi* (shavings of dried bonito) and the dark, strongly flavoured *koikuchi* soy sauce favoured in Edo.

Kanto taste still runs to *soba*, while the Kansai favourite is generally *udon*, and the styles of preparation also differ somewhat between the regions. A person from Osaka or Kyoto might have this to say about Tokyo-style *soba*: 'The *soba* already looks blackish and unappetizing compared to pure-white *udon*, and that red broth they put on it makes it too salty to eat.' Whereas a Tokyoite confronted with Kansai-style *udon*, which is served in a pale broth seasoned with mild *usukuchi* soy sauce, might say: 'The soup looks so weak you would think the cook forgot to put in the flavour. And the noodles are so big you can't really slurp them down, which is the whole point of eating them. The way Kansai people chomp on their thick *udon* is quite vulgar.'

The area around Nagoya, the major city that lies about midway between Kanto and Kansai, has its own local favourite, the wide, flat and thin wheat noodles called *kishimen*. They are eaten in broth seasoned with *hatchô* miso, a local speciality that has a deep red-brown colour and astringent taste because it is fermented from soybeans only, without the rice or barley that is usually added in making miso. This dish is a good example of the distinctiveness that can easily be found in the regional cuisines of Japan.

A noodle soup is made by boiling the noodles in water, scooping them out with a colander, placing them in a *donburi* bowl, adding the topping and other ingredients, and finally ladling in the broth. There are a large variety of toppings for soups. One of the most common is tempura, usually a prawn, creating the dish called tempura *soba* or tempura *udon*. A speciality of the Kansai area is *kitsune udon* ('fox' *udon*), named for the reddish colour of the topping, which is thin slices of deep-fried tofu (*abura-age*) that have been simmered in *dashi* stock with soy sauce and sugar. Besides the main topping, a green vegetable such as boiled spinach or welsh onion is usually added. Most people eat their soup after adding a pinch of seven-spice chili powder (*nanairo tôgarashi* or *shichimi tôgarashi*), which contains red pepper, Japanese pepper (*sanshô*), sesame seeds, dried citrus peel and other ingredients.

Soba may also be served cold. The most common type is *zaru-soba*, which is eaten with a cold dip made from soy sauce and *dashi* stock. The boiled *soba* is rinsed in cold water, and served on a draining screen of finely split bamboo set on a square or round lacquered wood frame. The noodles are topped with shreds of dried laver (*nori*), and the dip is accompanied by sliced welsh onion and grated wasabi horseradish which the diner adds to taste. This dish is named after the *zaru*, a colander that is traditionally made of bamboo. An older name is *seiro-soba*, using the term for a steaming basket that was used to cook *soba* in the days when the noodles consisted entirely of buckwheat flour, which made them too fragile for boiling. The bamboo screen used for serving is a vestige of the original cooking style. *Mori-soba* is identical to *zaru-soba* except that it is served without the laver topping or the *wasabi* condiment, and is therefore slightly cheaper, although in recent years some restaurants have begun serving this dish with wasabi.

Sômen wheat noodles (described in Section 3.8) are usually eaten cold, as *hiyashi-sômen*. The thin dried noodles are boiled, rinsed in cold water and served in a glass bowl of fresh water. Now that refrigerators are common, ice is usually added as well. The dip of soy sauce, *dashi* and *mirin* is typically garnished with grated ginger, welsh onion, and green perilla (*aojiso; Perilla frutescent var. crispa*) which has a fragrance like basil and spearmint combined. *Hiyashi-sômen* is a summer food only, while cold *soba* is eaten throughout the year.

The Chinese-style *râmen* noodles of Japan are more elastic and hence chewier than the traditional Japanese wheat noodles (*udon*, *sômen*, and *kishimen*). The difference results from the Chinese technique of adding alkali to the salty water that is used to knead the wheat dough. This also gives the noodles a pale yellow hue and a particular aroma. They were served in Chinese restaurants and by street peddlers from about 1920 as a dish called *shina soba* (China *soba*), but because that name had a derogatory nuance it was changed after the Second World War to *chûka soba* (Chinese *soba*) or, more commonly, *râmen*. The word *râmen* probably came from the Chinese *lâ miàn* ('handmade noodles') although there are other theories. The dish consists basically of noodles in a pork or chicken broth seasoned with black pepper and topped with slices of pork and various other items. In the post-war years, many Japanese who had returned from living in Manchuria or other parts of China opened *râmen* shops with great success. It was a time of food shortages in Japan, and not only did Chinese food in general have a reputation for high nutrition, but *râmen* with its meat broth and meat topping offered more protein than most traditional Japanese noodle dishes. *Râmen* shops have remained common throughout the country ever since.

Many distinctive local versions of *râmen* were established as the shops in each region concentrated on the varieties of soup seasonings and toppings appreciated by local people. Among the best known is Sapporo *râmen*, from the large city in Hokkaido, which features heavy noodles (kept elastic by increasing the alkali in the dough), a rich thick broth seasoned with miso instead of the more common salt and soy sauce, and locally produced toppings of butter and maize. The other Hokkaido cities of Asahikawa, Hakodate and Kamikawa, and the Kyushu cities of Fukuoka (Hakata), Kumamoto and Kagoshima all have their names attached to well-known *râmen* recipes which have become part of the local cuisines. This proliferation of regional varieties is remarkable, as it runs counter to the strong national trend toward standardization of food which has accompanied the growth of nationwide distribution networks and the mass media since the 1960s. Now the local *râmen* dishes have themselves gone national, as chains of *râmen* shops specialized in particular styles have developed in the large cities. This relatively new Japanese food has indeed developed with great dynamism.

The word *râmen* is also associated with instant noodles, an international phenomenon which originated in Japan in 1958 with a product called Chicken Râmen. Mass-produced noodles were permeated with chicken bouillon and then deep-fried at a temperature high enough to evaporate all the moisture, leaving the noodles porous and dry, ready to absorb water. Placed in a bowl and covered with boiling water, the noodles become soft and turn the water to broth. The catch phrase for Chicken Râmen, 'Just wait three minutes', instantly entered the language and the factory could not keep up with the demand, and other manufacturers jumped into the market. It was just at that time that Japan was finally breaking loose from the after effects of the war and prosperity was coming into sight. People were busy, and readier than ever to minimize their time in the kitchen – the perfect conditions for selling instant food. The man behind Chicken Râmen, Andô Momofuku, went on to develop Cup Noodle in 1971. This is instant noodles plus dehydrated toppings of meat or seafood and vegetables, in a styrofoam container with a plastic spoon. Just add boiling water, and the disposable cup functions as both cooking pot and serving bowl. The classic East Asian noodle soup contains a substantial amount of broth, requiring a large bowl, which is difficult to eat noodles from without chopsticks. Cup Noodle broke through that limitation by changing the forms of the container and the ingredients, and so reached out to markets around the world that were not accustomed to noodle soups.

9.9   Pickles and Preserved Seafood

Preserved foods are an important part of most dietary traditions. Classical Japanese cuisine may lack the cured meats and cheeses of Europe, but its pickles and preserved seafood are at the core of dietary practice. To begin with, every authentically Japanese meal includes pickles, to accompany the equally indispensable rice.

Pickles – food stored away with a quantity of salt and transformed, through the action of the salt and the effects of lactic acid bacteria and yeast, into sour–salty products that will keep for a long time – are called *tsukemono*. The term technically includes pickled seafood, but usually refers to vegetable products. *Tsukemono* first developed in the snow country, the northern regions of Hokkaido, Tohoku and Hokuriku where preserved vegetables are essential because no food can be gathered from the land for several months each winter. Both cultivated vegetables and wild edible plants were pickled. Drying has also been a vital technique of preserving vegetables and other foods. Removing moisture from food also allows it to be transported much more easily. Dried kelp, laver and other seaweed such as *wakame* have been distributed on a national scale since ancient times.

The city of Kyoto produces many famous pickle specialities which were developed during the centuries when it was the capital and the headquarters of high culture. Vegetables were emphasized in

Kyoto cuisine, partly because the inland location made it difficult to get fresh seafood on a daily basis, and many unique or improved varieties were developed in the surrounding countryside to serve the city's refined tastes.

There are eight main techniques of pickling in Japan: (1) *shiozuke* (salt pickling), the simplest technique, in which vegetables are sprinkled with salt and placed in a container with a weighted inner lid; (2) *nukazuke* (rice-bran pickling) using a salted paste of bran (3) *shôyuzuke* (soy-sauce pickling); (4) *misozuke* (miso pickling); (5) *kasuzuke* (sake-lees pickling), using the remains of rice from brewery vats; (6) *suzuke* (vinegar pickling), with salt added; and (7, 8) two types of *kôjizuke* (rice-mould pickling), one in which the yeasty mould is mixed with salt, and another in which it is mixed with brine and mustard powder. All of these basic techniques use either salt or a salty seasoning (soy sauce or miso). In addition there are a few unusual *tsukemono* made in other ways, without salt.

In addition to the different techniques and many local variations, the main ingredients are myriad, some of the most typical being leafy greens, radishes, turnips, eggplants, and cucumbers. Altogether, there are several thousand kinds of pickles available. Among them are two which have spread throughout the country and may be considered the quintessential Japanese pickles: *takuan* and *umeboshi*.

Takuan is *daikon* radish pickled with rice bran. Its production has flourished since the seventeenth century. The *daikon* are harvested in the last days of autumn and hung to dry, uncut, in a sunny and airy place. In the days when large farming families prepared their own pickles for the whole year, a hundred or more of the large vegetables – typically at least 30 cm long and 5 cm in diameter – might be processed at once. Those to be eaten soon would be left to dry for about a week, and those to be kept the longest for three to four weeks. The dried *daikon* are packed tightly together in a wooden cask, and each layer is sprinkled with a mixture of rice bran and salt before being covered with another layer. The cask is then covered with an inner lid pressed down with a heavy weight. Some households add extra ingredients to impart special flavour and aroma, such as dried persimmon or mandarin orange peels, or dried aubergine leaves. *Takuan* has a pale yellow colour that comes from the pigment in the rice bran. It is served in slices about half a centimetre thick.

Umeboshi is a Japanese apricot (*ume*) that has been dried and pickled in salt. The Japanese have traditionally set great store by this very salty and acidic red pickle. Merely mentioning the name will cause many people's mouths to water as they recall the sharp, sour taste. A small amount is considered effective in supplying the body with salt and quenching thirst, and the *umeboshi* has been used in military rations since the civil wars of the sixteenth century. Ordinary citizens routinely use its preservative effect by placing it on rice in a box lunch, or at the centre of a rice ball (*nigirimeshi* or *o-nigiri*). In China the unripened fruit has been used medicinally since ancient times, either smoked or salted before drying. In Japan it is said to prevent food poisoning, and in premodern times it was believed to prevent infection during a plague.

Ume for pickling are gathered in June when they have just begun to lose their green colour and acquire a yellow tinge. The completely unripe fruit will not make a tasty pickle, while the fully ripened apricots are too soft and would lose their shape. They are covered with a large amount of salt and placed in a container with a heavy weight on the lid for about two weeks, by which time a pool of *umezu* ('apricot vinegar') has collected inside the container. At that point, the leaves of the red perilla (*akajiso*; *Perilla frutescent*) are in season and available at the market, and these are rubbed with salt and added to the *umezu*, turning the liquid a vibrant red. The *ume* are pickled (and dyed) in that liquid for three to four weeks and then, during the hottest part of the year, taken out and dried in the sun for about three days. Next they are put back in the liquid for a week to ten days until the flesh of the fruit is soft, and finally transferred to an airtight container. The red juice is set aside for use as a sour seasoning. After six months the *umeboshi* will be edible, but the full taste takes several years to mature. They keep extraordinarily well; occasionally a jar of *umeboshi* over a hundred years old is found in a storehouse, and the pickles are still edible. *Umeboshi* preserved for a long time lose their moisture and are covered with wrinkles, and a wrinkled old woman might be called an *umeboshi* hag.

In general, *tsukemono* are ready-to-eat foods that need no cooking or preparation. Most are simply cut into pieces that can be grasped with chopsticks before being eaten in small quantities with rice. Some people season them with soy sauce, but this is hardly necessary as it is adding one salty food to another. However, in the snow country where they originated, *tsukemono* were preserves to be

255

eaten in quantity, and were cooked as part of a winter meal after first soaking them in water to remove the salt.

Pickle shops first appeared during the Edo period in the large cities, while in the countryside *tsukemono* continued to be made in the home. As recently as the 1930s, 80 per cent of all pickles were produced in the home, but today the majority are factory made. Even in the snow country, imported or hothouse vegetables are available year-round, and few people rely on *tsukemono* as ingredients for cooking. In any case, the pickles themselves can be bought at supermarkets any time, and hence the necessity of preserving vegetable foods for long periods is no longer felt at the household level. As a result of changes in dietary habits and awareness, foods preserved in salt for long periods are now seen as a potential source of illness, and pickles with reduced salt content are gaining popularity. In other words, preserved foods are being transformed into fresh foods.

The same may be said for preserved fish, which are still common in the marketplace despite the increased availability of fresh fish and thawed frozen fish. Preserved fish today are mostly either lightly salted or partially dried with much of the moisture intact. Yet the traditional, more thorough preservation methods still exist. The technique of smoking fish has long been known in Japan but never came into wide use, except in the case of *katsuo-bushi*, where it was actually a refinement of an established drying process (see Section 9.1). In early times fish was preserved through fermentation into *shiokara* or *narezushi*, which are still available as delicacies (see Section 2.5). Juicy types of fish may be preserved through heavy salting, while other kinds of fish and shellfish are sun-dried until they are thoroughly dehydrated. More than a hundred varieties of sea fish are dried and marketed in Japan, along with various shellfish and quantities of squid and octopus. By weight, the dominant *himono* (dried fish) products are sardines, anchovies, horse mackerel and other small fish which are caught in large volume and have too low a market price to merit fresh distribution.

Lightly salted fish and dried fish are usually grilled and then eaten plain, although soy sauce may be added to the less salty varieties. Preserved foods including dried fish have traditionally been the core of the Japanese breakfast menu because they can be prepared quickly and easily. The typical breakfast at a traditional inn

256

consists of salted salmon or small dried fish, *nattô* (in eastern Japan), a few small sheets of dried *nori*, a raw egg, miso soup, rice, and pickles. Most of these foods are preserved, and only the soup requires real cooking. The raw egg is broken and mixed with a little soy sauce and then poured over the rice.

The minimum meal in the Japanese pattern is *ichijû-issai*, or one soup and one side dish (plus rice). In that case the side dish will be pickles. The humblest version of all is *chazuke*, a one-bowl meal consisting of green tea poured over rice – with pickles, for *tsukemono* is an irreducible cornerstone of the rice-based meal.

9.10   Mochi, Confectionery and Tea

The food which is at the heart of the rituals in the most important of Japan's annual festivals, the New Year, is of course rice, and it is rice in a special form that symbolizes the deep connections the Japanese feel with nature and agriculture. It is *mochi*, rice cakes made from a very glutinous type of rice. The rice is first steamed and then kneaded to a viscous paste, traditionally by placing it in a wooden mortar and pounding with a large, long-handled mallet. Many Japanese families still pound *mochi* by hand on one of the last two or three days of the year. The effort is repaid when the freshly pounded *mochi* is torn into pieces and eaten warm, with a covering of *kinako* (a yellowish flour made from parched soybeans), a dollop of grated *daikon* radish with soy sauce, a coating or filling of sweet adzuki-bean paste (*an*), or a filling of *nattô*. Freshly pounded *mochi* is soft and easy to eat, but it quickly hardens and must be grilled or otherwise reheated to become edible. Reheated *mochi* is very sticky and difficult to chew and swallow. The majority of the population that does not pound its own *mochi* for New Year buys the mechanically kneaded product in shops.

Cakes of *mochi* are served on New Year's Day in *zôni*, the celebratory soup eaten at breakfast. They are also used to make the standard New Year decoration called *kagami-mochi* or 'mirror-mochi' due to its shape – not a glass mirror but the polished bronze disc mirror of old East Asia. The bronze mirror is a Shinto symbol for the presence of divine spirits, and is usually placed in the inner sanctuary of a shrine as the receptacle for the deities that come from the other world to listen as people pray. Displaying stylized 'mirrors' of *mochi*, two cakes piled one on the other, on the household altar sanctifies the home as a ritual site for the New Year festivities. Praying to *kagami-mochi* is recorded as early as the tenth century, but is likely much older, for the *toshigami* or New Year deity that is believed to reside in it rules over rice growing for the year, and is thus associated with the oldest of farming rituals.

Shinto rice deities are believed to reside in every manifestation of rice, and the steaming and smashing together of many thousands of grains of rice into a single sticky mass symbolizes the amalgamation of countless divine spirits. This is why *mochi* is regarded as a holy food, and is closely associated with many of the large and small annual festivals in Japan. In addition, eating *mochi* is believed to provide more energy and power than eating other foods. As physiological reasons for that belief, a high amount of calories can be assimilated from a small amount of *mochi*, and *mochi* takes longer to digest than most foods and hence more time passes before feelings of hunger return. On the psychological level, eating *mochi* is viewed as a means of taking on the supernatural force of the rice spirit.

When *mochi* is eaten at a meal it is the staple, but when eaten with tea between meals it falls in the category of sweets called *mochi* confections. Fresh *mochi* is white, viscous and very plastic, which facilitates various kinds of secondary processing, and there are numerous *mochi* confections. It is sometimes kneaded together with vegetables, wild plants, or seaweed to impart a green hue, or with red or yellow colouring agents. It is formed into every kind of shape – discs, balls, ovals, rectangles, diamonds, flower petals – and may be filled with sweet bean-jam paste. *Mochi*-style dumplings (*dango*) are also made by mixing rice flour, from either glutinous or non-glutinous rice, with water and moulding it into little balls which are steamed. They are eaten with coatings of sweetened soybean flour, sesame seeds, bean jam or soy sauce.

The word *kashi* now means confectionery of all kinds, but in ancient times it referred to fruits and nuts that were eaten as refreshments between meals, such as peaches, persimmons, melons, mandarins, chestnuts and walnuts. This class of foods was also known in ancient times as *kudamono*, the term that is used today to mean fruits. During the Edo period, cakes and candies made mainly from sweetened grain or beans became popular, and *kashi* changed its meaning from delicacies found in nature to those created by human hands.

There is a record reporting that in CE 643 an aristocrat who had immigrated to Japan from Korea tried unsuccessfully to set up beekeeping. Over the next thousand years beekeeping seems to have been unknown. In the eighteenth century, farmers in several parts of the country gathered honey as a sideline, mainly from the hives of wild bees, but their production was small and the honey was too expensive to become established as a food ingredient. It was used instead as medicine. The Meiji government introduced Western honeybees and beekeeping techniques in 1877, and the industry flourished, with honey production high enough at one point to support exports.

A syrup called *amazura*, made by tapping and boiling the sap of an ivy vine (*Parthenocissus tricuspidata*), was used to concoct sweet refreshments for nobles at the Heian court during the tenth century. In the summer it was placed over ice that had been kept since the winter and served in metal bowls. It was also used in a yam porridge. Chinese-style cakes (*tōgashi*), kneaded from wheat or rice flour and deep-fried in sesame oil, were made in Japan from about the eighth century, but as a rule sweeteners were not added (see Section 3.6).

Sugar was a rarity in Japan, imported from China and used only in medicine, until the merchant trading boom of the sixteenth century. Japanese merchant shipping to China and Southeast Asia flourished, and Portuguese, Dutch, English and Chinese trading ships called regularly in Japan. Sugar imports increased, and European-style sweet cakes (*nanban gashi*) began to be made in Japan (see Section 4.3). There was also further spread of Chinese-style sweet buns (*manjū*) which had previously been made in Buddhist monasteries. Quite popular in Japan today, *manjū* consists of bean jam wrapped in a crêpe-like shell made from flour, folded into a rounded shape and steamed. After Japan closed its borders in 1639, Dutch and Chinese ships continued trading through Nagasaki, and sugar was one of the major imports. Sugar production began in Japan during the seventeenth century, using sugar cane cultivated in the Ryukyus and southern Japan. As sugar became more easily available, confectionery shops opened in the cities, and one of them in Edo published a catalog in 1683 listing 172 kinds of sweets.

Nowadays, a cup of green tea might be accompanied by a sweet, but usually not. The connection is not particularly strong since green tea has come to be seen mainly as a way to quench thirst or change one's mood. It was different in the seventeenth century, when tea and sweets were closely associated and developed in parallel. On one level, creation of the finest confectionery was supported by the practice of the tea ceremony, in which sweets are used to balance the astringent taste of the concentrated green tea. As with every other aspect of the tea ceremony, excellence and subtlety are demanded. The sweetness must not be so strong that it spoils the flavour of the tea, and the aesthetics of colour and shape are also important. Just as it gave rise to the refined *kaiseki* cuisine (see Section 4.2), the tea ceremony spawned a long and continuing tradition of elegant sweets in the cities where it thrived, especially Kyoto, Kanazawa and Matsue.

The tea ceremony and its powdered tea (*matcha*) were enjoyed only by an elite. The common people acquired the custom of eating sweets along with the spread of leaf tea, which is much simpler to prepare. Powdered tea is made by picking the tender young leaves of the tea plant, steaming them while still green and then drying them with warm air, and grinding them in a small mortar. To brew the tea, a small amount of powder is put in an individual bowl, water that has boiled and cooled somewhat is added, and a bamboo whisk is used to whip the mixture to an even, slightly foamy texture. Even without all the special implements and elaborate etiquette of the tea ceremony, *matcha* is rather troublesome to brew. Leaf tea is simpler. The leaves are steamed and dried, and used whole. The tea is brewed by the pot, by putting the leaves in a teapot and adding hot water. Alternatively the leaves may be steeped in a kettle, or put into water that has boiled. Before leaf tea became popular in the early seventeenth century, the everyday beverage of the common people was water, served either hot or cold, and sometimes hot water was poured over the scorched remains of boiled rice for a weak grain tea. Tea cultivation proved possible in many parts of Japan, and as leaf tea caught on, many farmers began cultivating a few tea plants for their own supply. It quickly became the national beverage.

The best grade of leaf tea, *gyokuro* ('jade dew'), is made with the tenderest young leaves, picked in May or June from tea bushes that are protected from direct sunlight by bamboo blinds. It is appreciated for its fragrance and for its flavour, which is a blend of mild bitterness and subtle sweetness. *Gyokuro* is the highest grade of *sencha*, the general name given to the standard grade of tea made from the first-growth and sometimes second-growth leaves. Both *sencha* and *gyokuro* are brewed in a small teapot with a straight protruding handle called a *kyûsu*. The tea is placed in the pot and water of about 60°C is added (boiling water is never used), after first warming the cups with a little hot water which is later discarded. There is a tradition of serving a high-quality sweet with a cup of *gyokuro* or *sencha*, but this is optional and not usually done. The general way of drinking leaf tea is to enjoy it as one pleases. There are a few aficionados who practice a 'way of *sencha*' (*senchadô*), which is modeled on the tea ceremony (*chadô*) and was founded in the seventeenth century.

The leaves that grow in after the early growth has been picked for *sencha* are clipped, and the next, brittle growth is harvested with the stems to make the coarse leaf tea called *bancha*. It has a yellow-brown tinge and slightly bitter taste. *Bancha* leaves are browned by roasting to make *hôjicha*, an aromatic tea that brews to a dark reddish colour with a robust taste. The tougher *bancha* leaves require boiling water to extract the flavour for drinking. *Bancha* and *hôjicha* were sometimes steeped in the kettle, but are made nowadays in either a *kyûsu* teapot or a *dobin*, which is larger with a non-ceramic carry-type handle and often made of earthenware.

The treats that traditionally accompanied the commoner's tea – *bancha* – were unaffected and inexpensive. Often they were unsweetened, such as the *senbei* rice crackers that are still found today. A popular version in Tokyo is the *shiosenbei*, a salty cracker made by grilling disks of kneaded rice flour over a charcoal fire while basting them with soy sauce. Until the middle of the twentieth century, the townspeople customarily bought sweet or savoury confections to enjoy with their tea, while farmers drank tea with homemade snacks such as salty pickles, boiled or baked sweet potatoes, or chestnuts. In the village life of the past, it was customary to take a break from work and have a snack at about three in the afternoon, and this became a tea break in the Edo period.

Western confectionery containing fat and dairy products (*yôgashi*), especially cakes, were widely introduced from the Meiji period and today their popularity rivals that of the traditional

Japanese confections (*wagashi*). Green tea is always served with Japanese sweets, and black tea or coffee, also quite popular, are served with the Western varieties. In modern life many people drink tea or coffee several times a day, and so the beverages are often not accompanied by a sweet or other snack.

9.11   The Dynamics of Sake and Tea

Since the 1980s it has become fashionable to drink *ginjôshu*, a refined type of sake, chilled like white wine to appreciate its fruity aroma. Otherwise, as a general rule sake is warmed for drinking. China also has the traditional custom of warming non-distilled drinks such as Shaoxing rice wine. In Japan, the nobility of the Heian period warmed their sake except during the hot season (from the fifth day of the fifth lunar month to the ninth day of the ninth month). During the Edo period it became the general practice to drink warm sake all year round. This may have been a consequence of innovation. A new technique came into use for producing sake with a higher alcohol content, in cedar casks with capacities of several tons rather than the previous earthenware jars, and the new product was probably well suited for drinking warmed.

Sake is heated in a *tokkuri*, a small ceramic bottle that is placed in hot water and then brought to the table for pouring. Most bottles hold one *go* (180 millilitres). Some people like their sake very hot, while others say that spoils the taste, and sake lovers may well debate this point at drinking parties. Researchers have found that a level somewhat warmer than body temperature – similar to the temperature of a Japanese bath – is best for appreciating the taste and fragrance. The sake cup (*choko*) is quite small and therefore frequently refilled. Except when drinking alone, the rule is never to fill one's own cup. When a nearby cup is empty, one picks up the *tokkuri* and offers to pour, and the receiver then returns the favour. The cup is always held in the receiver's hand while the sake is poured. In some bars and restaurants, hostesses (or in the most exclusive traditional restaurants, geisha) do the pouring as part of their duties of entertaining the customers.

Figure 20   A serving vessel and cup for sake.

There is a custom of drinking sake from another's cup at formal parties, although it is dying out due to young people's objection on grounds of hygiene. One asks a senior, 'Please allow me to drink from your cup,' and that person then empties the cup and passes it to the junior, who receives it respectfully with both hands. The cup is filled and drained, then returned, and the junior refills it from the flask, which completes the process of exchange. One might perform this exchange with many persons of senior status at the same party, and sometimes a bowl of water is furnished for rinsing the exchanged cups. The antecedents of this practice include the formal drinking party of the Heian period, which began with the ritual of three rounds of sake in which everyone, starting with the guest of honour, would sip from the same large cup. The custom of sharing drink originated as a religious observance, still practised at some Shinto festivals, in which sake that has been offered to the deities is poured into a large cup and passed along according to the order of seating. Becoming intoxicated from the same cup is clearly a means of establishing solidarity among the drinkers. In the early tea ceremony, too, the custom of drinking from a common bowl was borrowed from the sake-drinking etiquette of the late sixteenth century.

The presence of those customs implies that sake and tea were for many centuries drunk mainly in group settings. Literary and historical records show that there were some nobles, high-ranking samurai, and wealthy people who regularly drank alone, but sake was consumed predominantly at festivals, community events and formal parties, that is, at ceremonial moments which were separate from the flow of normal life. The essence of the tea ceremony is a spirit of giving and receiving in a shared moment, and it is held for a small group in a special room that is separated from ordinary life.

In the Edo-period, cities that group nexus began to weaken. Drinking powdered tea was an involved and social process, but the spread of leaf tea made it easy and practical for people to drink tea alone without any ceremony. Sake was no longer kept only in the community for special occasions, but became a commercial commodity available at a growing number of shops. Taverns (*izakaya*) also appeared, providing a space for individuals or groups to drink sake when they pleased, independent from any ceremonial event. Thus beverages for extraordinary occasions began to be transformed into daily drinks, and what had been drunk in a group setting came to be consumed independently.

Alcohol brings intoxication and tea brings awakening, and various cultures have recognized the antithetical relationship. It was masterfully expressed in a Chinese work from the ninth or tenth century, *Chá-jiu lùn* (On tea and wine), in which personifications of the two argue their respective merits and exploits to a standoff, and water steps in as the mediator to heal the breach. In Japan, one's fondness or disinclination for alcohol leads to classification as either the drinking type or the sweet-tooth type – *karatô* or *amatô*. *Kara* means spiciness or saltiness, as in the salty snacks usually served with alcohol, and *ama* means sweetness. The beverage for a sweet-tooth is tea, which historically has been mainly an everyday drink, whereas alcohol in Japan has historically been associated mainly with festivals and special occasions – another aspect of antithesis.

Offerings of sake are a part of almost every Shinto festival, in line with the saying, 'No god refuses holy sake' (i.e. none of the myriad Shinto deities). When the rites are finished the celebrants gather for a meal and drink the consecrated sake, which thus becomes a means of communion between the human and the divine. In contrast, in Buddhist temples, where alcohol is not tolerated and where tea drinking first took root, offerings of tea are often placed at the altar during religious rites. Likewise, sake is the appropriate gift at weddings, which are observed with Shinto rites, while tea is given at funerals, which are generally conducted with Buddhist rites.

An additional aspect of the opposition is that a person who can drink large amounts of alcohol is judged as manly, while those devoted to sweets and tea tend to be seen as effeminate.

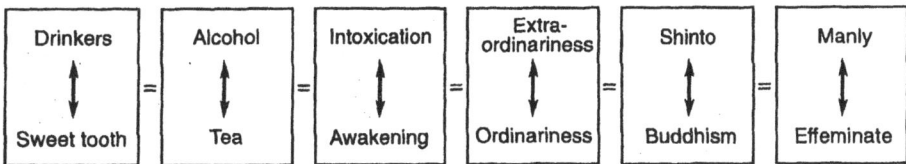

Drinkers ↕ Sweet tooth	=	Alcohol ↕ Tea	=	Intoxication ↕ Awakening	=	Extra-ordinariness ↕ Ordinariness	=	Shinto ↕ Buddhism	=	Manly ↕ Effeminate

Figure 21   Cultural polarities of sake and tea.

Until the late nineteenth century, the major beverages in Japanese culture were only two, sake and tea. Then Japan opened to the outside world and turned a new page in its beverage history. Drinks that were unknown little more than a century ago are now part of the daily lives of most of the population. How have these new drinks, some with deep roots in Western or global civilization, been positioned within the context of the value structure of Japanese culture?

In many respects, alcoholic beverages from the West (beer, wine, whisky and other spirits) have acquired an image similar to that of sake. They are served with the same kinds of salty snack foods, and the ability to drink a large amount is associated with manliness. However, none of the 'foreign' beverages has gained the status of a ceremonial drink for special occasions, or come to be perceived as connected to the divine realm. At banquets or parties it is common to raise a glass of beer in a toast. Nonetheless, the formal beverage for a ceremonial occasions such as a wedding or festival is without exception sake.

Non-alcoholic drinks that have arrived on the scene since the Meiji period include coffee, black tea, carbonated soft drinks, and juices, as well as milk which, though not unknown, had never been customarily consumed. Coffee and black tea naturally fall into the stimulant category with green tea (which also contains caffeine). Soft drinks including juices generally have a very feminine image, but these beverages do not fit into the traditional rubric defined by sake and tea.

Drinking glasses, unknown until Meiji times, are generally viewed as unsuitable for sake, and conversely ceramic cups or serving vessels are never used for beer, wine or spirits. The ceramic teacups, bowls and pots for green tea are still universally of the traditional designs. A handled cup with saucer would be unthinkable for green tea, but is required for Western tea or coffee, unless it is iced in a tumbler. Likewise soft drinks and milk are served in glasses and never in ceramic cups. In short, when it comes to the vessels used for beverages, the lines between old and new are still strong.

REFERENCES

Adachi Susumu. 1980. *Gyûnyû – gyûnyû kara nyûseihin made* [Milk – from milk to dairy products]. Tokyo: Shibata Shoten.

Aoki Masaru. 1970. Yôshi kippan kô [On eating rice with spoons]. In *Aoki Masaru zenshû 9 kan* [Collected works of Aoki Masaru, volume 9]. Tokyo: Shunjusha.

Bull, N. I. and Buss, D. H. 1980. Contributions of foods to sodium intakes. London: *Procedures of the Nutrition Society* 39: 30A.

Chen Wen Hua and Watabe Takeshi. 1989. *Chûgoku no inasaku kigen* [The origin of Chinese rice growing]. Tokyo: Rokkô Shuppan.

Dore, Ronald. Blackburn and Kishiwada: Proletarian Towns and Middle-Class Towns. In *Japanese Civilization in the Modern World II -- Cities and Urbanization*, ed. Tadao Umesao et al. Osaka: National Museum of Ethnology, 1989.

Etchû Tetsuya. 1982. *Nagasaki no seiyô ryôri: yôshoku no akebono* [Western cuisine of Nagasaki: the dawn of Western-style food]. Tokyo: Dai-ichi Hôki Shuppansha.

Frois, Luis. [c. 1590] 1982. *Nichiô bunka hikaku* [Comparison of Japanese and European culture], Japanese translation by Okada Akio. Tokyo: Iwanami Shoten.

Fukuo Takeshirô. 1979. *Nihon kodai no 'hishio' no seishitsu ni tsuite – sono shôyu taru koto no teishô* [On the nature of hishio in ancient Japan – an essay on the soy sauce of the time]. In

REFERENCES

Nihon shi senshû [Anthology of Japanese History], ed. Fukuo Takeshirô, 455–70. Osaka: Fukuo Takeshirô Sensei Koki Kinenkai.

Fukuzawa Yukichi. [1899] 1978. *Fukuô jiden* [The autobiography of Fukuzawa Yukichi]. Tokyo: Iwanami Shoten.

Haginaka Mie et al. 1992. *Kikigaki: ainu no shokuji* [The diet of the Ainu, verbatim]. Tokyo: Nôsangyoson Bunka Kyôkai.

Harada Nobuo. 1985. *Nihon chûsei ni okeru nikushoku ni tsuite* [On meat eating in medieval Japan]. In *Higashi ajia no shokuji bunka* [Dietary cultures of East Asia], ed. Ishige Naomichi. Tokyo: Heibonsha.

_____. 1989. *Edo no ryôri shi--ryôrihon to ryôri bunka* [History of Edo cooking – cookbooks and culinary culture]. Tokyo: Chûô Kôronsha.

Hirata Mario. 1985. *Edo jidai ni okeru gaikoku ryôri no sho* [Documents on foreign cooking in the Edo period]. In *Higashi ajia no shokuji bunka* [Dietary cultures of East Asia], ed. Ishige Naomichi. Tokyo: Heibonsha.

_____. 1992. *Edo no inshokuten* [Restaurants of Edo]. In *Tabemono nihonshi sôran* [Japanese food history compendium]. Tokyo: Shinjinbutsu Ôrai Sha.

Ishige Naomichi. 1968. *Nihon inasaku no keifu* [Genealogy of rice-growing in Japan]. *Shirin* 51(5):130–50. Kyoto: Kyoto University.

_____. 1975. *Shokuji patân no kôgengaku* [Researches on contemporary eating patterns]. *Seikatsugaku* 1:165–80. Tokyo: Nihon Seikatsu Gakkai

_____. 1986. *Beishoku minzoku hikaku kara mita nihonjin no shoku seikatsu* [Dietary patterns of the Japanese in light of a comparison of rice-eating nations]. In *Seikatsugaku no hôhô*

[Methodologies for the study of living patterns], ed. Chûbachi Masayoshi, 10-26. Tokyo: Domesu Shuppan.

_____. 1990. Développement des restaurants Japonais pendant la période Edo. In *Les restaurants dans le monde et à travers les âges*, ed. Alain Huetz de Lemps and Jean-Robert Pitte, 19–82. Grenoble: Edition Glénat.

_____. 1991. *Bunka menruigaku koto hajime* [Elements of a cultural noodle-ology]. Tokyo: Fûdiamu Komyunikêshon.

_____. 1993. Cultural Aspects of Fermented Fish in Asia. In *Fish Fermentation Technology*, ed. Lee, Steinkraus and Reilly, 13–32. Tokyo, New York, Paris: United Nations University.

Ishige Naomichi and Inoue Tadashi. 1991. *Gendai nihon ni okeru katei to shokutaku* [Change and transformation in table setting: home dining in modern Japan]. Osaka: *Bulletin of the National Museum of Ethnology* 16.

Ishige Naomichi and Kenneth Ruddle. 1990. *Gyoshô to narezushi no kenkyû: monsûn ajia no shokuji bunka* [Studies on fermented fish: the eating culture of monsoon Asia]. Tokyo: Iwanami Shoten.

Itô Kinen Zaidan. 1990. *Nihon shokuniku bunka shi* [Cultural history of meat-eating in Japan]. Nishinomiya: Itô Kinen Zaidan.

Kanagaki Robun. 1871 [1967]. *Aguranabe*. Tokyo: Iwanami Shoten.

Kanzaki Noritake. 1989. *Daidokoro no bunmei to bunka – hi o chûshin to shite* [Civilization and culture of the kitchen – The fire as centre]. In *Katei no shokuji kûkan* [The space for the meal in the home], Yamaguchi Masatomo and Ishige Naomichi, ed., 35–9. Tokyo: Domesu Shuppan.

Katô Momoichi. 1987. *Nihon no sake 5,000 nen* [5,000 years of Japanese sake]. Tokyo: Gijutsudô Shuppan.

Kawamura Y. and Kare M. R. 1987. *Umami: A Basic Taste.* New York and Basel: Marcel Decker Inc.

Kitô Hiroshi. 1983. *Edo jidai no beishoku* [The rice diet of the Edo period]. *Rekishi kôron* 89. Tokyo: Yûzenkaku.

Kôseishô Hoken Iryô Kyoku Kenkô Zôshin Ka [Ministry of Health and Welfare, Health Promotion Division]. 1993. *Heisei gonendo han: kokumin eiyô no genjô* [The state of the nation's nutrition, 1993]. Tokyo: Dai-ichi Shuppan.

Koyama Shûzô. 1984. *Shoku seikatsu o kaeta doki no shutsugen* [How the advent of earthenware changed eating habits]. In *Asahi hyakka: sekai no tabemono* 12. Tokyo: Asahi Shimbunsha.

Koyama Shûzô and Gotô Toshiko. 1985. *Nihonjin no shushoku no rekishi* [A history of staple foods of the Japanese]. In *Higashi ajia no shokuji bunka* [Dietary cultures of East Asia], ed. Ishige Naomichi. Tokyo: Heibonsha.

Kumakura Isao. 1976. *Honzen kara kaiseki e* [From honzen to kaiseki]. *Bessatsu taiyo* 14:85–92. Tokyo: Heibonsha.

_____. 1990. *Chanoyu no rekishi: Sen no Rikyû made* [History of the tea ceremony up to Sen no Rikyû]. Tokyo: Asahi Shimbunsha.

Lee Sung Woo. 1980. *Kankoku no tabemono no shakaishi (kan)* [A social history of Korean food (conclusion)]. *Ajia kôron* 12. Kyoto: Kankoku Kokusai Bunka Kyôkai.

_____. 1990. *Kankoku no gyunyû riyou ni kansuru shiteki kôan* [Historical ideas concerning the use of milk in Korea]. *Shoku no kagaku* 151:48–54. Tokyo: Kôrin.

Lévi-Strauss, Claude. 1977. *The Roast and the Boiled*. In *The Anthropologists' Cookbook*, ed. Jessica Kuper, London and Henley: Routledge and Kegan Paul.

Miura Sumio. 1993. *Mana ita to hôchô--kirikizamu chôrigu no rekishi* [Chopping board and kitchen knife--a history of cookery cutting tools]. In *Shokuseikatsu to mingu* [Dietary life and articles of everyday use], ed. Nihon Mingu Gakkai. Tokyo: Yûzankaku.

Mitani Kazuma, *Edo shomin fûzoku zukai*, Miki Shobo, Tokyo, 1975

Miyamoto Tsuneichi. 1977. *Shoku seikatsu zakkô* [Thoughts on dietary life]. *Miyamoto Tsuneichi chosakushû* [Collected writings of Miyamoto Tsuneichi], Vol. 24. Tokyo: Miraisha.

Miyazaki Akira. 1987. *Shokutaku o kaeta nikushoku* [How meat-eating changed the dining table]. Tokyo: Nihon Keizai Hyôronsha.

Mizutani Tadashi et al. 1987. A Chemical Analysis of Fermented Fish Products and Discussion of Fermented Flavors in Asian Cuisines. Osaka: *Bulletin of the National Museum of Ethnology* 12:3, 814-827.

Nakano Masuo. 1989. *Zanryû shibousan ni yoru kodai fukugen* [Reconstructing the ancient past with residual fatty acids]. In *Atarashii kenkyûhô wa koûkogaku ni nani o motarashita ka* [What new research techniques have come from archaeology?], 'Daigaku to Kagaku' Kôkan Shinpojiumu Soshiki Iinkai, ed. Tokyo: Tabapro.

NHK Yoron Chôsabu [NHK Opinion Survey Bureau]. 1984. *Nihonjin no suki na mono* [What the Japanese like]. Tokyo: Nippon Hôsô Shuppan Kyôkai.

_____. 1986. *Zusetsu: Nihonjin no seikatsu jikan 85* [Lifestyles of the Japanese, 1985 – Charts and Graphs]. Tokyo: Nippon Hôsô Shuppan Kyôkai.

REFERENCES

Okada Akio. 1979. *Chûshaku 'nanban ryôrisho'* [The annotated 'Nanban recipe']. *Inshoku shirin* 1:38–67. Tokyo: Inshoku Shirin Kankôkai.

Oyamada Tomokiyo. 1909. *Matsunoya hikki* [Matsunoya journal]. Tokyo: Kokusho Kankôkai.

Rodrigues, João. [1608] 1967. *Arte da Lingoa de Japam*, Japanese translation by Rodrigues Nihon Kyôkai in *Nihon kyôkai shi*. Tokyo: Iwanami Shoten.

Sahara Makoto. 1991. *Kodai no shoku 7: saiko no kondate / hashi no kigen* [Food in ancient times, part 7: the oldest menus and the origin of chopsticks]. *Vesta* 7, 25–31. Tokyo: Ajinomoto Shoku no Bunka Sentâ.

_____. 1992. *Kodai no shoku 12: Shokki o mittsu ni wakeru* [Food in ancient times, part 12: the three types of tableware]. *Vesta* 12, 34–41. Tokyo: Ajinomoto Shoku no Bunka Sentâ.

Sakai Toshihiko. [1903] 1979. *Shinkazokuron* [A new theory of the family]. Tokyo: Kodansha.

Sei Shônagon. 1967. *The Pillow Book of Sei Shônagon*, tr./ed. Ivan Morris. Harmondsworth: Penguin.

Shimabukuro Masatoshi. 1989. *Okinawa no buta to yagi – seikatsu no naka kara* [Pigs and goats of Okinawa in the context of daily life]. Naha: Hirugisha

Shinoda Osamu. 1968. Tofukô [Thoughts on tofu]. *Fûzoku* 8, 30–37.

Tanaka Seiichi and Ôta Hiroyasu. 1981. *Shoku ni kan suru nenjû gyôji* [Annual observances connected with food]. In *Higashi ajia no shokuji bunka* [Dietary cultures of East Asia], ed. Ishige Naomichi. Tokyo: Heibonsha.

Terasawa Kaoru and Terasawa Tomoko. 1981. *Yayoi jidai shokubutsusei shokuryô no kisoteki chishiki: shoki nôkô shakai kenkyû no zentei to shite* [Basic information on Yayoi-period vegetable foodstuffs: premises for the study of early farming society]. *Kôkogakuron* 5. Nara: Kashiwara Kôkogaku Kenkyûjo.

Wani Kômei. 1987. *Sorakukô* [A study of dairy foods]. *Inshoku shirin* 7:21–38. Tokyo: Inshoku Shirin Hakkôkai.

Watanabe Makoto. 1964. *Nihon shoku seikatsu shi* [History of Japanese dietary patterns]. Tokyo: Yoshikawa Kôbundô.

Zokugun Shoruijû Kanseikai. 1933. *Rôshôdô Nihon kôroku* [Rôshôdô chronicle of Japan]. Tokyo.

Lightning Source UK Ltd.
Milton Keynes UK
UKOW06f0404170915

258727UK00005B/100/P